Your Healing Stars: Volume II
The Integration of Ayurveda and Vedic Astrology

by Radhe

© 2016 by Susan (Radhe) Pfau

All rights reserved. No part of this book may be used or transmitted in any form or by any means, electronic or mechanical, including photocopying, recording, or by an information storage retrieval system, without written permission from the Publishers.

Published by

Shree Ganapati Productions
June 1, 2016

Ayurvedic and Vedic Astrology consultations and services are available from Radhe at celestialgazing.com

Printed in the United States of America by
CreateSpace, an Amazon.com Company
Charleston, SC

ISBN-13: 978-1517512286

Invocation

Gaṇānāṃ tvā gaṇapatiṃ havāmahe, kaviṃ kavīnām upamaśravastaman jyeṣṭharājam brahmaṇām brahmṇas pata, ā naḥ śṛṇvann ūtibhiḥ sīda sādanam. (Rigveda 2.23.1)

We invoke you, the Lord of hosts (Ganesha) over the hosts (of divine powers), the seer of seers with the highest inspired knowledge, the greatest king of the expressive powers of the soul, O Lord of the soul. Hearing us, sit down upon the seat (of our embodied being) with your powers of expansion.

Gratitudes and Acknowledgments

With deep respect and honor, I thank my instructors who have freely shared their wisdom of Ayurveda, Jyotisha and the Vedic scriptures. They include Dr. Vasant Lad, Dr. K. S. Charak, Vladimir Yatsenko, Penny Farrow, Dennis Flaherty and James Kelleher. With some exceptions, the graha condition methodology and many of the yoga qualification requirements presented in *Your Healing Stars: Volume I and II* have been taught to me by Penny Farrow, a long time student of Hart deFouw.

I am grateful for the encouragement and valuable advice received from friend and editor, Barbara Cook. Barbara is a New Zealand based Ayurvedic practitioner, Sanskrit instructor, and freelance editor.

Illustrations are graciously provided by Aaron Staengl of Ayurveda Posters and the Ayurvedic Institute located in Albuquerque, New Mexico.

About the Cover

On the cover is Lord Dhanvantari, the Vedic god of Ayurveda. Dhanvantari carries in his hands the scriptures of Ayurveda, a healing herb, a leech (used In Ayurveda for blood purification) and a vessel filled with the divine nectar of immortality (soma) uncovered from the bottom of the ocean by the gods and demons.

Books by Radhe @ celestialgazing.com

Your Healing Stars, Volume I: Fundamentals of Vedic Astrology

Your Healing Stars, Volume II: The Integration of Ayurveda and Vedic Astrology

The Divine Forces of the Lunar Nakshatras, as portrayed in the Vedas

Contents

SECTION I: Evolution of Health and Healing 1
    Chapter 1: Imagine the Unimaginable 2
    Chapter 2: The Notion of Karma in Ayurveda and Jyotisha 7

Introduction to Section II and III 9

SECTION II: Dosha Prakruti and Physical Health 11
    Chapter 3: Dosha Prakruti 12
    Chapter 4: Graha Archetypes 21
    Chapter 5: Constitutional Strength and Vitality 29
    Chapter 6: Vikruti and the Trik-Dusthanas 39

SECTION III: Samprapti and Disease Formation 53
    Chapter 7: The Ayurvedic Concept of Samprapti 54
    Chapter 8: The Kalapurusha of the Birth Chart 59
    Chapter 9: Identifying Khavaigunyas 66
    Chapter 10: Dhatus-Srotamsi and the Grahas 76
    Chapter 11: Evaluating Dhatus using Graha Karakas 82

Introduction to Section IV 88

SECTION IV: Manas Prakruti and Mental-Emotional Health 90
    Chapter 12: The Interplay of the Trigunas and Tridoshas 91
    Chapter 13: Emotional Health and Wellbeing 100
    Chapter 14: Intelligence and Discernment 109
    Chapter 15: Life Factors and Timing Considerations 118

Introduction to Section V 122

SECTION V: Spiritual Welfare & Dharma 125
    Chapter 16: Purusharthas and the Birth Chart 126
    Chapter 17: Uncovering Your Dharma 131
    Chapter 18: Yogas for Spiritual Growth 136
    Chapter 19: Chakras, Energetic Portals for Graha Consciousness 143
    Chapter 20: Enlightenment through the Stars 153
    Chapter 21: Chakra Evaluation Process 157

Introduction to Section VI 161

SECTION VI: Healing through the Grahas 162
    Chapter 22: Celestial Prayers to the Grahas 163
    Chapter 23: Choosing the Right Gemstones 167
    Chapter 24: Other Important Gemstone Considerations 176
    Chapter 25: Planetary Aromatherapy 180
    Chapter 26: The Sacred Nature of Plant Life 187
    Chapter 27: Nakshatra Rasayana Chikitsa 192
    Chapter 28: Health Aspects of the Nakshatras 238

Appendix Material 243

Appendix A: Summary Graha Condition and Terminology 244
Appendix B: Determining Your Prakruti 247
Appendix C: Determining Your Vikruti 250
Appendix D: Determining Your Mental Constitution 253
Appendix E: Summary Bhava Classifications 256
Appendix F: Channels of Nourishment and Elimination 257
Appendix G: Ayurvedic Significations of the Grahas 260
Appendix H: Navagraha Van and Rashi Van 264
Index 265

Introduction

My first glimpse of a seamless integration of a Vedic birth chart and an Ayurvedic consultation occurred in 2008 when I attended Dr. Vasant Lad's Ayurvedic Gurukula program in India. Each week, hundreds of clients from around the world arrive at Dr. Lad's free Pune clinic in search of a holistic approach to healing. Diet and lifestyle advice, Ayurvedic herbs, marma therapy, pranayama, meditation and Vedic birth chart interpretation are essential protocols for Dr. Lad. As a recent graduate of the Ayurvedic Institute and one who had practiced Jyotisha (Vedic Astrology) for over a decade, I reveled at the ease by which Dr. Lad assimilated Jyotisha and Ayurveda.

I have come to appreciate that both sciences offer tremendous wisdom and insight in the field of healing. When Ayurveda and Jyotisha are practiced together, the accuracy of the Ayurvedic evaluation process increases. Using Jyotisha, a health practitioner can also predict periods of health-risk years in advance. This gives the client the gift of time to make diet and lifestyle changes that can mitigate and/or defer sickness and disease. With its comprehensive set of planetary remedial measures, Jyotisha expands the practitioner's set of tools he or she can use to support clients' achieving a state of optimal health.

Since that fall in 2008, my professional practice has incorporated both of these divine sciences. It is my sincere hope that *Your Healing Stars: Volume II* will inspire other Ayurvedic practitioners and Jyotishis to do the same.

Note to the Reader

Your Healing Stars: Volume II is written for the Ayurvedic practioner or Jyotishi who wishes to integrate the health and healing aspects of Vedic Astrology (referred to in this book as Jyotisha, 'science of light') and Ayurveda. Although certain key Ayurvedic principles are summarized, it is recommended that a reader who is unfamiliar with Ayurveda purchase one of several excellent books on the topic, such as *Textbook of Ayurveda Fundamental Principles*, by Dr. Vasant Lad.

If you are new to the science of Jyotisha or would like a refresher on basic concepts and terminology, please read *Your Healing Stars: Volume I, Fundamental Principles of Vedic Astrology*, available at Amazon or at a reduced price at Celestial Gazing. Volume I contains important Jyotisha principles, concepts and chart interpretation techniques that are applied throughout Volume II.

Your Healing Stars: Volume II is written in a comprehensive but concise manner and includes many client chart examples that illustrate important concepts and techniques. However, oral traditions such as Ayurveda and Jyotisha are traditionally studied with the guidance of a well-versed instructor. For the reader who wishes to supplement the information contained in Volume I or Volume II with one-on-one instruction, the author offers personal and/or group instruction on Ayurveda and Jyotisha.[1]

Note, if you are interested in purchasing a Jyotisha software program, the author highly recommends *Shri Jyoti Star*, developed and maintained by Andrew Foss, PhD.[2]

---

[1] Visit celestialgazing.com
[2] See vedicsoftware.com.

SECTION I: Evolution of Health and Healing

Chapter 1: Imagine the Unimaginable

An Ancient Vision of Health

It is commonly believed that the *Atharvaveda* is the first Indian medical text. An arcane scripture composed around 1500BC, it is the last of the four Vedas and mostly dedicated to the topic of health and disease.[1] Yet, several thousand years earlier, the ancient rishis of the *Rigveda* acclaimed the unimaginable by foretelling a time when humankind would no longer be plagued by pain, suffering and disease. As utopic as this vision seems, the rishis fully comprehend the dauntless task at hand—immortality of the body.

Like other divine avatars that have descended to earth at critical times in history, the Rigvedic rishis incarnated to assist humankind in its evolutionary progress. They appeared in an ordinary manner, as generational family units. These rishis are the Atharvan, Angirasas and Bhrigu families of rishis, along with many others. One by one, they tell their messages in the one thousand-hymned *Rigveda*, India's earliest codified spiritual scripture and the first of the four Vedas.

The inspired sages also inspired others with their vision of immortality of the body. Indeed, the purpose of their descent was to remind humankind of this possibility, and of the work we can do to fully illuminate the soul (consciousness) within our material existence. This is the ancient notion of the Vedic sacrifice, referred to as *karma* (the work). It includes the concept of *seva*, the privilege and obligation that we have as embodied beings to serve the world, one another and the gods. The desired result of this glorious *yajna* (sacrificial performance) is the full, complete expression of consciousness within the flesh, so that our bodies transcend the realm of sickness and death.

Sacrificial Worship for the Attainment of Heaven

The *Rigveda* is a holy scripture cognized by hundreds of rishis who carried the torch for immortality. They set out humanity's goals for the current Vaivasvan *manvantara* and prophesized mankind's accomplishments.[2]

One-thousand years later, around 3000BC, the Brahmanic era was well underway. This was a period steeped in sacrificial ceremonies performed by the Brahman (priestly) caste, a caste one is born into. The period covered approximately 2,000 years, during which time the *Yajurveda*, the 'knowledge of sacrificial worship' and the third Veda, was codified.[3]

---

[1] The four Vedas in chronological sequence are: *Rigveda*, *Samaveda*, *Yajurveda* and *Atharvaveda*.

[2] Each manvantara lasts 306.7 million years and consists of a period of activity in which Brahma engages in the process of creation, followed by a period of rest, when Vishnu sleeps afloat the cosmic ocean on thousand-hooded snake, Ananta Shesha (infinite remainder). Fourteen manvantaras form a day and night of Brahma. At the end of fourteen manvantaras, all the worlds and regions of space are consumed by fire. After another period of rest, the next set of fourteen manvantaras and another day and night of Brahma commences. A new vision is delivered by the rishis at the opening of its commencement. One hundred days and nights equal the lifespan of Brahma.

[3] The *Samaveda*, codified prior to the *Yajurveda*, consists of hymns from the *Rigveda* composed in song (*sama*) format. Its hymns are sourced principally from *Rigveda* Mandala 9, a mandala dedicated to Lord Soma.

The grand Brahmanic ceremonies involve hundreds of minute and exacting rites. As many as sixteen priests, each a specialist in his own peculiar field of sacrificial knowledge and its duties, conduct these elaborate ceremonies. Certain worships, such as the Somayajna (Soma sacrifice), extend over a year's period. The *Yajurveda* and its supporting texts document the intricate ways of the sacrifice. It is concerned with spiritual attainment, but includes sovereign sacrifices that protect the King's powers and fortify his rulership over the kingdom.

During this early developmental stage in India, before the invasion of outside influences, an intimate connection to and reverence for the celestial forces existed. The Brahmin priests meticulously prepared the sacrificial grounds in accordance with principles of astronomy as well as the cardinal directions and elemental forces. Their ceremonies were performed to honor the sun's path during the course of a year and the resulting changes in seasons. New and full moon ceremonies were also routinely done.

The *Yajurveda* stipulates auspicious nakshatras for various sacrificial rites and the building of sacred fires. For example, the elaborate Agnichayana (construction of the sacrificial fire altar) instructs on how to arrange the topmost layer of the fire altar: 28 bricks (one for each nakshatra, including Abhijit) are to be placed closely together in a circle. The *Taittiriya Brahmana*, supporting text of the *Yajurveda*, lays out the rites for a 28-day lunar sacrifice. Each day during the sacrifice, oblations are offered to one of the nakshatras, and mantras are sung to the glory of its ruling devata.

It seems that during the remote Brahmanic times, the knowledge of healing was separate from the priestly knowledge of how to perform sacrificial rites. The *Yajurveda* lacks any reference to medicinal or sacrificial remedies for sickness and disease. The healers of India were most likely agrarian village people treating diseases with plants and techniques that were unique to their location. They practiced a shamanic-type of healing that would have included practices of divination.

The Atharvaveda

In search of answers to human beings' struggle with illness and disease, the *Atharvaveda* first and foremost addressed a multitude of health issues. Fever, dropsy, leprosy, leukoderma and hereditary disease, to mention a few, are the life-threatening concerns of its time. Nearly 4,000 of its 6,000 hymns are invocatory mantras asking the gods for aid in sickness and disease, or to medicinal plants that are administered orally or topically, or worn as amulets. The *Atharvaveda* identifies more than one hundred herbs, many of which come to occupy a significant place in the later classical Ayurveda texts. Magical spells and incantations, pacifying rites and fasting are interlaced with herbal applications, and curative procedures are combined with spiritual rituals.

The *Atharvaveda* postulates a holistic approach to healing, one that later informs Ayurveda. In addition to the physical conditions plaguing society, it addresses mental and emotional imbalances, such as jealously, anger, possession by spirits, familial discord and strife, and so on.

As in the previous era of Brahmanism, the worship of the grahas and nakshatras and, in this case, knowledge of their role in the healing process, remains at the forefront. The nakshatras are worshiped and adorned in an *Atharvaveda* hymn entitled "To the Lunar Nakshatras for Blessings".[4] In another hymn, a baby's birth under Mula nakshatra is described as a most inauspicious event, and the parents of the child are advised to implore the gods to protect their baby from Nirriti's (the devata ruler of Mula) harm.[5] An elaborate "medical ritual" is prescribed in the *Kausika Sutra* for such occurrence. The *Kausika Sutra* is an axillary *Atharvaveda* scripture.

The *Shantikalpa Parisista*, another important supplementary text to the *Atharvaveda*, prescribes a lengthy shanti offering (peace offering) to the nakshatras. This *kalpa* (law book) offers many insights into the nature and qualities of the nakshatras and their ruling devatas. Certain passages are accompanied by the recitation of particular *Atharvaveda* verses.[6]

In another *Atharvaveda Parisista*, the 120-verse *Nakshatrakalpa*, the nakshatra devatas are eulogized and their ritualistic worship methods specified. This kalpa even stipulates the number of days a disease will endure based on the transiting moon's nakshatra at the time of illness.[7]

Ritualistic Medicine and the Scientific Worldview

The *Charaka Samhita* tells of a time in which the human race is overcome by the darkness of illness and disease. The rishis are gravely concerned for, preoccupied by their dire state, people no longer adhere to their spiritual practices. The great sages approach Brahma for a solution. He imparts the vidya of Ayurveda to the Ashwini Kumars, divine twins who are the sons of Surya (the sun). In turn, they instruct Indra on the sacred ways of healing, and Indra passes the knowledge on to the rishis.[8] One such seer is Agnivesha, who codifies the wisdom of Ayurveda in a text called *Agnivesha Tantra*, acclaimed as the first text on Ayurveda.

Here, Sage Agnivesha and other rishis receive the "official" knowledge of Ayurveda from Indra, the most hymned-to godhead in the *Rigveda*, by way of the Ashwini Kumars. In this *sampradaya* (lineage), no connection to the *Atharvaveda* is described, nor are the seers (Angirasa and Atharvan) of this Veda named among those Indra instructs on Ayurveda.

With the passage of time, parts of the *Agnivesha Tantra* become corrupt, while other parts are lost. Charaka, a student of Agnivesha, restores the lost knowledge and scripts the *Agnivesha Tantra* in a language suitable for the lay physician. The *Agnivesha Tantra* is renamed the *Charaka Samhita*. The time period is roughly 300-100BC and India, along with the rest of the world, is at the beginning of a scientific revolution.

That India's budding medical community all but disclaims any influence on its profession from the ritualistic and seemingly superstitious healing ways of the *Atharvaveda* is not surprising. Mystical knowledge is often ignored, lost or tucked away into the background as a civilization advances from a magical-mythological time to one founded on mental constructs

---

[4] See *The Divine Forces of the Lunar Nakshatra* written by the author.
[5] Ibid.
[6] Ibid.
[7] See Chapter 28: "Health Aspects of the Nakshatras".
[8] *Charaka Samhita, Angivesha's treatise refined and annotated by Charaka and redacted by Dridhabala*, Prof. Priyavrat Sharma (ediotr-translatory), Chapter 1:4-5. Chaukhambha Orientalia, 2005.

and scientific postulates.

But make your way through the *Charaka Samhita* and you will uncover an adamant endorsement of the *Atharvaveda* and its arcane approaches to sickness and disease. Here, Charaka gives curative mantras, *upayas* (remedial measures) and ritualistic medical practices their due.

> Therefore, by the physician who has inquired about (*which Veda an Ayurvedic practitioner should follow*), devotion to the Atharvaveda is ordered from among the four (*Vedas*): Rgveda, Samaveda, Yajurveda and Atharvaveda. For it is stated that the sacred knowledge of the fire priests (*Atharvans*) is medical science because it encompasses the giving of gifts (dana), invoking blessings (savasti), sacrifice to deities (ayana), the offering (bali), auspicious observances (mangala), the giving of burnt offerings (homa), restraint of the mind (niyama), atonement (prayascitta), fasting (upavasa) and the recitation of mantras; and medical science is taught for the benefit of long life. (*Charaka Samhita* Volume I, 30.20-21)

It is likely that this passage is one of many that survived from the *Agnivesha Tantra* which was composed in a time closer to that of the *Atharvaveda*. Charaka may have retained this passage because he understood that an Ayurvedic physician must access all available means to aid the health and wellness of his client.

Some argue that this passage is merely a pacification script to minimize tensions between those quasi-religious healers that remained loyal to the *Atharvaveda* and those that lead the way into the scientific era of medicine and sought to advance surgical procedures.

But the above citation is not an isolated passage, and the classical Ayurveda texts do emphasize the importance of astrological timing, recommend appropriate remedial gemstones, stipulate that a small statue of a man will help change the sex of a fetus to male, call attention to the importance of dreams and omens, and so on.[9] Moreover, in his elaborate descriptions of different types of insanity, Charaka includes those caused by evil spirits and those caused by the gods.[10] Despite all this, it is also clear in the Charaka Samhita that a significant transition was underway in India from ritualistic healing to a decidedly scientific approach.

In more modern times, Ayurveda continues to prescribe the use of mantras as well as color therapy and other remedial measures that harness *prabhava* (supernatural power). Ayurveda uses the term prabhava to describe an effect that is currently unexplainable by scientific laws.

As in previous times, the grahas and their influence in the healing process are still validated by India's medical community. Rasashastra (alchemy), a special Ayurveda branch of medicine, correlates the healing effects of the grahas to various metals and precious and semiprecious stones. For example, gold is associated with the properties of the sun, and the

---

[9] *"Science" vs. "Religion" in Classical Ayurveda*, Steven Engler, Numen, Vol. 50, No. 4 (2003), pg. 436.
[10] *Charaka Samhita, Angivesha's treatise refined and annotated by Charaka and redacted by Dridhabala*, Prof. Priyavrat Sharma (ediotr-translatory), Volume II, Chapter 9, 18-20. Chaukhambha Orientalia, 2005.

sun is described as the signature graha for the heart. A person with a weak heart is recommended to wear a gold bracelet or drink water from a gold cup.[11] This is another example of prabhava, health practices whose benefits are currently beyond modern scientific explanation.

In many parts of India, herbs are harvested and medicinal remedies prepared when the moon transits certain nakshatras understood to be auspicious for such activities. The proper timings for commencing medicines or having surgery are also determined by the moon's transit through certain nakshatras.

Today, nearly all U.S. Ayurveda schools offer courses in Jyotisha and encourage their students to integrate the principles of these two sister sciences.

---

[11] Refer to Chapter 23: "Choosing the Right Gemstone".

Chapter 2: The Notion of Karma in Ayurveda and Jyotisha

Jyotisha clients often ask: "Is my destiny fated?" To answer this question requires an understanding of karma based on a commonly accepted Hindu perspective. This perspective identifies three types of karma: *sanchita*, *prarabdha* and *kriyaman*.

Sanchita means 'accumulated'. Sanchita is the totality of actions performed in previous lifetimes whose *karma phala* (fruits of action) are yet to fructify but will do so in this and future incarnations.

The second type of karma is prarabdha, which means 'to commence or set in motion'. Prarabdha is that portion of sanchita karma that one is destined to experience in this lifetime. Prarabdha karma creates the urges, desires and forces that activate or ripen the fruit of past life actions. Taken collectively, the twelve bhavas of the birth chart show the prarabdha karma that is likely to unfold during the person's present incarnation.

Prarabdha karma sets our destiny in motion. Yet, each moment we have the opportunity to modify our fate. Kriyaman (being made) karma is action we perform in the present that will bear fruit in current or future lifetimes. Kriyaman describes our ability to augment or change our destiny, for better or worse.

Kriyaman karma can be viewed as that portion of karma that comes from free will. The amount of free will one has in a lifetime varies in each area of life (e.g., marriage, health, career, education) and from one birth chart to the next. The more ingrained a particular event or experience is in the birth chart, the less freedom a person has to modify its outcome or prevent it from happening.

In the Ayurvedia text *Charaka Samhita*, Charaka posits this same viewpoint when declaring that karmas can be classified as strong (fixed), weak (unfixed) or somewhere in between strong and weak (fixed-unfixed).[1] Charaka states that because certain health conditions represent fixed karmas, they persist despite even an ardent effort to avoid or mitigate them. In other words, they allow for little free will. On the other hand, most health conditions represent unfixed or fixed-unfixed karmas. Charaka asserts that in these cases, a proper diet, appropriate lifestyle and the cultivation of a sattvic mind will enhance a person's health and well-being.

To illustrate, assume a birth chart shows a mix of fixed and unfixed karmas (i.e., fixed-unfixed) in relation to diabetes. If the person is alerted to the possibility of becoming diabetic, he or she can benefit right away by exercising and following a reasonable diet (actions constituting free will). Some of the symptoms of diabetes may still manifest but, due to the individual's persistent attention and action, he or she will be much less likely to experience the full impact of the disease. Even if the karma is extremely fixed, a person who

---

[1] *Charaka-Samhita, Agnivesa's treatise refined and annotated by Charaka and redacted by Drdhabala*, Priyavrat Sharma (editor-translator). Chapter 3.3.31, 33-34. Chaukhambha Orientalia, 2005.

becomes aware of this can plan to meet the need for medical management, and work to keep himself as healthy as possible.

Several Jyotisha techniques help us evaluate the degree of free will related to particular events and areas of life. In *Your Healing Stars: Volume I, Fundamental Principles of Vedic Astrology* a comprehensive discussion of graha condition is presented.[2] The condition of a graha is a prime indicator of its ability to influence a person's life. Certain graha conditions suggest fixed karmas and others suggest unfixed or fixed-unfixed karmas.

Confluence techniques are other methods used to evaluate the degree of fixed karma concerning a particular area of life. An event or experience that involves multiple reinforcing factors in the birth chart is far more likely to occur than an event with only one or two indicators. Graha karakas, rashi confluence, chart rotation, Surya and Chandra Lagna confluence are just a few such techniques.[3] These confluence methods are demonstrated in many client case illustrations in this book.

Lastly, *yogas* (particular planetary configurations) are typically involved in scenarios of fixed karma. Yogas enhance the probability that certain experiences will play out in the individual's life, whether they relate to wealth (*dhana yogas*), fame (*raj yogas*) or misfortune (*daridra yogas*). These yogas were presented in *Your Healing Stars: Volume I, Fundamental Principles of Vedic Astrology*. In this volume, yogas for health and those for disease are described.

Events representing fixed-unfixed karma involve more free will, for they *may or may not* occur. Hence, these events are far more difficult to predict with certainty. To ensure such an event unfolds requires conscious intent and effort. Focused intention and persistent effort can be effective in manifesting a desired experience, be it a happy home life, fruitful career or satisfying marriage. In a similar manner, an unwanted experience or outcome such as ill-health, financial hardship or the loss of a relationship may be modified.

Our responsibility as Jyotishis is to make the individual aware of those areas where there is more choice or free will. Here, awareness and dedicated focus can be vehicles for modifying karma. Yet, even in cases where only fixed karma is present, never underestimate the power an individual has to use his or her intelligence and determination to redirect the ship into new waters—no matter how powerful the undercurrent. This is particularly true when the Lagna and its Lagnesha are well-conditioned.

As professionals, we can be direct and honest with a client without being fatalistic. This means discussing difficult life areas in a solution-oriented way that encourages the client to take ownership for his or her situation and make life-enhancing decisions. When we communicate birth chart findings in this manner, we do justice to the individual and to the science of Jyotisha.

---

[2] For a summary of graha conditions and related terminology, see Appendix A.
[3] Refer to *Your Healing Stars: Volume I, Fundamental Principles of Vedic Astrology* for a detailed discussion and illustration of these confluence techniques.

Introduction to Section II and III

Ayurveda is that science where what is useful and detrimental (to health and life), the happy and unhappy (states of) life, what is good and bad for life, its measurement (life span) and life itself are described. (Charaka Samhita, 1.41)

Ayurveda appreciates the uniqueness of each individual and uses personalized approaches to health and healing. For an Ayurvedic practitioner, this begins with an assessment of the individual's constitution or *prakruti*. The classical Ayurveda texts identify seven major prakruti types: *ekadosha* or single *dosha* dominant (vata, pitta, kapha), *dvidosha* or dual dosha dominant (vata-pitta, vata-kapha, pitta-kapha) and *samaprakruti* or the equal balance of all three doshas (vata-pitta-kapha).

A person's prakruti is an expression of his unique anatomical, physiological and psychological make-up. By understanding a person's prakruti, we can better understand which doshas are more likely to affect the person's health, what habits he or she is inclined to adopt and what type of diet and therapies are most appropriate.

Each graha and rashi is associated with a particular dosha, so we can use the grahas of a birth chart to make both a quantitative and qualitative assessment of a client's prakruti. A client's predominant dosha is determined by evaluating the strength and placement of grahas and specific graha-rashi configurations that influence health, constitution, and character. Jyotisha also recognizes seven planetary body-types and archetypal personalities, each represented by one of the grahas (except Rahu and Ketu) in accordance with its doshic constitution and anthropomorphic form. Our quantitative birth approach of assessing the condition of a graha[1] and its rashi relationships can be supplemented with this more qualitative method of determining prakruti.

Secondly, we must assess the client's constitutional strength and inherent resistance to sickness and disease. When the person has a robust constitution, diseases indicated in the birth chart tend to be resolved more quickly and be less complex. Alternatively, they may occur as part of the natural ageing process at the later stage of an otherwise healthy life.

When a person deviates from his inherent prakruti, he becomes subject to ill-health. Thus, a client's tendency towards doshic imbalance (*vikruti*) plays an important role in his overall wellbeing. The trik-dusthanas[2] and their bhaveshas are significant here, for they represent acute (6B-6B bhavesha) and chronic (8B-8B bhavesha) disease and the wasting of bodily

---

[1] See Appendix A for a summary of graha conditions and related terminology. This is an important topic that is presented and illustrated in *Your Healing Stars: Volume I, Fundamental Principles of Vedic Astrology*.
[2] See Appendix E for the classification of the 12 bhavas of the birth chart as discussed in detail in *Your Healing Stars: Volume I, Fundamental Principles of Vedic Astrology*.

tissues and organs or the need for prolonged bedrest (12B-12B bhavesha).[3] These topics are the subject matter of Section II.

Our focus shifts in Section III to the Ayurvedic notion of *samprapti*. According to this concept, the disease process typically occurs over an extended period of time during which its original cause (doshic aggravation) develops in several stages. An aggravated dosha reaches a certain level of intensity in its main site before spilling over and spreading to one or more other tissues and organs. Important Ayurvedic concepts related to samprapti are also presented in this section.

Next, we methodically examine the birth chart for potential *khavaigunyas*. These are inherently vulnerable spaces in the body where aggravated doshas lodge and produce disorder and disease. The Jyotisha notion of Kalapurusha is central to how we identify and prioritize khavaigunyas. Kalapurusha means 'cosmic being'. It is pictured as a person whose limbs and organs overlay the stellar rashis. When mapped against the birth chart, Kalapurusha helps to highlight specific khavaigunya sites, be it an organ (heart, liver, colon, stomach), bodily function (fat metabolism, hormone production, bile production) or limb (arms and legs).

Ayurveda identifies seven basic tissues (*dhatus*) that maintain and nourish the body: *rasa dhatu* (blood plasma, including white blood cells and lymph fluids), *rakta dhatu* (red blood cells), *mamsa dhatu* (muscle tissue), *meda dhatu* (adipose tissue), *asthi dhatu* (bone tissue), *majja dhatu* (nerve tissue) and *shukra and artava dhatus* (male and female reproductive tissue, respectively). Each graha (except Rahu and Ketu) serves as the primary significator or *karaka* (producer or creator) for one of the seven dhatus. This assignment is based on the gunas, dosha and psychological attributes of the graha and those of the dhatu. The health of each dhatu can be evaluated by a systematic assessment of its graha karaka, a technique illustrated in Section III.

---

[3] Bhava 1 and its bhavesha are referred to as the "Lagna-Lagnesha", Bhava 2 and its bhavesha, "2B-2B bhavesha", Bhava 3 and its bhavesha, "3B-3B bhavesha", and so on.

SECTION II: Dosha Prakruti and Physical Health

Chapter 3: Dosha Prakruti

Vata, Pitta and Kapha

Vata, pitta and kapha are the three Ayurvedic doshas. They arise from the *mahabhutas* (great elements): earth, water, fire, air and space. All five elements are in everything, but each dosha is related mainly to two. For example, air and ether are the predominant elements of vata dosha. The light, mobile, cool, dry and subtle qualities of air and ether work together as vata dosha to promote and support all movements in the body, be that the movement of the breath, blood and nutrients, muscles and limbs or urine and feces. Vata also fills all empty spaces within the body (e.g., the bones, joints, brain, spinal column).

Figure 1: Elements and Doshas

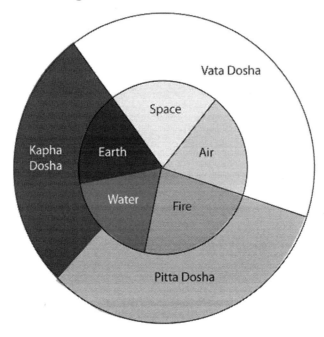

In a similar manner, water and fire are the primary elements of pitta dosha. With its hot, sharp, light, slightly oily, liquid and spreading qualities, pitta performs the transformational processes within the body: food into chyme, light into visual impressions, information into comprehension, and so on. This transformative function is facilitated by a series of chemical reactions such as those that involve digestive enzymes (gastric acid, pepsin, intrinsic factor, hydrochloric acid) and bile. Without water as its medium, fire (and its resultant chemical reactions) could not function in the body. Importantly, pitta is also responsible for the regulation of body temperature through the production of heat, a principal by-product of its metabolic function.

Lastly, earth and water are the most predominant elements in kapha dosha. Earth is solid and immovable. Its nature is one of caution, persistence, strength and dependability. In contrast, water lacks the solidity of the earth element. It is fluid and adaptive and flows down the path of least resistance. Similarly to the fire and water elements of pitta dosha, these two seemingly opposing elements work hand-in-hand in the form of kapha dosha. Kapha is the cementing force within the body that provides structure and strength (earth) and lubricates and nourishes all organs and tissues (water). When earth and water work together as kapha dosha, anabolic processes take place in the body, such as building, repairing and healing of organs and tissues.

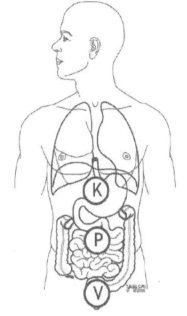

Each dosha has a bodily location or "seat" from which it initiates its actions and generates its humors. The primary seat of vata is the colon, the seat of pitta is the small intestine and that of kapha is the stomach. Thus, the gastro-intestinal system is the primary field of influence for all three doshas. This is why Ayurveda stresses the importance of a proper diet.

Prakruti

We are each born with a particular ratio of vata, pitta and kapha, which remains the same throughout life. This ratio establishes our prakruti, or unique constitutional make-up, including physical and physiological characteristics and personality traits.

For example, a person with a vata prakruti is typically slender and has one or more disproportionate features. His appetite varies between strong and weak and the bowels tend to be constipated. He or she is restless, alert and quick to grasp new concepts. In contrast, the pitta individual is of medium height and frame, prone to early greying or baldness and has sharp and penetrating eyes. His or her appetite is strong but the bowels are often loose. A pitta-dominant person is ambitious, courageous and competitive, and has a sharp and piercing intellect. Lastly, a person with a kapha prakruti has a rounded but firm physique, large, attractive eyes and thick and plentiful hair. Digestion is slow but strong, and he or she possesses physical and mental stability and endurance. Kapha individuals are known for their benevolence, patience and loving ways, but they are often slow to initiate or accept change.

To support and maintain our inborn prakruti, Ayurveda stipulates appropriate lifestyle routines (*dinacharyas*), such as diet and exercise programs, proper climates and even customized spiritual practices (*pranayama*, mediation and *yoga asanas*).

Several qualitative and quantitative diagnostic methods are available to assist Ayurvedic practitioners in their evaluation of a client's dosha prakruti. These include pulse diagnosis, client questioning and observation of the client's physical attributes. (For an example of a standard set of client questions used for this purpose, see Appendix B.) Most Ayurvedic practitioners combine these methods. Results gleaned from taking the pulse and observing the physical features of the individual can be compared to those obtained from a client questionnaire.

Jyotisha also offers a qualitative and quantitative approach based on the underlying dosha prakruti of the grahas. The quantitative method involves examining the birth chart for prominently placed and strongly conditioned grahas as well as particular graha-rashi configurations. This methodology is illustrated in the following sections. In addition, we can use a qualitative approach based on the scriptural archetypal personalities and anthropomorphic characteristics of the grahas. This approach is presented in the next chapter.

As complementary sciences, Jyotisha and Ayurveda are intended to supplement one another. We get optimal results when we compare and contrast our pulse diagnosis, physical examination and/or client questionnaire with our Jyotisha results.

Graha and Rashi Doshas

Each graha has a predominant prakruti that corresponds to its inherent nature. For example, the two fiery grahas, Surya and Mangala, are pitta predominant. Translated as 'heavy', Guru is the major kapha graha, while Shani, anthropomorphized as tall, skinny and aging, is the main vata graha. Chandra's cool, watery nature and ever-changing appearance explains its kapha (primarily) and vata (secondarily) prakruti. However, when the moon is dark at the time of birth, Chandra is vata (primary) and kapha (secondary).

Budha is a fast-orbiting graha that is never more than 45° from the sun. This affords Budha a vata (primarily) and pitta (secondarily) prakruti. Shukra (a word that is translated as 'semen') represents the watery reproductive fluids of the body, giving this other quick-orbiting inner graha a kapha (primarily) and vata (secondarily) prakruti.

Lastly, Rahu and Ketu are similar to Shani and Mangala, respectively. Yet, as unstable vortices of energy, Rahu represents imbalanced vata and Ketu is imbalanced pitta.[1]

For the sake of simplicity, we will initially consider only the primary dosha of a graha when assessing prakruti. However, more advanced Jyotishis are encouraged to incorporate, where applicable, a graha's secondary dosha into the prakruti evaluation.

---

[1] Refer to *Your Healing Stars: Volume I, Fundamental Principles of Vedic Astrology* for a description of Rahu and Ketu.

Table 1: Graha Dosha Prakruti

Graha	Primary	Secondary
Surya	pitta	
Chandra	kapha	vata
Mangala	pitta	
Budha	vata	pitta
Guru	kapha	
Shukra	kapha	vata
Shani	vata	
Rahu	vata	
Ketu	pitta	

Each rashi also has a prakruti, which comes from a combination of its elemental representation and planetary rulership. The air rashis of Gemini, Libra and Aquarius are vata rashis, along with Virgo (ruled by Budha, a vata graha) and Capricorn (ruled by Shani, a vata graha). The fire rashis of Aries, Leo and Sagittarius are pitta rashis. The water rashis of Cancer, Scorpio and Pisces are kapha rashis, along with Taurus (ruled by Shukra, a kapha graha).

Table 2: Rashi Dosha Prakruti

Lagna	Dosha Prakruti	Lagna	Dosha Prakruti
Aries	pitta	Libra	vata
Taurus	kapha	Scorpio	kapha
Gemini	vata	Sagittarius	pitta
Cancer	kapha	Capricorn	vata
Leo	pitta	Aquarius	vata
Virgo	vata	Pisces	kapha

Dosha Prakruti as Shown in the Birth Chart

The Lagna and Lagnesha represent the constitutional make-up, physical attributes and personality characteristics of the individual. This is the basis for our fundamental rule: the prakruti of the individual is denoted by the dosha of the rashi that rules the Lagna (primarily) *and* that of the Lagnesha (secondarily).

To illustrate, assume for an Aries-ruled Lagna that the Lagnesha (Mangala) occupies Aquarius. In this case, the individual's prakruti is pitta (Aries-ruled Lagna) and, secondarily, vata (Lagnesha placed in Aquarius).

Chapter 3: Dosha Prakruti

Both Ayurveda and Jyotisha recognize that individuals are unique. This means that we must incorporate into our dosha prakruti evaluation distinctive planetary placements and graha conditions. As might be imagined, there are countless birth chart configurations. But by supplementing the above fundamental rule with a few simple principles, we can refine our birth chart-based prakruti assessment. This requires that we prioritize the dosha of those grahas that meet the following criteria.

1. Strongly conditioned grahas[2] that influence the Udaya Lagna (primary)[3] or its Lagnesha (secondary) or occupy the kendras (primary).

   Illustrated in *Your Healing Stars: Volume I*, strong grahas manifest their mundane significations visibly in a person's life. When such a graha influences the Lagna or the Lagnesha, its doshic nature, anthropomorphic features and personality traits (e.g., tall, round-faced, strong appetite, creatively inclined, competitive) are imprinted upon the individual.

   For example, if Shani is exalted in the Lagna, as is the case for a Libra-ruled Lagna, it indicates a vata constitution. The person will be thin and slender-framed, with dry skin or prominent bones. He will tend towards stiff or cracking joints, thin hair and brittle nails.

   This same notion is true for strong grahas that occupy kendras, even when they do not influence the Lagna or Lagnesha. Kendras are twice as large as other bhavas, and this symbolizes their importance. Grahas placed in kendras, particularly when strong, inscribe their physical characteristics, personality and inclinations prominently on the individual. In fact, the influence that such a graha has on a person's prakruti supersedes even that of a strong graha that influences the Lagnesha (i.e., along with strong graha influences on the Lagna, such graha becomes a primary determinant of prakruti).

   In our above Libra-ruled Lagna example, should Guru occupy the Cancer-ruled 10B (i.e., Guru is strong (exalted) and occupies a kendra), the person will have a dual-doshic constitution of vata-kapha.

   Importantly, do not consider the prakruti of any graha that is mixed in condition. Mixed conditioned and weak grahas often indicate vikruti, or an imbalance of the dosha they represent.

2. If #1 above does not apply, consider strongly conditioned grahas that influence the Chandra Lagna (primary) or its Lagnesha (secondary) or occupy the kendras (primary) from this Lagna.[4]

---

[2] Appendix A contains a summary of graha conditions and terminology.
[3] The Udaya (rising) Lagna is that space in the sky that was rising on the eastern horizon at the time of birth.
[4] To view the Chandra Lagna, simply rotate the chart until natal Chandra becomes the lagna. This technique is demonstrated in *Your Healing Stars: Volume I, Fundamentals of Vedic Astrology*.

The moon gives form to earthly matters and things tend to flourish under its influence. Thus, Chandra is the graha karaka for newborns and is also a significant determinant of a person's bodily appearance.

The same principles stipulated in #1 above also hold true from the Chandra Lagna. Of course, from this lagna, Chandra itself occupies a kendra. Hence, when strong (e.g., bright moon, sva rashi or exalted), it contributes towards a kapha prakruti.

3. Should #2 also not apply, give priority to ordinary grahas that influence the Udaya Lagna (primary) or its Lagnesha (secondarily).

If none of the above criteria is met, we are left with our fundamental rule: the dosha prakruti of the individual is that of the rashi that rules the Lagna (primarily) and that of the Lagnesha (secondarily).

In *Your Healing Stars: Volume I*, we saw that confluence adds certainty to one's birth chart predictions. The value of confluence in determining a client's prakruti is illustrated in the following section.

Client Case Illustrations

Our first client is Frank, a 52 year-old male with a Gemini-ruled Lagna.

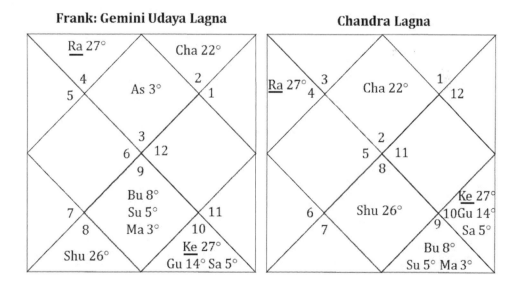

Applying the first principle, we notice that neither the Lagna nor its Lagnesha (Budha) are influenced by strongly conditioned grahas. Moreover, there are no strongly conditioned grahas in kendras. Therefore, we must consider the Chandra Lagna. From the Chandra Lagna, Chandra is the only qualifying graha, for Chandra has two factors of strength: it is both bright and exalted. Chandra is a kapha graha, indicating that Frank's prakruti is kapha. Notice that Shukra (a kapha graha, but ordinary in condition) aspects Chandra, which provides confluence for Frank's kapha prakruti.

Our next client is a 58-year old female named Katrina. Katrina has a Taurus-ruled Lagna.

Chapter 3: Dosha Prakruti

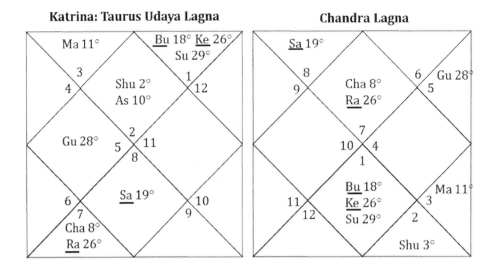

In Katrina's chart, the Lagnesha (Shukra) occupies the Lagna, but is of mixed condition (sva rashi and combust). Therefore, we cannot consider the prakruti of Shukra. Shani (a vata graha) has two factors of strength (dig bala and retrogression) and influences the Lagna *and* Lagnesha (Shukra). There are no other strong grahas occupying the kendras from the Udaya Lagna. Hence, Kaṭrina's dosha prakruti is vata.

For our third illustration, we turn to Terrance, a 63 year-old male with a Cancer-ruled Lagna. Terrance is a good example of a client with a dual-doshic constitution.

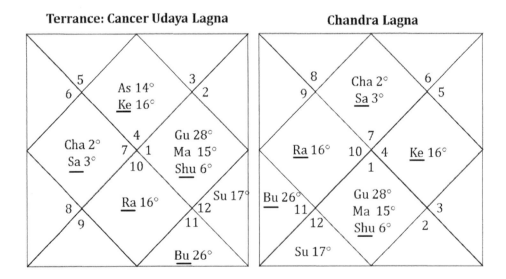

Both the Lagna and its Lagnesha (Chandra) are influenced by strongly conditioned (sva rashi and dig bala) Mangala, a pitta graha, and strongly conditioned (exalted and retrograde) Shani, a vata graha. Shukra, a kapha graha, is also strong (retrograde) and placed in a kendra. But Shukra has only one factor of strength and influences only the Lagnesha. Thus, Terrance has a vata-pitta prakruti.

For our next example, we will examine Sandra's birth chart. Sandra is a 45-year old female who also has a Cancer-ruled Lagna.

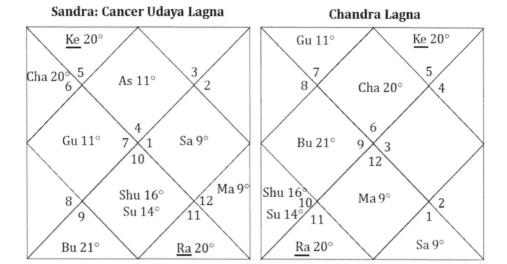

No strongly conditioned grahas influence the Udaya Lagna or its Lagnesha (Chandra) nor the Chandra Lagna and its Lagnesha (Budha). As well, no strongly conditioned grahas occupy a kendra from either Lagna.

Are there any grahas of ordinary condition that influence the Udaya Lagna or Lagnesha? Surya (a pitta graha) aspects the Lagna, while Mangala (also a pitta graha) aspects the Lagnesha. Here, we have two factors of confluence for a pitta constitution. (Notice that we cannot count Shukra's influence on the Lagna, for Shukra is combust.)

For our final client example, we have the birth chart of Alexandra, a 60-year old woman with a Capricorn-ruled Lagna. (See chart on the following page.)

The Lagna is aspected by strongly conditioned (retrograde) Shani (a vata graha), who is also the Lagnesha. The Lagnesha (Shani) is in association with strongly conditioned (exalted) Rahu (also a vata graha). In this case, we have two factors of confluence indicating a vata constitution. Budha is of mixed condition (retrograde and combust) and Chandra is eclipsed by Rahu.[5] Thus, we cannot count either's influence on the Lagnesha.

---

[5] On the day Alexandra was born, a lunar eclipse was visible from her birth location.

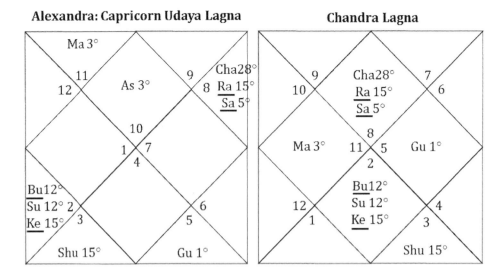

Summary

As illustrated in this chapter, we can apply a few simple rules based on Jyotisha principles of graha condition to assess a client's prakruti from the birth chart. Just as Ayurveda recognizes that a person's prakruti may be dual-doshic, the same is true of Jyotisha. This was demonstrated in Terrance's chart, where strongly conditioned Shani (a vata graha) and Mangala (a pitta graha) occupy kendras and influence the Udaya Lagna and its Lagnesha.

At times, the prakruti evaluation may not seem so straightforward, due to conflicting birth chart configurations or lack of confluence. In these cases, supplement your Jyotisha evaluation with the graha profiles provided in the next chapter. You can also corroborate your evaluation with the results you obtain from the questionnaire in Appendix B.

Chapter 4: Graha Archetypes

Introduction

Classical Ayurveda texts categorize prakruti into seven major types.[1] In a similar manner, Jyotisha recognizes seven archetypal categories; each represented by one of the grahas (except Rahu and Ketu) and based on their unique doshic constitution. Jyotisha shastra illuminates these archetypes by describing a graha's peculiar anthropomorphic nature, personality traits and inclinations. The seven psycho-physical graha types are described in this chapter.

The subtle qualities (*gunas*) of the mind (described in more detail in Chapter 12) are sattva, rajas and tamas. Sattva guna promotes clarity and harmony, qualities that support wisdom and truth. Rajas guna creates desires and inspires constant activity. It promotes change and movement. Lastly, tamas guna gives fixity in mind, causing resistance to change, inertia and attachment.

In an individual, the ratio of the three gunas determines his or her *manas prakruti*, or mental blueprint. Although a person's manas prakruti may change over the course of a lifetime, this is rare. Still, because of the subtle nature of thoughts and emotions, a person's superficial mental state (*manas vikruti*) can change moment-to-moment. These modifications are triggered every day by transiting grahas and, on a longer-term basis, by shifting dashas and bhuktis. Thus, even a sattvic person experiences periods of rajasic hyperactivity, indecisiveness and excess desire, or tamasic inclinations such as intolerance, self-criticism, fear of failure, anger and hostility.

The following sections focus on the graha's doshic archetype, but they include its sattvic potential, while also noting its rajasic and tamasic tendencies. For a detailed discussion of manas prakruti and the inherent guna of each graha, see Chapter 12: "The Interplay of the Trigunas and Tridoshas".

---

[1] Refer to "Introduction to Section II and II" for the seven major prakruti types.

Chapter 4: Graha Archetypes

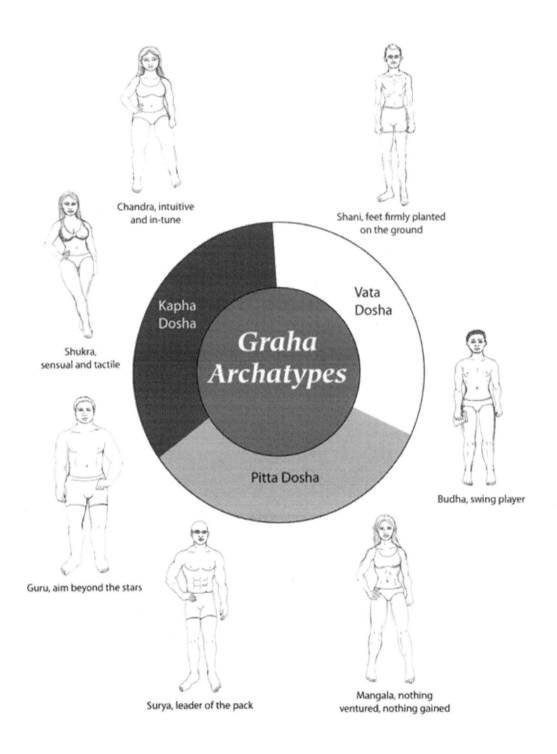

Vata Graha Archetypes

Budha: swing player

Dosha: vata-pitta
Guna: rajas

A well-proportioned but somewhat unisex body is the hallmark physical feature of the Budha-type. Typical of their vata nature, they have smaller than normal eyes and mouth.

Personality-wise, Budha-types can be hard to identify at first, for their adaptability camouflages their true nature. One minute they are engrossed in a deep philosophical discussion; the next minute, they are engaged in competitive sports, leading-edge research, or just plain fun and games. Indeed, Budha-types win the award as "swing player" on the team.

Yet, catch Budha-types alone and you are most likely to find them with their nose in a book, preparing for a lecture or taking stock of their mental skills. Nothing builds their confidence more than having a ready and able mind. Their intellectual ingenuity comes from their natural curiosity, their openness to new ideas and their willingness to experiment.

Since Budha-types also have a healthy dose of pitta (i.e., pitta is their secondary dosha), they are also inspired by intellectual challenges, which they generally meet, due to their cerebral acumen. Learning is the most important thing for these people, whether through formal education or self-study. As they mature, they share their knowledge with others as teachers. Creativity for Budha-types means artistic verbal expression and imaginative and/or clever use of words, including humor.

Budha-types are the quickest of the planetary personalities to adapt to new situations, and they are almost always first to complete an assignment or task. Their physical and mental quickness and dexterity can be truly remarkable.

Mental inclinations: Budha-types are naturally rajasic, for they are active, change-oriented and demand constant stimulation. However, when in excess, rajas creates hyperactivity, indecisiveness and overstimulation. They can sometimes experience excessive mental chatter, and can be spacey or scattered. In contrast, when tamas overtakes the mind, mental confusion sets in and the person struggles to adapt to the ever-changing circumstances of daily life. The person my even use their cleverness to manipulate others.

Shani: feet firmly planted on the ground

Dosha   vata
Guna   tamas

Here is your typical vata person: thin and slender-framed, with dry, cool skin and prominent bones. They tend towards stiff or cracking joints, thin hair and brittle nails. One or more "crooked features", such as crooked teeth, nose or smile, mark the Shani-type. They are sensitive to the cold, wind and dry weather and their appetites are erratic.

Reserved Shani-types can appear detached and austere, but they are also dependable, responsible and loyal. Indeed, their reserved ways hide many stellar virtues. They understand the value of hard work; they have great inner strength and can analyze any situation in a systematic and detached manner. Hence, contrary to popular belief, Shani-types are just as likely to excel in the mundane world as other graha types.

Shani-types match the determination and ambition of Mangala-types, but they are more deliberate, strategic and focused. Having the gift of patience, they take time to map out each and every step required to reach a goal—a process that impatient Mangala-types could never endure.

When it comes to spirituality, Shani-types have a leg up on most other planetary types. They approach spiritual practice with dedication and consistency. If ever a yogi or yogini can control his/her senses to achieve deep states of meditation, it is the Shani-type.

Mental inclinations: Jyotisha scripture assigns Shani the mental guna of tamas, for Shani-types often have a sense of being overburdened with responsibilities and obligations. Furthermore, they can be suspicious, manipulative, rigid or controlling in their ways. Let rajas instead dominate the mindset of the Shani-type and excessive fear and anxiety sets in and insecurities surface.

Yet, all stellar attributes described earlier are prominent in Shani-types when a sattvic mindset is maintained. The person is secure, practical and grounded in thought and responsible and accountable in action. The mind is deep and adept in profound philosophical thought.

Pitta Graha Archetypes
Surya: leader of the pack

Dosha   pitta
Guna   sattva

Surya-types are of medium but squarish build, moderate muscle tone and medium-size. Their skin is soft and warm and has an oily hue to it. The hair is fine and soft. Early greying or balding are typical signs of a Surya-type.

Surya-type individuals are natural born leaders. They are endowed with charisma and have an air of royalty. With their warmth and vitality, they instantly attract the attention of those around them. Indeed, behind every Surya-type is a loyal retinue. This is important to extroverted Surya-types, for they thrive on recognition. Confident, independent and accomplished, they epitomize solar power.

Having strong paternal instincts, Surya-types are drawn to roles that require wisdom and maturity. They may be an elder in the community or a leader of a state or nation. They are likely to assume this same position within their immediate and extended family. People seek their advice and leadership.

Their exuberance bubbles up from a seemingly endless supply of energy. With their sunny outlook, they inspire and motivate others. Most importantly, Surya-types place a high value on "right" living. Hence, they are naturally spiritually inclined.

Mental inclinations: Surya is one of the three sattvic grahas. Thus, Surya-types are well known for their consistency and steadfastness, strong sense of independence and self-reliance, love of truth and intellectual acumen. They exude a sense of warmth and friendliness.

Yet, even sattvic Surya-types can display rajasic or tamasic tendencies. When rajas overtakes their naturally sattvic mentality, there can be excessive pride, a sense of superiority and egotism. At times, this is accompanied with the desire for power, name and fame and delusions of grandeur. Let tamas prevail and, instead, resentfulness and envy, lack of confidence and fear of failure or intolerance are displayed.

Mangala: nothing ventured, nothing gained

Dosha	pitta
Guna	tamas

Mangala-types are of average build, slender waistline and with good muscle tone. Their skin has a rosy tint to it and there is a tendency towards rashes or moles. The eyes are of average size but are piercing.

Self-assured and strong-willed, Mangala-types eagerly take on challenges that come their way. Rarely recoiling from a threat, they march onto the battlefield of life with vigor and courage. They seek out adventure and take risks. "Nothing ventured, nothing gained" is their catch-call. Their resourcefulness and adeptness fuels their determination to succeed where others have failed.

You can spot a Mangala-type by their spirited, upbeat attitude and passion for life. As with their Surya-type cousins who are also energized by the fire element, Mangala-types are self-sufficient, assertive and independent. But, more intense than radiant and warm Surya-types, They embody the sharp and heating qualities of fire. Mangala-types thrive on competition and are bold, adventurous and direct.

However, their physical strength and courage is secondary to their enterprising minds and mental endurance. Mangala-types are willing to roll the dice, so they are usually the first to break new ground or venture into unchartered territory. They are often innovators and pioneers of scientific advancements.

With so much mental and physical power, Mangala-types are unstoppable once they focus on something.

Mental inclinations: Despite the nobler sattvic qualities mentioned above, Mangala-types must be constantly on guard, for they are frequently overtaken by inherent tamasic tendencies. In a tamasic Mangala-type mindset, this shows as hostility, extreme intolerance, destructive behavior and rage or hatred. Alternatively, under more rajasic circumstances, their courageous ways can turn reckless and impulsive; their sharp, penetrating intellect can become critical and self-centered; or their self-motivated ways may promote selfishness and unnecessary competitiveness.

Kapha Graha Archetypes
Chandra: intuitive and in-tune

Dosha	kapha-vata, but more vata when a dark moon
Guna	sattva

Chandra-types are one of the easiest to spot. They have a firm, round physique, full face, and large, wide, charming eyes. Their skin is thick, smooth, moist and cool to the touch. Their hair is thick, soft and wavy. Along with the Shukra-types, they are natural beauties.

While Surya-types are characteristic of the fire element, Chandra-types reflect the soothing water element. They are adaptable and intimately tuned in to their environment. Just as a river seeks to merge with the ocean, Chandra-types seek union with others. Relationships, especially familial ones, are a top priority, and home and family are central to domestically-oriented Chandra-types.

Chandra-types live in the realm of emotions and feelings. They sensitively connect with others and nature, and gain insights and wisdom through these connections.

No doubt a distinguishing feature of Chandra-types is their nurturing and protective manner. Being kind-hearted and compassionate, they love to help others. Thus, they are frequently involved in community support programs. Alternatively, they may take up the cause of protecting Mother Earth, her resources and her creatures.

Mental inclinations: Due to their loving, patient and nurturing ways, Chandra-types are naturally inclined toward sattvic thoughts and actions. At their best, they live in the moment, are connected to the world around them and sensitive to the needs of others.

Should a more rajasic nature surface, emotions become unstable and the person may be preoccupied with feelings and become excessively sentimental. The rajasic Chandra-type often fits the descriptive of "drama queen". Under tamasic influences, apathy or self-pity surfaces, along with mental dullness and cloudy thinking. The person may experience frequent states of moodiness, often attributable to his or her unwillingness to forgive and forget the hurtful actions of others.

Guru: aim beyond the stars

Dosha	kapha
Guna	sattva

Guru-types have bulky bodies and deep melodious voices. Their chests are prominent and their bone structure large. Indeed, everything about Guru-types is larger than life: their voice, wisdom, enthusiasm, optimism and often even their physical stature. You notice them easily, for their jovial persona fills the room.

Morally inclined, they tend to live according to the rules and regulations of society. It may appear that Guru-types are rather conventional. Indeed, this is usually true of their outer life. However, their profound wisdom and fascination with uncovering the truth affords them a novel philosophical perspective that originates from deep introspection and wisdom.

Nothing seems impossible for Guru-types, particularly if it involves defending justice, protecting the underdog or just changing the world. No cause is too grandiose, no odds too minuscule, to incite Guru-types to action. In their optimism, they reach for the stars and beyond. However, their approach in such endeavors is teamwork. Along with Shukra and Chandra-types, Guru-types insist on collaboration and the subordination of personal acclaims for the overall eminence of the group.

Their inborn sagacity, extraverted manner and amicable appearance allow Guru-types access to privileged circles. Hence, they easily procure generous support and funding for their numerous philanthropic causes.

Mental inclination: Guru is the last of the three sattvic grahas (Surya and Chandra are the other two). In addition to the above noted sattvic qualities, Guru-types are deeply grateful for all that life offers them. They are tolerant and peaceful-loving people.

Should all this sound too good to be true, perhaps it is. Sooner or later a stressful transit or challenging dasha comes along and rajas or tamas overtakes the sattvic mind. Rajas creates greed and hoarding, pretentiousness and/or the need to hold firmly onto excessively orthodox principles. Tamasic traits exhibited in Guru-types can include spiritual apathy or complete lack of faith, insensitivity towards others or an overwhelming sense of despair and gloom.

Shukra: sensual and tactile

Dosha   kapha-vata
Guna   rajas

True to their kapha nature, Shukra-types tend to have heavy thighs, arms and belly. Their voice is pleasant and their eyes, soft and charming.

Having great social grace, Shukra-types easily connect with all types of people. In fact, no one enjoys being with others more, whether at an important social gathering or in a simple conversation with a friend. With their diplomacy, charm and power of persuasion, they are at their best when working a crowd. Always knowing the right people to bring together for a cause or project, Shukra-types are expert in the field of human resources and just as notable for their skill in giving advice.

Sensual and tactile, they have a good eye for color and design and envision a world in which all things are artistically arrayed to appeal to the senses—beginning with themselves. Their search for beauty and love leads them to nature, as well as to truth and meaning.

While Guru-types are famed for their optimism and enthusiasm, Shukra-types are renowned for their idealistic, relational, and romantic perspective on life. They live to share life with others, particularly an intimate partner. Their self-worth and confidence blossoms when they are part of a caring, committed relationship.

As creators of music, dance, poetry and other forms of expression, Shukra-types make the world a more delightful place.

Mental inclinations: Like Budha, the other fast-orbiting inner graha, Shukra is inherently rajasic. When rajas dominates in a Shukra-type, there is overindulgence in the senses and an excessive emphasis on materialism. Love becomes conditional and, at times, possessive. There is insensitivity to the needs of others and lack of diplomacy. In contrast, the tamasic side of Shukra-types manifests as laziness and outright disrespect for others. When it comes to matters of love, tamasic Shukra-types are expert in the use of personal charisma and sexual or verbal manipulation to get their way.

Chapter 5: Constitutional Strength and Vitality

Introduction

The great Vedic astrologer, Sage Parashara, instructs on the importance of the Lagna: "O Brahmin, first of all, estimate the evils and other factors through the ascendant before declaring the effects of the twelve bhavas."[1] According to this enlightened seer, the effects of *all* other bhavas are predicated on the Lagna. This dictum is particularly true when evaluating health. Thus, our discussion on the inherent strength of one's constitution focuses on the Lagna and its Lagnesha.

In this chapter, important yogas for health and ill-health are introduced. We saw in *Your Healing Stars: Volume I*, that yogas are powerful planetary combinations that can override other birth chart configurations. As such, yogas are indicators of fixed karma and can enhance the accuracy of our birth chart interpretations. Also recall from Volume I, that the karma phala (fruits of actions) of yogas are at times described in exaggerated ways by shastra. This technique, known as *artha vada*, is illustrated in the following sections.

The Importance of the Lagna and Lagnesha

The body, its hue (complexion), its form, its characteristics and qualities, fame, happiness or unhappiness, residence abroad,[2] splendor and strength and weakness are the products, say the wise astrologers, of the Lagna of the birth chart.[3]

The *sva sthana* (place of self), or Lagna, is that space in the sky that is rising on the eastern horizon at the time of birth. Together with the Lagnesha, it represents one's physical constitution, psychological orientation, personality construct, confidence, self-esteem and overall health and wellbeing. The individual's quality of life and his overall sense of purpose and momentum are delineated by the Lagna and its Lagnesha ("Lagna-Lagnesha").

When the Lagna-Lagnesha are well-conditioned, one's life force is vibrant and his constitution strong. In this case, potential diseases shown in the birth chart are less serious and infrequent or more readily overcome. On the other hand, a poorly-conditioned Lagna-Lagnesha indicate a constitution that is more susceptible to ill-health. Moreover, the person's capacity to recover quickly from sickness and disease is impaired.

Hence, as with any birth chart assessment, the first step in our health evaluation process is to ascertain the condition of the Lagna and its Lagnesha. Using our bhava-bhavesha condition spectrum that we established in *Your Healing Stars: Volume I*, determine where along this continuum the Lagna-Lagnesha fall.

---

[1] *Maharshi Parashara's Brihat Parashara Hora Sastra*, R. Santhanam (translator), Vol. 1, Chapter 9.1. Ranjan Publication, 2000.
[2] In ancient times it was considered unfortunate if a person had to leave their motherland and take up residency in a foreign country. Hence, "residence abroad" means one's misfortunes in life.
[3] *Vaidyanatha Dikshita's Jataka Parijata*, V. Subramanya Sastri (translator), Vol. III, Chapter XI.13. Rajan Publications, 2004.

Figure 2: Bhava-Bhavesha Condition Spectrum

poorly-conditioned bhava-bhavesha
(i.e., bhavesha is weak, destabilized and poorly-placed; bhava is destabilized)

well-conditioned bhava-bhavesha
(i.e., bhavesha is strong, stabilized and well-placed; bhava is stabilized)

ordinary bhava-bhavesha
(i.e., bhavesha is ordinary; bhava has no factors of stabilization or destabilization)

Yogas for Health and Illness

Next, our attention turns to yogas that support (or deny) a robust and healthy constitution as indicated by the Lagna and its Lagnesha. Two sets of yogas are presented: *parvata* (mountain or rock) and *kahala* (large) *yoga* and *chamara* (an insignia of royalty) and *ava* (bring down or lower) *yoga*.

Parvata and kahala yoga

Parvata yoga emphasizes the condition of the dispositor (i.e., the bhavesha) of the Lagnesha. A strongly conditioned dispositor supports the affairs of its bhava and those of any grahas occupying its bhava. Hence, when the dispositor of the Lagnesha qualifies for parvata yoga, it adds strength to the Lagnesha and all that it represents, including health.

Requirements for parvata yoga are: the dispositor of the Lagnesha must be sva rashi or exalted *and* placed in a kendra or trine. Phala Deepika calls our attention to several auspicious results of this yoga: "Those born with Parvata yoga possess limitless wealth, happiness and perpetual gains. He commands authority over the earth."[4]

Terrance: Cancer Lagna

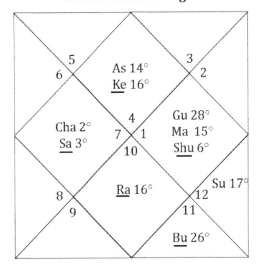

When we extend these same qualifications to the dispositor of the dispositor of the Lagnesha, then kahala yoga forms: such dispositor must be sva rashi or exalted *and* placed in a kendra or trine. Kahala yoga is one step removed from the Lagnesha, which means that it will have less impact. Still, it has a positive influence on the person's health and all other Lagna affairs. Phala Deepika describes the karma phala of this yoga: "The native born with a kahala yoga in his birth chart is wise, prosperous, cheerful, benevolent, noble, kind and propitious."[5]

Let us examine the Cancer-ruled Lagna chart of our client Terrance, who is in his mid-sixties. (Terrance's birth chart was presented in

---

[4] *Mantreswara's Phala Deepika*, S.S. Sareen (translator), Chapter 6.35. Sagar Publications, 2001.
[5] Ibid.

Chapter 3.) First determine where on our condition spectrum the Lagna-Lagnesha fall. The Lagnesha (Chandra) is strong (dig bala and bright moon) and well-placed in the kendra 4B. Despite its stabilization by Guru and Shukra, the Lagnesha (Chandra) *as well as* the Lagna is greatly destabilized by strongly conditioned Shani and Mangala, and Ketu occupies the Lagna. Still, since the Lagnesha has two factors of strength, we would place the Lagna-Lagnesha to the right of center on our condition spectrum. How far to the right will depend on the presence of other yogas for heath and ill-health.

For parvata yoga, Shukra (the dispositor of the Lagnesha) must be sva rashi or exalted and placed in a kendra or trine.[6] In Terrance's chart, Shukra occupies the kendra 10B and is strong (retrograde) but not sva rashi or exalted.

Next see if there is kahala yoga. Kahala yoga requires that the dispositor of the Lagnesha's dispositor is sva or exalted and placed in a kendra or trine. We just identified Shukra as the dispositor of the Lagnesha. Now we must determine if Shukra's dispositor meets these same criteria. Shukra is placed in Aries and its dispositor Mangala is sva rashi and occupies a kendra. This qualifies for kahala yoga and adds support to Terrance's overall constitution.

Chamara and ava yoga

Chamara and ava yoga draw attention to the combined condition of the Lagna and its Lagnesha.

The auspicious chamara yoga forms when the Lagnesha is strong and well-placed *and* the Lagna *or* the Lagnesha is stabilized by the influence of a shubha graha.[7] According to Sage Mantreswara, chamara yoga supports longevity and health, among other things: "The person having chamara yoga gains more and more importance day by day like the waxing Moon and is of a virtuous disposition. He is reputed, a leader of mankind, *enjoying longevity* and abundant prosperity."[8]

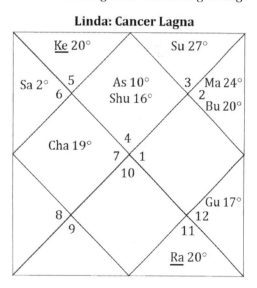

In contrast, ava yoga adversely impacts health. Ava yoga forms when the Lagnesha is weak and poorly-placed *and* the Lagna *or* the Lagnesha is destabilized by the influence of a papa graha.[9] The result of ava yoga as described by Mantreswara is: "The man born in ava yoga is insignificant, suffers from the extremes of poverty, from humiliation, is *short-lived* and associates himself with wicked people. He is of

---

[6] Note that we can extrapolate from the underlying principle of parvata yoga, that when the dispositor of the Lagnesha is weak and poorly placed, the health is harmed.
[7] Generally, Chandra, Budha, Guru and Shukra are considered shubha grahas. Refer to *Your Healing Stars: Volume I, Fundamentals of Vedic Astrology* for exceptions to this general rule.
[8] *Mantreswara's Phala Deepika*, S.S. Sareen (translator), Chapter 6.45. Sagar Publications, 2001.
[9] Surya, Mangala, Shani, Rahu and Ketu are considered papa grahas.

Chapter 5 Constitutional Strength and Vitality

poor character and disabled. *His condition* (i.e., life and health) *is mostly unsteady."*[10]

By way of illustration, let us take a look at the Cancer-ruled Lagna chart above that belongs to Linda, a 65 year-old female client. Firstly, notice that Linda's prakruti is kapha: strongly conditioned (sva rashi) Guru (a kapha graha) influences the Lagna, while the placement of Shukra (also a kapha graha) in the Lagna adds confluence.

Does parvata or kahala yoga form in Linda's chart? The dispositor of the Lagnesha (Chandra) is Shukra. Shukra occupies a kendra, but is not sva or exalted. Shukra's dispositor is Chandra. Chandra is strong (dig bala) and placed in a kendra, but is not sva or exalted. Thus, parvata and kahala yoga are not present in Linda's birth chart.[11]

Does chamara or ava yoga exist? The requirements for chamara yoga are met: the Lagnesha (Chandra) is strong (dig bala) and well-placed (4B) *and* the Lagna is stabilized by shubha grahas Shukra and Guru. Chamara yoga supports Linda's physical constitution and promotes good health.

Jody: Cancer Lagna

```
           Bu 10° Shu 11°
           Ke 17° Su 28°
    Sa 10°     5       As 12°    3
              6        Ma 24°      2
                     4
                  7 \ 1
                    10
                              Gu 18°
              8                12
              9          11
                       Ra 17°
                       Cha 25°
```

In contrast is Jody's birth chart, also a Cancer-ruled Lagna chart. Jody is a 61 year-old client with a kapha prakruti: strongly conditioned (sva rashi and retrograde) Guru (a kapha graha) aspects the Lagna. Pitta is the secondary dosha because strongly conditioned (sva rashi) Surya aspects the Lagnesha (Chandra).

Notice that parvata and kahala yogas are not present in Jody's chart. Does chamara or ava yoga exist in Jody's chart?

A lunar eclipse occurred on the day of Jody's birth which was visible at her birth location.[12] Thus, the Lagnesha (Chandra) is weak and poorly-placed in the trik-dusthana 8B and both

---

[10] *Mantreswara's Phala Deepika*, S.S. Sareen (translator), Chapter 6.58. Sagar Publications, 2001.

[11] However, notice that the Lagnesha (Chandra) is *parivartana* (exchanges) with the 4B bhavesha (Shukra). When two bhaveshas ruling positive bhavas are parivartana, the bhava affairs associated with each are strengthened. It is almost as if each bhavesha occupies its own bhava. Parivartana and other mutual and non-mutual graha relationships are described in *Your Healing Stars: Volume I, Fundamental Principles of Vedic Astrology*.

[12] Consistent with the principle of pratyaksha introduced in *Your Healing Stars: Volume I, Fundamental Principles of Vedic Astrology*, for an eclipse to be significant, the birth location must have been in the path of the eclipse. This information is available on the NASA website. Although the moon is full during a lunar eclipse, because it is invisible, we do not consider Chandra to be strong on that day (i.e., Chandra is not of mixed condition).

Chapter 5 Constitutional Strength and Vitality

the Lagna and Lagnesha are destabilized by the weak papa graha Mangala.[13] This is a good example of ava yoga.

Shubha and ashubha yoga

The next two sets of yogas involve the stabilization and destabilization of the Lagna.

Shubha (benevolence, splendor) and *ashubha* (unpleasant, disagreeable) *yoga* are based upon the familiar principle that shubha grahas influencing a bhava stabilize the affairs of that bhava, while papa grahas destabilize its affairs. Parashara awards yoga status to such influences when the all-important Lagna is involved: a shubha graha *occupying* the Lagna forms shubha yoga and a papa graha *occupying* the Lagna forms ashubha yoga.[14] Shubha yoga supports the general health of the individual and ashubha yoga adversely impacts health.

Any ordinary or strongly conditioned shubha graha occupying the Lagna technically forms shubha yoga. However, graha stabilization and bhava rulerships must be considered.

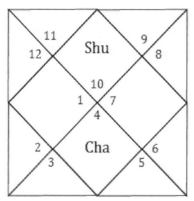

To illustrate shubha yoga, imagine a Capricorn-ruled Lagna occupied by Shukra and aspected by Chandra. Shukra is ordinary, stabilized and the bhavesha for the positive 5B and 10B. This is a powerful shubha yoga that supports a healthy physical constitution.

What if, instead, Guru occupies this same Capricorn-ruled Lagna? In this case, Guru is of mixed condition (dig bala and debilitated) and the bhavesha for two dusthana bhavas (3B and 12B). As you can imagine, this configuration harms the individual's health.

In contrast to shubha yoga, ashubha yoga qualifies when a papa graha of any condition occupies the Lagna. Most inauspicious is a weak papa graha, for its condition greatly destabilizes the Lagna. Once again, secondary factors of stabilization and bhava rulerships should be considered. A weak papa graha that is destabilized and the bhavesha for two dusthana bhavas is particularly detrimental to health.

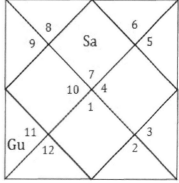

To illustrate ashubha yoga, let us assume for a Libra-ruled Lagna, that Shani occupies the Lagna and Guru aspects it from the 5B. Despite Guru's stabilizing influence, strongly conditioned (exalted) Shani forms ashubha yoga.

Still, since Shani is the bhavesha for two positive bhavas (4B and 5B), the individual will derive certain benefits from

---

[13] Notice that Budha and Shukra are in a planetary war. Because of its relative brightness on the day of Jody's birth, Shukra wins the planetary war. As the winner, Shukra is destabilized but not weak. (See *Your Healing Stars: Volume I, Fundamental Principles of Vedic Astrology*.)
[14] When qualifying yogas, Surya is considered a papa graha.

this planetary configuration. For example, innate intelligence (Shani as the 5B bhavesha) is a key attribute of this person. He also has a sense of responsibility and accountability (exalted Shani) that developed from his early childhood environment (Shani as the 4B bhavesha). Furthermore, Shani's karaka significations are compelling forces in the person's life. He will be disciplined and possess great fortitude and ambition.

These benefits do not override the karma phala of ashubha yoga, but they do provide intelligence, a sense of accountability and discipline which will help to mitigate the effects of ashubha yoga on the health of the individual.

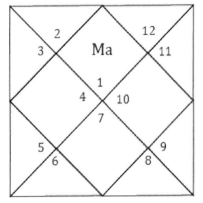

Let us look at one more birth chart example of ashubha yoga. What if for an Aries-ruled Lagna, Mangala occupies the Lagna? Since strongly conditioned (sva rashi) Mangala is also the Lagnesha, we would expect a healthy and vibrant constitution.

Yet, even under this scenario, Mangala forms ashubha yoga. A papa graha that is the bhavesha for the bhava it occupies harms the sensitive affairs (including the internal organs of the body) associated with its bhava placement and does so in a manner consistent with its papa nature.[15] In this way, despite a healthy constitution, the person will experience the effects of ashubha yoga. Perhaps the person's impulsive and daring nature (Mangala in Aries) causes accidents that injure the head (represented by the space of the Lagna) and/or pitta-type conditions (Mangala), such as migraines or early hair loss (also represented by the space of the Lagna).

However, since Mangala is the Lagnesha, the individual will have tremendous self-confidence, a strong sense of individuality and great enthusiasm for life. He will approach adverse situations in a courageous manner, while all the time passionately pursuing his aspirations. All these are characteristics of Mangala in Aries.

Let us now return to Jody's birth chart, which we examined in the last section. In addition to ava yoga, notice that ashubha yoga forms due to the placement of Mangala in the Lagna. Most detrimental is its debilitation status, i.e., Mangala is weakly conditioned. For Jody, there is not one (ava yoga), but two (ashubha yoga) yogas that adversely affect the strength of her constitution and ability to resist disease.

Recall that yogas are indicators of fixed karma. This is especially true when multiple yogas with similar karma phala are present in the birth chart. However, even in cases of fixed karma, it is important to encourage the client to take responsibility for his or her health by following an Ayurvedic diet and health-promoting daily practices.

---

[15] The general rule stipulated in *Your Healing Stars: Volume I, Fundamental Principles of Vedic Astrology* is as follows. A papa graha influencing (by aspect or occupation) its own bhava fortifies the affairs of the bhava. For this rule to apply, the papa graha must not be weak. Still, because of its papa nature, the graha harms the *sukshma* (subtle) or most delicate aspects of the bhava. This includes the happiness that one gains from the matters represented by the bhava as well as the personal relationships and health aspects of the bhava.

Lastly, at times, both shubha *and* ashubha yoga are present. In these cases, the fruits of both yogas manifest.

Shubha kartari and papa kartari yoga

The importance of a stabilized Lagna is emphasized in a second set of yogas know as *shubha kartari* (auspicious scissors) and *papa kartari* (inauspicious scissors) *yoga*. When the Lagna is flanked by shubha grahas, shubha kartari yoga forms and, when flanked by papa grahas, papa kartari yoga forms. Once again, important graha qualifiers include condition and, secondarily, stabilization and bhava rulerships.

Sage Mantreswara includes the impact on health when citing the karma phala of these two yogas: "A person born in shubha kartari yoga is *long-lived*, fearless, *free from sickness*, without foe, happy and rich. Those born in papa kartari yoga are poor, unclean, miserable, bereft of wife and children, *disabled and* of *short life*."[16] (Here is a perfect illustration of artha vada, or an exaggeration of yoga results.)

In our Leo-ruled Lagna chart example, the Lagna is flanked by shubha grahas Budha and Shukra. This forms shubha kartari yoga. Notice that Budha is strongly conditioned (sva rashi) and the bhavesha for the neutral 2B and positive 11B. Shukra is ordinary in condition and the bhavesha for the mild-dusthana 3B and positive 10B.

However, since ashubha yoga is also present (Mangala occupies the Lagna), we can expect the karma phala of both yogas to manifest.

Parvata and kahala and chamara and ava yogas are more rare than shubha/ashubha and shubha kartari/papa kartari yogas. Hence, these latter yogas are to be interpreted within the context of the former ones.

To illustrate this concept, let us return to Linda's Cancer-ruled birth chart. We noted earlier the presence of chamara yoga, which supports Linda's general health and wellbeing. Notice that Shukra forms shubha yoga, another yoga for wellness. This shows additional fixed karma concerning Linda's health. But how should we interpret the impact of the papa kartari yoga (Ketu and Surya flank the Lagna) in light of chamara yoga? The harmful effects of papa kartari yoga are mitigated by Linda's overall vibrant health.

Still, we learned in *Your Healing Stars: Volume I* that the results of any yoga plays out in the person's life to a greater or lesser degree based on other natal factors, and under conducive dasha-bhuktis and transits.[17] In the next chapter, we will revisit Linda's birth chart and examine the health events triggered by the papa kartari yoga and the offsetting effects of

---

[16] *Mantreswara's Phala Deepika*, S.S. Sareen (translator), Chapter 6.11. Sagar Publications, 2001.
[17] The Vimshottari system and planetary transits are covered in *Your Healing Stars: Volume I, Fundamental Principles of Vedic Astrology*.

chamara and shubha yoga.

It is often tricky to predict the results of yogas. Even when a planetary configuration qualifies as yoga, other birth chart indicators and yogas may suggest that its results will only partially or not at all fructify. At other times, the strict requirements for yoga are not met, but there are certain compensating factors that support its results in part or fully. Here, the experience of a Jyotishi is critical for accurate birth chart predictions.

Surya, Graha Karaka for Health

A graha's role as a bhavesha is more chart-specific than its role as a karaka because its bhava rulership will vary according to the Lagna. Therefore, when interpreting any aspect of life, including health, primary importance is given to the bhavesha and its bhava (or Lagna and its Lagnesha), and secondary importance to the graha karaka.

Surya is the planetary ruler of Leo, the natural 5B rashi of the zodiac. The central fire of the stomach and small intestine (jathara agni) and the fire of the liver (bhuta agni) are represented by this bhava and rashi.[18] Thus, Surya represents the principal digestive functions of agni, which convert food we eat into the energy that powers everything we do. The heart and the circulatory system, responsible for carrying oxygen and nutrients to each cell, are represented by this same bhava and graha. As well as giving life, Surya-related bodily systems defend the body against disease, making Surya the graha karaka for overall health.

Surya's essence is *tejas* (radiant light), the foundation for all transformational processes in the physical and subtle bodies. In the mental realm, tejas allows for digestion and transformation of information into comprehension and right knowledge. It supports mental clarity and provides fortitude and intellectual courage so one may penetrate deeper truths. Hence, Surya imparts the capacity for brilliant self-expression and visionary intelligence, other 5B attributes.

On the subtlest level, tejas is the fervor of spiritual practice, or *tapas*, which cleanses and purifies the subtle bodies. Under the Sankhya system of tattvas, this graha represents purusha, or enlightened awareness.[19] Thus, Surya is responsible for our spiritual aspirations and the unfolding of consciousness.

Surya is depicted in Jyotisha shastra as a swift, restless courser who mounts the heights of the sky on a well-decorated golden chariot furnished with golden yokes and drawn by seven white-footed bay steeds. According to Shri Aurobindo, the horse "is an image of the great dynamic force of Life, of the vital and nervous energy, and is constantly coupled (*in the Vedas*) with other images that

---

[18] See Chapter 8: "The Kalapurusha of the Birth Chart" for a complete listing of the organs, limbs and bodily functions represented by the twelve bhavas.
[19] See "Chapter 12: "The Interplay of the Tridoshas and Trigunas" for a description of Sankhya and its 25 tattvas.

symbolize consciousness."[20]

Sphujidhvaja, author of the Jyotisha text, *Yavanajataka*, describes the many imperial attributes of Surya and its anthropomorphic form: "The Sun is a handsome, square-limbed man, whose spares hair is soft and curly and has loose ends. His eyes are sweet and wide; his body gleams like molten god. It is his nature to be inscrutable and firm; he is a fierce, steadfast hero who is hard to assail, a powerful leader whose body-hair is yellow like purified gold and whose deeds are swift and righteous. His essence is of bone (*i.e., Surya is the karaka for the asthi vaha srotas, i.e., bone tissue and its pathway*)."[21]

Important facets of the personality, such as confidence, self-worth and strength of character, are other significations related to Surya. Along with health, these factors impact our ability to withstand difficulties and live life with consistency and steadfastness. In the above scriptural passage, Sphujidhvaja assigns asthi vaha srotas to Surya. An important function of this srotas is to provide support (*dharana*) and protection to the body, just as the life-giving golden rays of the sun promote a healthy and disease-resistant constitution.[22]

When natal Surya is well-conditioned, one's digestive fire and metabolic functions are hardy and the heart and circulatory system are strong. Thus, the person's constitution is robust and resistant to disease. The person approaches life with confidence. He is consistent and assumes ownership for actions and their results. His intelligence serves as a dharmic asset in life.

When Surya is poorly-conditioned, the digestive fire is low and one's ability to overcome or resist sickness is compromised. Often, self-esteem and confidence suffer, causing lack of consistency and courage. These attributes harm the health of the individual and his sense of purpose.

Evaluate the condition of graha karaka Surya and determine where along our graha condition continuum it falls. Use this information to confirm or modify your Lagna-Lagnesha and yoga findings.

Figure 3: Graha Condition Spectrum

poorly-conditioned graha	**well-conditioned graha**
(i.e., weak, destabilized, poorly-placed)	(i.e., strong, stabilized, well-placed)

Summary

In summary, after determining your client's prakruti, the next step in the health evaluation process is a methodical assessment of his or her constitutional strength and general vitality. For this purpose, consider the following.

---

[20] *Secret of the Veda*, Sri Aurobindo, pg. 93. Lotus Press, 1995.
[21] *Yavanajataka of Sphujidhvaja*, D. Pingree (translator), pg. 7, Harvard University Press, 1978.
[22] Refer to Chapter 10: "Dhatus-Srotamsi and the Grahas".

1. Condition of the Lagna-Lagnesha
2. Yogas for health: parvata and kahala yoga (primary), chamara yoga (primary), and shubha and shubha kartari yoga (secondary)
3. Yogas for ill-health: ava yoga (primary), papa and papa kartari yoga (secondary)
4. Condition of Surya, graha karaka for health

Chapter 6: Vikruti and the Trik-Dusthanas

Introduction

The Lagna and its Lagnesha represent a person's physical constitution and personal characteristics (prakruti). Hence, along with yogas for health, they are the most important gauges for a person's overall physical health and wellbeing. These concepts are presented and illustrated in the previous chapter.

A person's prakruti does not vary in the course of his lifetime. But people are subject to a host of internal and external factors that can create a temporary or longer-term shift away from their underlying prakruti. This shift or variation from prakruti is called vikruti, which means 'deviation'. When a person deviates from his or her inherent doshic constitution, he or she becomes vulnerable to disease and sickness. (For an example of the standard set of client questions that can be used by Ayurvedic practitioners to assess a client's vikruti, see Appendix C.)

Improper diet, lack of exercise, insufficient sleep, stress and worry are examples of internal factors that promote doshic imbalance. External influences such as seasonal changes, environmental conditions and socio-economic circumstances can also cause vikruti. When doshas become disturbed, pathological changes can happen and toxins (*ama*) often build up. Left untreated, these changes eventually put various bodily tissues (dhatus) and their channels (srotamsi, plural for srotas) at risk.

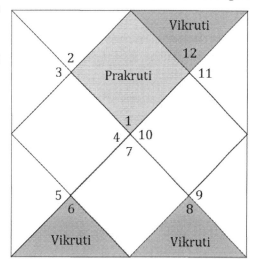

The trik-dusthana bhavas (6B, 8B, 12B) function just like other bhavas, in that they represent the health of certain bodily organs and limbs. This is the topic of Chapter 8: "The Kalapurusha of the Birth Chart". However, the trik-dusthana bhavas play another important role in health and disease because these bhavas and their bhaveshas are indicators of vikruti.

In this chapter, a general framework is established to help us determine the unique impact of the trik-dusthanas on the health of the individual. Conclusions that you draw from applying this process are valid *only* when considered within the broader context of the birth chart, particularly the condition of the Lagna-Lagnesha and yogas for health and ill-health.

The Tricky Trik-Dusthanas

Vedic sacrifices are often performed at transitional points (*sandhis*) of the day or year. For example, Chaturmasyas (seasonal ceremonies) are performed as one season ends and another commences; the New and Full Moon ceremonies, as the moon transitions from its waxing to waning and waning to waxing phases, respectively, and the New Year Celebration, as the sun begins its northerly path. These sacrificial ceremonies help ensure the smooth continuance of the month, season and year during sensitive and unstable transition periods.

In a similar manner, the transitional times of the day represent sandhi points, or vulnerable gaps. These "gaps" are knit together through sacrificial acts, such as the Agnihotra (performed immediately before sunrise and after sunset), to ensure the continuance of another day. These gaps are represented by the trik-dusthana bhavas. The 12B is immediately after sunrise, the 8B, immediately before sunset, and the 6B, immediately after sunset. Although not considered a dusthana bhava, the 2H is also located in a transitional place in the sky (immediately before sunrise).

6B-6B bhavesha

An astrologer ought to divine diseases, enemies, bad habits and hurts that a person may have from the 6th house...[1]

The combative nature of the 6B qualifies it as a place of opponents and enemies. Yet, sometimes the most daunting adversaries of the 6B are not external, but rather the internal enemies of sickness and disease. Thus, when emphasizing the importance of the trik-dusthanas in predicting ill-health, Mantreswara, author of the well-known astrological text *Phala Deepika*, places particular importance on the 6B and its bhavesha. This makes the 6B-6B bhavesha primary indicators for doshic imbalances. "Anything about disease and sickness should be ascertained through those grahas occupying the 6th bhava, the bhavesha ruling the 6th bhava and grahas in association with the 6th bhava as well as grahas posited in the 8th and 12th bhavas."[2,3]

A *roga sthana* (place of sickness), the 6B represents various types of acute illness and disease. These health conditions are characterized by sudden onset and finite duration, such as many types of fevers, ulcers, influenza and inflammation due to injury or acute infection. This 6B *kshata sthana* (place of injuries) also denotes wounds, scars and various types of minimally invasive medical procedures (chiropractic manipulation, physical therapy, endoscopy, etc.). As *the* bhava of competition, it also indicates extreme physical exertion. Thus, all types of sport injuries (muscle injuries, torn ligaments, bone fractures, aches and pains) are 6B health issues.

These examples of 6B-related acute conditions and their treatments are quite common, and many can be remedied by medication or simple changes in diet, exercise and lifestyle. This is because the 6B is the only trik-dusthana that is also an upachaya bhava. With proper attention and effort, 6B affairs improve, including those related to health. Still, if ignored, 6B doshic imbalances can eventually intensify, spreading to dhatus and their srotamsi. The concept of progressive dosha disturbance is called *samprapti*, an Ayurveda theory that describes the dosha-based model of pathogenesis.

Importantly, the 6B and its bhavesha show not only our tendency towards acute disease, but also our ability to mitigate, delay or prevent such conditions by following health-sustaining

---

[1] *Vaidyanatha Dikshita's Jataka Parijata*, V. Subramanya Sastri (translator), Vol. III, Chapter XIII.71. Rajan Publications, 2004.
[2] *Mantreswara's Phala Deepika*, S.S. Sareen (translator), Chapter 14.1. Sagar Publications, 2001.
[3] Due to their adverse nature, Jyotisha assigns the term *chhidra* (defect or blemish) to grahas functioning as trik-dusthana bhaveshas and those that occupy their bhavas.

practices such as a proper dinacharya (daily routine) and daily exercise.[4] When strongly conditioned, the 6B-6B bhavesha indicate the individual's ability to adhere to these lifestyle practices that promote health and minimize doshic imbalance. When the 6B-6B bhavesha are poorly-conditioned, we can expect more frequent occurrences of acute ill-health and the person is less likely to embrace a healthy daily regime. Notice in the above opening quote that Jataka Parijata assigns "bad habits" to the 6B.

In summary, the dusthana nature of the 6B qualifies it as one capable of producing suffering from acute disorders and disease. Yet, its upachaya nature suggests that with persistent effort and proper daily routines, we can resist, defer or overcome such conditions.

The 2B is closely connected with the 6B, for it relates specifically to one's diet and its impact on vikruti. This *anna-panaka sthana* (place of food and drink) indicates our food choices and habits as well as our predisposition to alcohol, drugs and smoking.[5] When the 2B-2B bhavesha are poorly-conditioned, the client makes improper food choices and may have eating disorders, alcoholism or addiction to legal, illicit or pharmaceutical drugs. The 2B-2B bhavesha also shows one's susceptibility to food allergies.

8B-8B bhavesha

From the 8th house the following should be examined: longevity, death, rectum, mode of death, enjoyment of food,[6] service, being bitten and defeat.[7]

Lacking the upachaya nature of the 6B, the trik-dusthana 8B relates to diseases that are more systemic or deeply rooted. Being third (willpower, strength, courage) from the 6B (acute illnesses), the 8B represents health conditions that require great courage and fortitude to overcome.[8]

Whereas the 6B signifies health conditions of a finite duration, the 8B encompasses diseases that persist over long periods and generally cannot be prevented by vaccines or cured by simple medications. In a similar manner, the 6B represents minimally invasive surgeries and the 8B, major ones, such as those involving removal of limbs and organs. The emotional worries and anxieties of the 6B are also amplified in the 8B, producing habitual fears and phobias. This makes the physical and mental-emotional health concerns of the 8B more intense and grief-producing. It also justifies its Sanskrit name, *klesha sthana* (place of hardship and distress).

---

[4] All self-improvement regimens and disciplines are represented by the 6B, including yoga, martial arts and nutritional programs.

[5] The 2B-2B bhavesha also shows a person's taste preference. Each graha is associated with one of the 6 rasas (tastes): Surya (pungent), Chandra (salty), Mangala (bitter), Budha (blend of tastes), Guru (sweet), Shukra (sour), Shani (astringent) and Rahu or Ketu (unusual or vitiated tastes). Look to graha influences on the 2B and its bhavesha to assess the taste preference of the individual.

[6] 8B grahas cast their drishti on the 2B, giving pleasure (or displeasure) in food.

[7] *Vyankatesh Sharma Sarvarth Chintamani*, J.N. Bhasin (translator), Chapter 7.1. Sagar Publications, 2002.

[8] The principle of bhavat bhavam correlates each bhava in the birth chart to the bhava the same number away from it as it is from the Lagna. Refer to *Your Healing Stars: Volume I* for additional illustrations of bhavat bhavam.

Chronic disabilities, relentless pain, incurable diseases, epidemics (e.g., yellow fever, plague, smallpox, malaria, leprosy, HIV), natural disasters and war are other 8B medical atrocities. With Scorpio as the natural ruler of this bhava, there is often a cloud of mystery or secrecy surrounding 8B health conditions.

The 8B is called the *ayus sthana* (place of longevity) and *mritya sthana* (place of death). This seemingly contradictory designation is easily explained. Just as the 6B represents acute health conditions *as well as* our ability to overcome or evade such conditions, the 8B shows our tendency towards chronic states of disease *as well as* our ability to avoid or mitigate them.

Since longevity is the subject matter of the 8B, this bhava and its bhavesha are primary constituents in yogas for early and/or untimely death. Interestingly, the great sage Parashara offers the following cautionary advice regarding these yogas: "O Brahmin, for the benefit of mankind I narrate methods (*yogas*) of ascertaining longevity, but know that longevity is difficult even for gods to predict."[9]

12B-12B bhavesha

It is through the 12th house … that an astrologer should divine a person's wandering far away, misfortune, evil doom, liberality, the comforts of the bed, dignity and waste of wealth.[10]

An interesting aspect of the 12B is its association with "comforts of the bed", as mentioned in the above citation. The 12B shows the pleasures that one receives (or not) in bed, i.e., sexual intimacy. When this connotation is taken to the extreme, 12B bed pleasures can turn into sexual addictions and obsessions or become the source of marital conflict. This is seen from the bhavat bhavam position of the 12B as sixth (inimical relationships, conflict) from the 7B of marital happiness.

"Comforts of the bed" can also imply "lack of bed comfort", i.e., bed confinement. Hence, this *vinashaka sthana* (place of annihilation) includes those places reserved for prolonged periods of recovery, confinement or isolation (mental wards, convalescence homes, longer-term care facilities). This is in contrast to the 6B of outpatient clinics and short-term care facilities and the 8B of critical care units (CCUs), rehabilitation centers and health facilities that provide intensive care medicine.

The 6B and 12B axis is an important one relating to sickness and disease. A reflection bhava for the 6B of known enemies, the 12B represents our secret or hidden enemies, including invisible pathogens that threaten our physical health.[11] Left undetected and untreated, these enemies cause a gradual wasting or expenditure of the body. This same bhava reflection principle explains why the 12B indicates the consequences that a person will experience because of poor health habits shown by the 6B.

---

[9] *Maharshi Parashara's Brihat Parashara Hora Sastra*, R. Santhanam (translator), Vol. 1, Chapter 43.2-3. Ranjan Publication, 2000.
[10] *Vaidyanatha Diskshita's Jataka Parijata*, V. Subramanya Sastri (translator), Vol. III, Chapter XV.73. Rajan Publications, 2004.
[11] Refer to *Your Healing Stars: Volume I* for an explanation of bhava reflection, along with illustrations of this principle.

Lastly, its connection with the bed makes the 12B one of sleep and dreams. Sleep disorders such as insomnia, nightmares and sleep-walking are indicated by this bhava.

As with the 6B and 8B, the 12B shows the possibility of prolonged hospitalization or extended bedrest *as well as* our ability to avoid such situations.

Mangala, Shani and the Nodes of the Moon as Graha Karakas for the Trik-Dusthanas

The trik-dusthanas are the only bhavas with multiple (and solely) papa grahas as their graha karakas. The karakas for the 6B are Mangala (primary) and Shani (secondary); the 8B, Shani (primary) and Rahu (secondary); and the 12B, Ketu (primary) and Shani (primary). These malefics must be strong in order to help us fight the battles associated with the trik-dusthana bhavas. The primary graha karakas for the 6B and 8B are discussed below, followed by a discussion of Rahu and Ketu.

Mangala is the primary karaka for the 6B, and Shani is its secondary karaka. Not surprisingly, Shani and Mangala are also karakas for *mamsa dhatu* (muscle tissue), which gives strength and power to the body.[12] The psychological attributes of mamsa dhatu are those necessary to conquer the minefield of health conditions represented by this trik-dusthana: fortitude, determination and accountability (Shani) and will-power and courage (Mangala).[13] Mangala is also the karaka for the adrenal glands (represented by the 6B) that are responsible for our fight-or-flight response.[14]

Mangala is the force that empowers us to meet challenges head-on, and it gives us confidence that where there is a problem, there is a solution. The ram, an animal that denotes action, force, determination, power and drive, is its celestial animal. No wonder that this red hot graha is dubbed a fierce warrior and dauntless fighter. For his valorous and daring ways, Mangala is assigned the celestial cabinet post of army-commander-in-charge.

In his Jyotisha text *Yavanajataka*, Sphujidhvaja describes Mangala's fierce ways: "Mars is a hot and passionate man with flaming curly hair and a terrible red body. The corners of his eyes are bloodshot and he shines like a blazing fire. He is powerful in his vehemence and terrifying like Kumara (*Shiva's son*) . . . He is a hero, used to killing, taking and opposing. Clothed in red, he commits acts of violence and strength. His essence is of marrow (*i.e. Mangala is the karaka for bone marrow, where red blood cells (rakta dhatu) are produced*)."[15]

Mangala tops the list of 6B karakas for many other reasons, including his goal-oriented and results-driven approach. You won't find this graha frittering the day away analyzing the safest way forward. Instead, Mangala opts for quick, innovative and ground-breaking

---

[12] Refer to Chapter 10: "Dhatus-Srotamsi and the Grahas".
[13] Ibid.
[14] Refer to Chapter 8 for a description of the organs and limbs associated with each of the 12 bhavas.
[15] *Yavanajataka of Sphujidhvaja*, D. Pingree (translator), pg. 8. Harvard University Press, 1978.

solutions. These attributes, along with its physical strength and willpower, justifies Mangala as the graha karaka for 6B health concerns.

When natal Mangala is strong, the individual has the energy, strength and courage to combat ill-health and disease. In search of a solution, Mangala directs his keen intellect and problem-solving skills to the task.

On the other hand, if natal Mangala is weak, the person may lack the willpower, energy and drive to tackle 6B challenges and obstacles, including those related to health. Or, perhaps, when in search of health solutions, even the smallest roadblock appears daunting. Under either scenario, Mangala becomes the karaka for accidents, inflammations, burns and burn-outs, injuries and surgery—all acute conditions of the 6B.

Shani is the natural first choice as the 8B graha karaka. Its methodical, structured and cautious approach is quite contrary to the sometimes impulsive, superficial and quick-and-dirty ways of Mangala. Like any reputable doctor, Shani is most concerned about uncovering the underlying cause of an ailment, rather than treating its symptoms. As a bhava that represents longevity, Shani is it for the long-haul.

Manning the post of servant on Surya's celestial cabinet, Shani is known for its hard-working ways. This graha offers many tools for maneuvering through and around the sometimes grave health concerns associated with the 8B. It gives discipline, structure, perseverance, concentration and detachment. When it comes to strategic alternatives, Shani outshines all other grahas. Its celestial animal is the black crow, a rather ominous bird. The crow is an audacious animal that symbolizes transformation, a major 8B affair.

The 8B represents the final stage in the elimination of metabolic waste products via the feces, for it is the rectum and anal orifice of the Kalapurusha, and Shani is the graha karaka for *purisha vaha srotas* (large intestines, sigmoid colon, rectum and anal orifice).[16]

Many significations of Shani noted by Mantreswara are intrinsic or extrinsic culprits of the complicated 8B ailments, such as debt, poverty and hard labor. "From Saturn guess everything regarding longevity, death, fear, defamation, misery, degradation, sickness, poverty, misery, labor and menial work, reproach, sin, impurity, censure, misfortune, constancy, sense of guilt, association with and shelter under the low, buffalo, drowsiness, debts, iron, servitude, agricultural tools, litigation and captivity."[17]

When natal Shani is strong, the person is all the wiser for having experienced and overcome great hardships, including health challenges. The person assumes responsibility for personal health issues and works through them with patience and fortitude, tackling any roadblocks in a willful, deliberate and serious manner.

---

[16] Refer to Chapter 8: "The Kalapurusha of the Birth Chart" and Appendix F: "Channels of Nourishment and Elimination".
[17] *Mantreswara's Phala Deepika*, S.S. Sareen (translator), Chapter 2.7. Sagar Publications.

But when natal Shani is weak, the person struggles with daily regimes, and can feel burdened and overwhelmed by self-care tasks. Lacking a sense of empowerment, the person may feel victimized by circumstances and unable to see opportunities to change these for the better. In this case, Shani functions instead as a karaka for chronic or degenerative diseases, removal of organs or limbs, strife, fear, grief or depression and even death—all 8B health conditions.

Lastly, when it comes to matters of extreme or unusual health conditions, the nodes of the moon have a special affinity for the trik-dusthanas.

Representing exaggerated vata, Rahu, the head of the demoness snake, is the karaka for chronic vata illnesses and diseases, such as paralysis, lameness, Parkinson disease, multiple sclerosis, vertigo, emaciation, insomnia, vata-type comas (those that come as a result of concussion, compression, contusion) and convulsions. On a psychological level, Rahu creates phobias, neurosis, hallucination and mental disturbances.

The lioness is Rahu's celestial animal, for his grandfather, Sage Kasyapa, and wife Diti (bounded, limited, divided) gave birth to Simhika (lioness), who then parented Rahu.

A pitta graha depicted as the tail of the snake, Ketu represents extreme conditions of aggravated pitta, such as chronic fevers, epileptic seizures, viral or infectious diseases, pitta-type comas (encephalitic, hepatic, meningitis, cerebral hemorrhage) and drug addictions. Like Rahu, Ketu is the karaka for a host of psychological issues, including psychiatric disorders.

The turkey vulture, a scavenger bird, is Ketu's celestial animal. These birds feed mainly on dead animals, using their keen sense of smell to find fresh carcasses.

Despite their apparent abhorrent nature, even Rahu and Ketu find a place on Surya's celestial cabinet. They form the planetary army. While Ketu guards the King's homeland and that of his people, Rahu expands the kingdom by conquering new territory.

Evaluating the Trik-Dusthanas

Arishta (disastrous or fatal) *yogas* are planetary combinations that involve the trik-dusthana bhavas and their bhaveshas. These are yogas for ill-health and can indicate a shortened lifespan or a life that is plagued by serious health issues. We can extrapolate the principle of arishta yogas to better understand special considerations of the trik-dusthanas and their adverse impact on the health of an individual. As discussed in this section, these considerations include the preferred placement and strength of a trik-dusthana bhavesha and graha occupation of the trik-dusthana bhavas.

Preferred placement of a trik-dusthana bhavesha
A trik-dusthana bhavesha that influences the Lagna or Lagnesha brings the unwelcome matters of its bhava directly into the individual's physical and mental-emotional life. This can

be particularly harmful to health when the trik-dusthana bhavesha and/or the Lagna-Lagnesha are weakly conditioned. Hence, it is preferable that trik-dusthana bhaveshas not influence the Lagna or its Lagnesha.

From a practical perspective, it is a rare chart in which this occurs, particularly when the 6B, 8B and/or 12B are ruled by grahas casting multiple aspects (e.g., Mangala, Guru or Shani). Therefore, we must rely on a basic principle: a well-conditioned Lagna-Lagnesha greatly mitigate the effects of adverse birth chart configurations, including those for disease and ill-health.

Because the kendras are bhavas of action and manifestation as well as important pillars of life, it is also preferred that the trik-dusthana bhaveshas not occupy these bhavas, particularly when weakly conditioned.[18]

Preferred condition of a trik-dusthana bhavesha

A strong bhavesha ruling a positive bhava manifests its auspicious affairs prominently, perhaps through a satisfying marriage, healthy children or prosperous career. Furthermore, each graha represents certain personality traits, personal relationships and various bodily organs and limbs. An example illustrated in Chapter 5 is a strong natal Surya, which imparts self-confidence, a robust constitution, clear, sharp intellect and a healthy heart and circulatory system. This same strong Surya reinforces a positive and/or influential relationship with the father and other male authority figures in the person's life. Hence, a graha must have strength in order to support its role as a bhavesha of a positive bhava *and* as a karaka for its significations.

Nonetheless, when this same graha also rules a trik-dusthana bhavesha, it powerfully imparts its adverse nature to the affairs of the bhava it occupies and aspects, and any grahas it influences. This includes acute health conditions, litigation, debt and formidable competitors (6B bhavesha), chronic health concerns, severe upheavals, scandals and financial distress (8B bhavesha) and prolonged hospital stay, isolation, loss and excessive expenditures (12B bhavesha).

So, what is the preferred condition of a bhavesha that rules at least one trik-dusthana? That depends on the condition of the Lagna and Lagnesha. When the Lagna-Lagnesha are well-conditioned, the overall health of the individual is fortified. He or she more readily withstands the physical and mental-emotional pressures created by the misfortunes and hardships of the trik-dusthana bhaveshas, and even leverages them to his or her advantage. Concurrently, the person reaps the rewards of the many positive qualities and life matters associated with a strong trik-dusthana bhavesha.

For example, a well-conditioned 6B-6B bhavesha give the capacity to make good lifestyle decisions that help the person avoid or mitigate acute health issues. It also promotes

---

[18] Since any weakly conditioned graha jeopardizes the individual's health, a trik-dusthana bhavesha should not occupy that bhava ruled by its debilitation rashi.

professional interests in areas of conflict resolution, the healing arts and certain financial arenas. It gives adeptness in competitive sports as well.[19]

A well-conditioned 8B-8B bhavesha provides the fortitude required to overcome or resist chronic health conditions. Similar to the 6B, it gives proficiency in various medical and financial fields as well as an interest in alternative healing modalities.[20] Notably, as a bhava that is twelfth (loss or negation) from the 9B of accepted societal ways, the 8B can also bring name and fame from cutting-edge innovations, pioneering research and novel inventions and discoveries.

Finally, there are many auspicious matters associated with a well-conditioned 12B-12B bhavesha, including an ability to avoid premature aging, enjoyment of foreign travel, distinction in foreign affairs (foreign ambassadorship, executive leadership in foreign subsidiaries, foreign policy-making, etc.), a love of wild animals, and so on.[21]

But, when the Lagna-Lagnesha are poorly-conditioned, the person's constitutional strength is jeopardized and he or she is more likely to be overcome by hardships and adversities. In this case, the difficulties presented by a strong trik-dusthana bhavesha can be debilitating, especially when that trik-dusthana bhavesha influences the Lagna or Lagnesha.

Hence, we can only ascertain the preferred condition of a trik-dusthana bhavesha by assessing the relative condition of the Lagna-Lagnesha, and only after considering the explicit trade-offs involved with a strong trik-dusthana bhavesha, as articulated above. However, as a general rule, it is best when the Lagnesha is of equal or greater strength than the trik-dusthana bhavesha. Under no circumstances is it preferred that a trik-dusthana bhavesha be weakly conditioned.[22]

Trik-dusthana bhavas

When a graha occupies a trik-dusthana, its affairs as a bhavesha *and* its significations as a karaka are compromised. This is particularly true if the graha is weak. For example, a weak 5B bhavesha placed in the 8B puts 5B organs at risk.[23] If the 5B bhavesha is Budha, graha karaka for the mind, we can also expect attacks of mental anxiety and nervousness. Thus, it is preferable that no grahas occupy the trik-dusthana bhavas.

There are two exceptions to this general rule. The first involves a Lagnesha or bhavesha that gains strength due to its trik-dusthana bhava placement. To illustrate, assume for a Libra-ruled Lagna, that the Lagnesha (Shukra) occupies the Taurus-ruled 8B. In this case, the Lagnesha (Shukra) is strong (sva rashi) due to its trik-dusthana placement. Alternatively, consider for this same Lagna, that the Lagnesha (Shukra) occupies the Pisces-ruled 6B. Once again, the Lagnesha (Shukra) is strong, for it occupies its exaltation rashi.

---

[19] See *Your Healing Stars: Volume I, Fundamentals of Vedic Astrology* for the detailed affairs and related professions of the 12 bhavas.
[20] Ibid.
[21] Ibid.
[22] Note that nicha bhanga will not modify or reduce the health impact of a debilitated trik-dusthana bhavesha. For the principles of nicha bhanga, refer to Chapter 18: "Yogas for Spiritual Growth".
[23] For a detailed discussion of the medical significations of each bhava, see Chapter 8: "The Kalapurusha of the Birth Chart".

The second exception is 6B papa grahas. Papa grahas that occupy the 6B and are not weak thrive in this upachaya bhava, for they are eager to fight back when confronted with "enemies" (illness and disease) and are significantly less rattled than shubha grahas by the dusthana nature of the 6B. Thus, papa grahas occupying the 6B help us to overcome 6B-related acute health conditions.[24]

Summary

Of course, even when all the above conditions are met, no one completely escapes the adverse health impact of the trik-dusthanas and their bhaveshas. Each of us has experienced a cold or flu, constipation, sinus headache and countless other mild health conditions, and most of us have also experienced some sort of more serious injury or disease. However, when the above criteria are met and the Lagna-Lagnesha are well-conditioned, most chronic or debilitating health conditions are unlikely to have a significant impact on the person's life and/or are deferred until later in life, as the body naturally and gradually losses its vitality.

Lastly, a cautionary note is necessary about the placement of the nodes of the moon across the 6B and 12B, an axis of disease and illness. Recall that the nodes of the moon are mathematical points in the sky where the orbit of the sun and that of the moon intersect, and where solar and lunar eclipses occur.[25] The bhava placements of the nodes indicate unusual, sudden or unexplained events. Furthermore, Rahu and Ketu can eclipse consciousness, creating lack of awareness, misunderstandings or wrong judgements. Thus, when the nodes are placed across the 6B and 12B axis (or 2B and 8B axis), disease may go undetected, be misdiagnosed or wrongly treated.

Although our focus in this chapter has been on health, we must consider the possibility of other hardships imposed by the trik-dusthanas, such as powerful enemies, bankruptcy, public scandal, isolation and so on. The trik-dusthanas are also capable of creating adversities for the important people in our life, like children, parents, a spouse or close friend.

To illustrate, suppose that the 9B bhavesha occupies the trik-dusthana 8B and Surya, graha karaka for the father, is debilitated. Rather than (or in addition to) experiencing 9B health issues such as sciatica pain, torn thigh ligaments or a broken femur, the person may have a difficult relationship with his father (9B relationship) and/or the father experiences severe upheavals, financial difficulties or chronic disease (all 8B affairs).

Client Case Illustration: Linda

To illustrate the unique principles of the trik-dusthanas as prescribed in this chapter, let us return to our client Linda and her Cancer-ruled Lagna birth chart presented in Chapter 5. Recall that Linda's prakruti is kapha and her constitution is strong, as evidenced by chamara and shubha yoga. However, as demonstrated below, Linda can also expect to experience the health impact of papa kartari yoga.

---

[24] However, we will see in Chapter 11: "Evaluating Dhatus using Graha Karakas" that 6B papa grahas can harm the Kalapurusha organs represented by the 6B.
[25] See *Your Healing Stars: Volume I, Fundamental Principles of Vedic Astrology* for a description of Rahu and Ketu.

As we methodically evaluate the trik-dusthanas in Linda's chart, our main focus in this chapter is on their capacity to create vikruti that leads to acute health conditions (6B), chronic medical issues (8B) and/or wasting of the body (12B).

We will also examine the health impact of grahas placed in the trik-dusthana bhavas, and that of bhavas occupied by trik-dusthana bhaveshas. Where necessary, bhava-specific organs and limbs are referenced below. However, some readers may prefer to first read Chapter 8, which includes a comprehensive discussion of the Kalapurusha significations of each bhava.

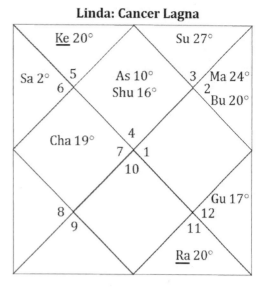

6B-6B bhavesha

We begin by identifying any grahas that influence the 6B. Recall that, except for papa grahas that are not weak, it is preferable that no grahas occupy this bhava. In Linda's chart, the 6B is destabilized by an aspect from Surya and Mangala, but no grahas occupy the bhava.

Next evaluate the condition and placement of the 6B bhavesha. The 6B bhavesha (Guru) is strong (sva rashi) but destabilized (aspected by Shani). Importantly, from its 9B placement, it influences the Lagna, not a preferred outcome. However, since the Lagnesha (Chandra) and 6B bhavesha (Guru) are of equal strength, this is not particularly detrimental to Linda's health. On the contrary, the strength of the 6B bhavesha indicates that Linda is able to minimize or overcome acute health conditions and to benefit from other, more positive qualities and life matters that are the domain of the 6B.

Still, any trik-dusthana bhavesha, particularly one that is strong or weak, has the potential to adversely impact the health of organs and limbs that are associated with its bhava placement. In Linda's case, we might expect acute health concerns relative to 9B medical significations (buttocks and thighs). Notice that the 6B bhavesha (Guru) *and* the 9B are aspected by the 8B bhavesha (Shani). This further highlights the potential for 9B health issues, but within the parameters of a chart that indicates an otherwise healthy individual.

When evaluating the 6B-6B bhavesha, be sure to assess the 2B-2B bhavesha for dietary habits that might contribute to vikruti. Here, we see that the 2B is destabilized by two papa grahas (occupied by Ketu and aspected by Mangala). The 2B bhavesha (Surya) is ordinary, of mixed stabilization (aspected by Shani and flanked by shubha grahas Budha and Shukra) and poorly-placed in the trik-dusthana 12B. On our bhava-bhavesha condition spectrum, this places the 2B-2B bhavesha slightly to the left of center, giving some concern that Linda's food choices are not supporting her health.

Adding confluence to this observation is the papa kartari yoga formed by the flanking of the Lagna by Ketu and Surya. To interpret more precisely the impact of this yoga, we can consider the nature of Ketu and the bhava rulership and karaka significations of Surya. Ketu, which forms one side of the papa kartari yoga, is placed in the 2B. This may show that Linda has a tendency to make improper or ill-informed dietary choices and may even have an eating disorder such as anorexia or bulimia. Recall that the nodes of the moon can eclipse consciousness, causing, in this case, poor food habits. The 2B bhavesha (Surya) participates in the papa kartari yoga by its 12B placement, suggesting that such choices have the potential over time to harm Linda's health and vitality (i.e., graha karaka Surya is poorly-placed in the 12B of slow wasting or expenditure of the body).

This is a good example of how yogas supersede by-bhava findings, a principle emphasized in *Your Healing Stars: Volume I*. In Linda's case, the condition of the 6B-6B bhavesha suggests that she will follow good daily routines but, specific to food choices and dietary habits, the papa kartari yoga overrides this finding.

8B-8B bhavesha

Let us begin by considering graha influences on the 8B. No grahas aspect the 8B, but Rahu occupies this bhava. Mentioned earlier, when either node of the moon occupies a trik-dusthana, diseases may be unusual, misdiagnosed, mistreated and/or go undetected for a period of time. This is especially a concern when Rahu or Ketu are exalted or debilitated, which is not the case in Linda's chart.

What about the 8B bhavesha (Shani)? This bhavesha is ordinary, stabilized (aspected by Guru) and placed in the mild-dusthana 3B. Significantly, from its bhava position, the 8B bhavesha (Shani) does not influence the Lagna or Lagnesha.

Based on Rahu's 8B placement and Linda's age (65), we would suggest that Linda schedule a colonoscopy, for the 8B represents the rectum and anal canal. Notice also that that the 8B bhavesha (Shani) is placed eight away from its own bhava and that Scorpio, the natural 8B rashi, is aspected by Shani and Mangala, giving confluence to potential 8B health issues.[26] We would also recommend that Linda receive a second opinion on any chronic health conditions diagnosed and have regular check-ups with her Ayurvedic practitioner and/or physician to mitigate the possibility of an undiagnosed health issue.

Lastly, because the 8B bhavesha (Shani) is placed in the 3B and aspected by the 6B bhavesha (Guru), we can expect Linda to incur health issues relating to the arms-hands, thyroid or upper respiratory system (i.e., 3B Kalapurusha significations) at some point.

Although our recommendations may sound ominous to Linda, we must remind her (and ourselves) that they are intended as preventative measures. Due to Linda's overall constitutional strength, should one or more of these health conditions manifest, it is unlikely to be debilitating or life-threatening until later in life.

---

[26] Rashi confluence and chart rotation techniques are explained in *Your Healing Stars: Volume I, Fundamental Principles of Vedic Astrology*. Surya Lagna and Chandra Lagna confluence techniques, also explained in *Your Healing Stars: Volume I, Fundamental Principles of Vedic Astrology* can, as well, be applied.

12B-12B bhavesha

Lastly, we need to evaluate the 12B and its bhavesha. The 12B has two factors of destabilization: Surya occupies the bhava and Shani (who is the 8B bhavesha) aspects it. Notice that there is also the stabilizing influence from shubha graha flanking. The 12B bhavesha (Budha) is ordinary, destabilized by Mangala and well-placed in the 11B. Importantly, the 12B bhavesha does not influence the Lagna or Lagnesha.

Here, again, our main concern centers on the potential health consequences of the papa kartari yoga. We noted earlier that Surya forms part of this yoga, implicating potential long-term consequences of poor eating or drinking habits. As well, we can expect some health issue relating to the feet, sleep disorders (both 12B medical significations) or vision (2B is vision and the right eye, 12B is the left eye). There is chart rotation confluence for these findings, as the 12B bhavesha is placed twelfth from its own bhava.

As with the 6B and 8B bhaveshas, the 12B bhavesha can indicate health concerns relative to its bhava placement. In this case, the 11B significations include the calves or ankles.

In summary, the most important thing to note in Linda's chart is that the Lagna-Lagnesha are well-conditioned and there are two yogas for health, chamara yoga and shubha yoga. The papa kartari yoga and our assessment of the trik-dusthanas must be interpreted within this broader context.

We all experience various health issues throughout the years and, as we advance in age, they tend to be more frequent, complex and/or longer in duration. Given Linda's age, we must take seriously the potential health concerns identified in her chart and recommend Ayurvedic practices and Jyotisha remedial measures to fortify these areas.

Linda's reported health issues

During the Ayurvedic consultation, Linda revealed that she suffers from sleep apnea, a chronic condition that disrupts her quality of sleep and, in turn, makes her tired during the day. Linda depends on Coca-Cola to sustain her energy level, consuming 3-4 large Cokes daily. This has led to Linda being overweight by 30-40 pounds. These conditions are supported by the papa kartari yoga in Linda's birth chart.

Linda confirmed that her ankles (11B) had been giving her problems and that she recently needed surgery to remove ankle bone spurs. For several years she has also suffered from sciatica (9B). Linda mentioned that during menopause, she developed Hashimoto's thyroditis. As explained in Chapter 8, the thyroid gland overlaps the 2B and 3B. In Linda's chart, a papa graha occupies both bhavas. Shortly after our session, Linda took my advice and scheduled a colonoscopy. Several pre-cancerous polyps were found and removed (8B).

Given the placement of Ketu and Rahu on the 2B and 8B axis, I was curious about any misdiagnosed or undetected health conditions. About 5 years ago, Linda had intense shooting pains up the right side of her face. Despite multiple visits to various doctors and dentists, the cause went undiagnosed for months. Eventually, a blood test showed that Linda had shingles, a viral infection of the nerve roots. Interestingly, the 8B represents debilitating pain (shingles qualifies) and the 2B represents the face.

Most of Linda's health issues have been acute or recent, as she approaches her mid-sixties.

This substantiates our chart finding that her constitution, in general, is strong and robust.

Although our focus is on health, it is interesting to note that the placement of the trik-dusthanas in Linda's chart have caused other hardships. A younger sibling has a debilitating illness (8B bhavesha placed in the 3B of siblings and aspected by a strong 6B bhavesha, Guru); Linda's relationship with her father was strained during early childhood (a strong 6B bhavesha placed in the 9B of father and Surya, graha karaka for the father, poorly-placed in the 12B) and one of her children has had multiple acute and chronic health issues (all three trik-dusthanas influence the 5B).

Summary

Ultimately, accurate predictions are highly dependent on our capacity to make sense of multiple birth chart factors. By practicing our birth chart skills and soliciting client feedback, our Jyotisha judgement is refined and birth chart interpretation becomes second nature, as a more fluid and intuitive process unfolds.

In the meantime, keep in mind that Jyotisha is first and foremost a science founded on specific concepts and principles. The art within the science flourishes when we understand and appreciate those fundamental principles.

SECTION III: Samprapti and Disease Formation

Chapter 7: The Ayurvedic Concept of Samprapti

Introduction

At the root of all disease is an imbalance of one or more of the three doshas: vata, pitta and kapha. This imbalance (or dosha vitiation) is referred to as vikruti. Vikruti begins with aggravation of a dosha's qualities within the GI tract. If not corrected, the aggravated dosha spreads beyond its GI tract site and into other dhatus and srotamsi, disturbing their functions and harming associated organs.

The Ayurvedic notion of samprapti, or the six stages of disease formation, illustrates how a simple doshic imbalance culminates into a full-fledged disease. These six stages are illustrated in the figure below.

Figure 4: Samprapti and the Disease Process[1]

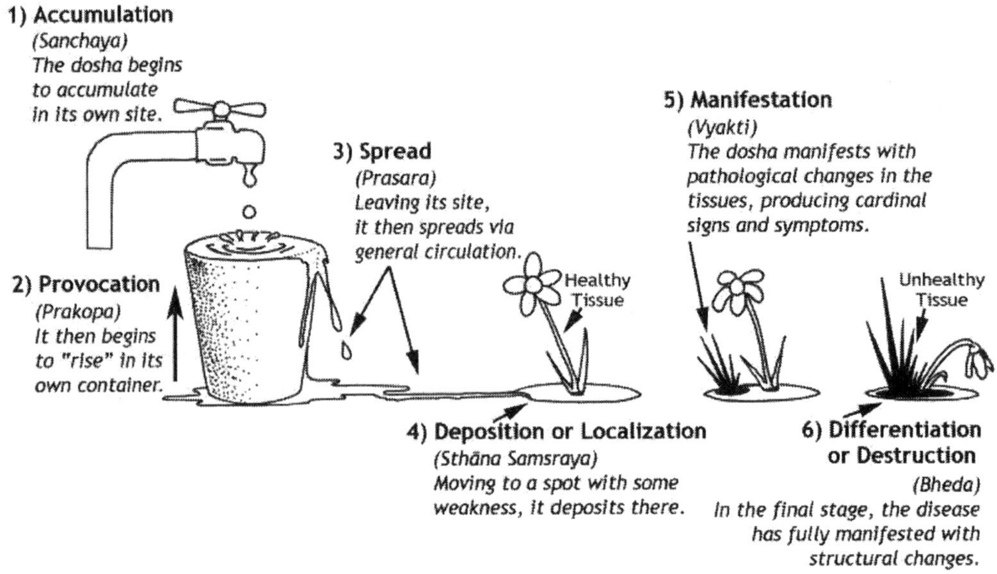

1) Accumulation
(Sanchaya)
The dosha begins to accumulate in its own site.

2) Provocation
(Prakopa)
It then begins to "rise" in its own container.

3) Spread
(Prasara)
Leaving its site, it then spreads via general circulation.

4) Deposition or Localization
(Sthāna Samsraya)
Moving to a spot with some weakness, it deposits there.

5) Manifestation
(Vyakti)
The dosha manifests with pathological changes in the tissues, producing cardinal signs and symptoms.

6) Differentiation or Destruction
(Bheda)
In the final stage, the disease has fully manifested with structural changes.

Doshas regularly progress through the first two or three stages of samprapti, because they are easily disturbed by minor, everyday dietary choices and lifestyle stresses. This explains why, in the course of a year, most of us experience minor digestive disturbances, as well as sinus headaches, chest colds, earaches, rough, flaking skin or mental restlessness. However, when dosha aggravation is prolonged, doshas can lodge in tissues and organs, causing more complicated problems.

Most critical during the initial stages of disease is the person's adherence to corrective measures, such as a proper diet, appropriate rest and remedial therapies. Recall that the 6B

---

[1] Lad, BAM&S, MASc, Vasant D. *The Textbook of Ayurveda: A Complete Guide to Clinical Assessment*, Volume Two. 2007, Stages of Samprapti, p 25.

and its bhavesha represent our ability to adhere to health-sustaining daily routines and the 2B and its bhavesha are specific to our dietary habits and food preferences.

When aggravated doshas enter the general circulation, they seek out weak or vulnerable areas of the body called khavaigunyas. Here, the aggravated dosha can lodge and create pathological changes in the tissues (dhatus) and related organs and systems (srotamsi). In the final stage of disease, doshas cause destruction of the tissue itself. This can be difficult to reverse.

In Section III: "Samprapti and Disease Formation", the birth chart is used to help identify inherently weak tissues and organs, or khavaigunyas, that are vulnerable to doshas in these later stages of samprapti.

Samprapti, the Etiopathogensis of Disease

1. Sanchaya (accumulation)

At the earliest stage of disease, one or more of a dosha's qualities become aggravated or vitiated, due to a host of extrinsic or intrinsic factors. This is called sanchaya stage. The aggravated dosha remains in its major site in the body: aggravated vata accumulates in the colon, aggravated pitta, in the small intestine, and aggravated kapha, in the stomach.

The individual experiences relatively mild symptoms, usually directly related to the digestive tract organs, but sometimes involving referred pain. In the case of vata sanchaya, symptoms may include gas or abdominal discomfort, pain in the GI tract and/or cravings for warm, liquid, slightly unctuous foods or hot drinks. Pitta sanchaya is often indicated by a slight rise in body temperature, sharp, localized pain or a feeling of heat in the GI tract, an increase in appetite (but not necessarily good digestion) and cravings for cool, mild, pitta-soothing things. Early symptoms of kapha sanchaya include sensations of heaviness and fullness, low appetite and a craving for light, warm and dry foods.

2. Prakopa (provocation)

If the cause behind sanchaya is not addressed, the aggravated dosha continues to build up and creates intensifying symptoms at its main site in the GI tract. This stage is called prakopa or provocation.

For example, the mild symptoms of aggravated vata dosha in the prakopa stage may now include burping, hiccupping, general abdominal distension or intensifying pain that moves. Pitta prakopa manifests as increased thirst, heat around the belly button, nausea, diarrhea and increased pain localized in the GI tract. Loss of appetite, mucoid nausea and physical lethargy are symptoms of kapha prakopa.

In these first two stages, the person still tends to crave things that have opposing qualities to those of the aggravated dosha. When properly addressed through the application of dissimilar qualities, the doshic imbalance is relatively easy to rectify.

3. Prasara (spreading)

Notice in the figure of the six stages of samprapti, that in the prasara or spreading stage, the "bucket" of aggravated dosha begins to spill over. The dosha spreads via the general circulation (rasa and rakta dhatus) and seeks to lodge in a tissue that is weak or vulnerable to doshic aggravation because of a previous lesion or constitutional predisposition. Doshas also tend to lodge in sites for which they have an affinity. For example, aggravated vata can spread to the nerves, muscles, bones or ears. Aggravated pitta might migrate to the eyes, skin or heart. Aggravated kapha enters the lungs, lymphatic system or sinuses.

Symptoms usually intensify at this stage, but they are not necessarily identifiable to a specific disease. For example, with aggravated vata, the person might get dry skin, cold extremities, heart palpitations, sciatic-type pain, and tinnitus. Increased pitta might cause symptoms such as increased sweating, hives, rashes, itching, hot flashes, intense heartburn or burning sensations. Increased salivation, whole-body heaviness and fatigue, water retention and sinus congestion are caused by increased kapha.

In a chart that shows an overall healthy constitution and the ability to adhere to a healthy lifestyle, the appropriate dinacharya and proper herbal remedies are generally sufficient to reverse dosha accumulation, even in the prasara stage. When contrary chart conditions exist, the aggravated dosha is likely to progress to the next stage of disease formation.

4. Sthana samshraya (localization)

At the sthana samshraya stage, the qualities of the aggravated dosha lodge in those organs and tissues that have a latent weakness. These vulnerable spaces are called khavaigunyas. The causes for khavaigunyas can include genetic factors, repressed emotions such as anger, grief or fear, or previous disease or injury. For example, a broken wrist from childhood that did not completely or correctly heal can become vulnerable to arthritis later in life.

Khavaigunyas are specific to each individual. For one person, an aggravated dosha may spread to the nervous system and manifest as moodiness or depression; for another person, an aggravated dosha may spread to the bones and manifest as spurs, and so on. Often we are not aware of tissues that are inherently weak, but they are apparent from the birth chart. The method for discovering vulnerable areas of the body is addressed in Chapter 9.

Once lodged in a khavaigunya site, the aggravated dosha disrupts the local tissue by imposing its own qualities. For aggravated vata, these qualities include light, cool, dry, rough, hard, subtle, clear or mobile; aggravated pitta imposes hot, sharp, light, slightly oily and liquid qualities and for aggravated kapha, the qualities may be heavy, slow, cold, oily, smooth, dense, soft, stable, liquid or cloudy. It is at this sthana samshraya stage that specific signs and symptoms of disease first begin to appear as precursors to a full-fledged illness.

5. Vyakti (manifestation)

By the vyakti stage, morbid changes in tissues are not just qualitative but quantitative—that is, they are readily observable through cardinal signs and symptoms. This is the stage in which a medical doctor can more easily name a specific disease based on standard diagnostic criteria. However, by the time tissue damage has taken place, the disease will probably not be as easy to treat. The vyakti stage typically requires stronger or more invasive treatments (Ayurvedic or otherwise) to prevent progression to the final stage of disease referred to in Ayurveda as bheda (diversification or destruction).

6. Bheda (destruction)

Lastly, in the bheda stage of disease, the peculiar pathological changes that began in the previous phase destroy the tissues that they have affected. The functions of the surrounding tissues and associated organs are also impaired and added complications may occur. Disease at this stage can be very difficult or impossible to reverse.

Chapter 8: The Kalapurusha of the Birth Chart

The Cosmic Being in the Sky

Kalapurusha refers to an image of a cosmic being whose body, limbs and organs overlay the stellar rashis. Each rashi in the birth chart corresponds to a particular part of this being, complete with physical, mental-emotional and spiritual aspects. In the following sections, the Kalapurusha significations of the rashis and bhavas are examined in detail. Their associated medical illnesses and diseases are also included.

Aries, the first rashi of the natural zodiac, represents the head, forehead and brain of Kalapurusha. But because the rashi of a particular individual's Lagna varies according to the time of birth, the limbs and organs of Kalapurusha begin with the rashi of the Lagna. For example, in a chart with a Virgo-ruled Lagna, Virgo and the space of the Lagna represent the head and brain.

Figure 5: Kalapurusha By-Bhava Limbs and Organs[1]

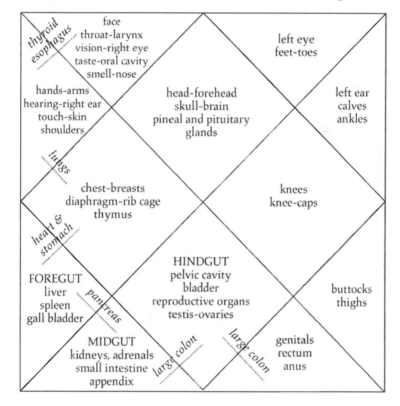

---

[1] There is also a nakshatra Kalapurusha which can be used for confluence. Refer to Chapter 28: "Health Aspects of the Nakshatras".

Chapter 8: The Kalapurusha of the Birth Chart

When the Kalapurusha is mapped to the birth chart, certain organs fall across two bhavas. In these cases, the first bhava corresponds to the first or upper part of the organ and the second bhava, to its latter or lower part. To illustrate, notice in the figure on the previous page that the stomach overlaps the 4B and 5B. The 4B is the uppermost, kapha-portion of the stomach (fundus) and the 5B is the middle and lower, pitta-portion (pylori-section) of the stomach, where sharp, penetrating digestive enzymes transform food. In a similar fashion, the 6B is the ascending and traversing colon, the 7B is the descending colon, and the 8B, the rectum.

The right and left sides of Kalapurusha are likewise mapped to the birth chart. From the middle of the Rising Sign (15°) to the middle of the 7B rashi (15°) is the right side of Kalapurusha and the remainder of the 7B rashi (15° to 30°) to the end of 12B rashi (30°) is its left side. This explains why the 2B is the right eye and the 12B is the left eye. Similarly, the 3B is the right ear and the 11B is the left ear.

Congruent with this representation, the internal organs of the body (e.g., lungs, heart, liver, intestines) are denoted by the right-side bhavas, while the external genitals, legs and feet are denoted by the left-side bhavas. The right side of the chart is that space in the sky that was invisible at the time of birth, just as our internal organs are hidden from view.

The spinal column is also overlaid onto the birth chart so that it corresponds to the twelve bhavas, beginning with the skull, which sits on top of the spinal column in the space of the Lagna. The right-side bhavas correlate to the anterior spinal column and the left-side bhavas correlate to the posterior spinal column. (By-bhava representation of the spinal column is presented in the next sections.)

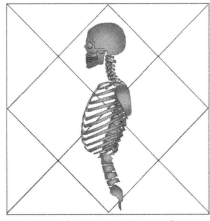

Anterior Spinal Column   Posterior Spinal Column

Bhava and Rashis Kalapurusha Significations
Lagna and Aries

The Kalapurusha significations of the *tanu sthana* (place of body) Lagna include the forehead, top of the head, hair, skull, brain and pineal and pituitary glands.

Illnesses and disease: Brain disorders (strokes, epilepsy, migraines, brain tumors), injuries to the head or skull (concussions, fractures), brain infections (meningitis, encephalitis), baldness, pineal malfunction (melatonin deficiency, immune suppression, insomnia) and pituitary gland disorders (tumors, growth hormone deficiency). Difficult and/or traumatic births are also seen from the Lagna.

2B and Taurus

The face is read from the 2B: its beauty, luster, shape, appearance, expression and markings. Other Kalapurusha significations include the following senses and their related organs: vision and the eyes, smell and the nose, and taste and the tongue. The 2B is specific to the right eye and the 12B, to the left eye.

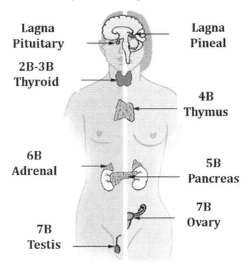

The mouth and oral cavity (lips, tongue, teeth), tonsils, upper esophagus and uppermost cervical vertebras are read from the 2B. The larynx, responsible for the pitch and volume of speech, and part of the thyroid gland are 2B organs.

Illnesses and disease: Poor eyesight, sinus conditions, diseases of the thyroid (goiter, hypo- and hyperthyroid), throat (mumps, tonsillitis, sore throat, laryngitis) and oral cavity (tooth decay, gum disease, oral infections and blisters), facial injury, disease of facial bones (TMJ), muscles (paralysis), nerves (Bell's palsy) and glands (parotid gland tumors). As the bhava of the voice, it includes all types of speech disorders (disfluency, articulation deficiency and voice disorders). Allergies are also 2B health issues.

3B and Gemini

The *vikrama sthana* (place of courage) 3B is the arms and hands of the Kalapurusha. It includes the remaining two senses and their related organs: touch and the skin and hearing and the ears. The 3B is specific to the right ear and the 11B, the left ear.

Other Kalapurusha organs, glands and limbs include the shoulders, clavicles, trachea and mid-to-lower cervical vertebrae. The thyroid and esophagus overlap the 2B and 3B, with the 3B representing the lower portion of both organs. Similarly, the lungs overlap the 3B and 4B. The 3B represents the upper portion of the lungs and the 4B, its lower portions.

Illnesses and disease: Upper respiratory diseases (common cold, laryngitis, asthma), injuries to the hands or arms (carpal tunnel, tennis elbow, fractures) and issues related to the ears and hearing (hearing loss, tone deafness, ringing in the ears).

4B and Cancer

The *vakshas sthana* (place of chest) 4B includes the breasts, chest, rib cage, thymus gland, lower respiratory system and upper thoracic vertebrae. It is mainly the upper fundus of the stomach that produces mucous secretions used to liquefy food. This is seen as a kapha function. The middle and lower pyloric section of the stomach are responsible for producing hydrochloric acid. This is considered a pitta function.

Notice in the natural zodiac, that kapha graha Chandra rules the 4B Cancer rashi and pitta graha Surya, the 5B Leo rashi.

The heart also overlaps the 4B and 5B. Its uppermost portion is represented by the 4B, but the majority of the heart is in the domain of the 5B.

Lastly, the 4B represents the womb when pregnant with child. This is because Chandra is the karaka for newborns and, in the natural zodiac, Chandra rules the 4B.

Illnesses and disease: Diseases of the breasts (breast cancer, fibrocystic disease, mammary dysplasia), lower respiratory illnesses (asthma, pneumonia, lung abscess, acute bronchitis and emphysema), fractured or broken ribs and illnesses requiring surgery in the chest area, such as heart surgery. Since the 4B also represents family, it denotes genetic predisposition to disease.

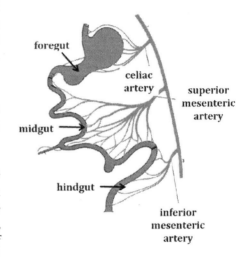

5B and Leo

The Kalapurusha organs and limbs of the 5B, 6B and 7B correspond to the foregut, midgut and hindgut, respectively.[2]

The foregut includes the majority of the stomach,[3] spleen, liver, gall bladder, bile ducts, initial portion of the duodenum and a large portion of the pancreas.[4] In addition to these vital foregut organs, the heart,[5] circulatory system and second half of thoracic vertebrae are assigned to the 5B, as well as the entire spinal cord.

Illnesses and diseases: Improper fat metabolism (diabetes, lipid storage disorders), diseases of the liver (hepatitis, jaundice, fatty liver, cirrhosis), gallbladder (gallstones, removal of gallbladder, inflamed bile ducts), upper duodenum (ulcers) and spleen (splenomegaly, enlarged spleen, asplenia and abnormal spleen functioning).

6B and Virgo

The 6B is the first of three bhavas involved in purification and elimination. It includes the

---

[2] At the *2008 New Mexico Medical Astrology Workshop*, Dr. K. S. Charak astutely extrapolated this bhava assignment based upon the embryonic development of the foregut, midgut and hindgut: "When the child is inside the body of its mother, its abdominal organs appear in the form of a tube which later on turns, twists and pouches out to form the various intra-abdominal organs. This tube (or gut) hangs from inside the back and three distinct blood vessels supply blood to it. The area supplied by each of these blood vessels is quite distinct. The first of the three segments is called the foregut, which pertains to the 5th bhava organs. The middle one is called the midgut and represents the 6th bhava organs, while the last one is called the hindgut and 7th bhava organs."
[3] See also section: "4B and Cancer" for a discussion of the stomach.
[4] The endocrine function of the pancreas is a 5B Kalapurusha signification and its exocrine function, a 6B Kalapurusha signification.
[5] See also section: "4B and Cancer" for a discussion of the heart.

latter section of the duodenum and balance of the small intestines (jejunum, ileum), cecum, appendix and ascending and transverse colon. The descending colon and sigmoid colon belong to the 7B and the rectum, to the 8B.

Foregut (5B)

Midgut (6B)

Hindgu (7B)

Rectum (8B)

The organs and bodily processes of the upper urinary system (kidneys, renal artery-vein, upper ureters), the lumbar vertebrae and part of the pancreas are the domain of the 6B.[6] This *ari sthana* (place of enemies) also includes competitors, adversaries and enemies. Hence, the 6B represents the adrenal glands, which are largely responsible for our fight-or-flight response.

Illnesses and disease: Issues of the intestinal tract (gas, malabsorption, constipation, diarrhea) and health concerns relating to the appendix (appendicitis), adrenals (adrenal fatigue) and kidneys (kidney infections, kidney stones, kidney failure).

7B and Libra

The *basti sthana* (place below the navel) 7B represents the female (ovaries, fallopian tubes, uterus, endometrium, cervix, vagina) and male (prostate gland, testis, seminal vesicle, vas deferens) reproductive organs, pelvic cavity, hip bones, sacrum, lower urinary system (bladder, lower ureters, urethra) and latter intestinal tract (descending colon, sigmoid colon).

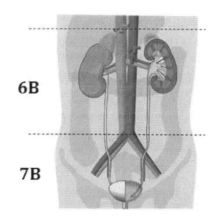

6B

7B

Illnesses and disease: Internal sexually transmitted diseases (STDs), interstitial cystitis, lower urinary issues (urinary incontinence, urinary tract infections), endometriosis, sexual dysfunctions (low libido, frigidity in women, impotence in men), reproductive issues, prostate concerns (prostatitis, benign prostatic hyperplasia, prostate cancer) and dislocation or replacement of hip joints.

8B and Scorpio

The *guhya sthana* (place of things private) 8B represents the genitals, rectum, perineum, anus, anal canal and coccyx.

Illnesses and disease: The 8B is one of external STDs (as opposed to the internal STDs of the 7B), hemorrhoids, rectum and anal canal.

9B and Sagittarius

The 9B through the 12B denotes the lower limbs and feet of the Kalapurusha. The 9B represents the buttocks, thighs and related muscles (quadriceps, hamstrings), bones

---

[6] See FN 4 in this chapter.

(femurs), veins, arteries and nerves (upper sciatica).

Illnesses and disease: Specific to the 9B is sciatica pain, broken femur, cancer of the femur and torn thigh muscles. However, one should consider all four bhavas (9B-12B) when assessing medical issues of the lower limbs, such as paralysis, leg cramps, paresthesia (numbness, burning, tingling), muscle aches of the legs, leg rashes and bites, leg length inequality and leg deformity.

10B and Capricorn

This bhava represents a complex array of joints, tendons (patellar), ligaments (collateral, cruciate), cartilage (articular) and bones (patella) in the knee region. The 10B *gamana sthana* (place of gait) also shows the gait or stride of a person.

It might at first seem odd that the 10B which represents the zenith of the heavens and is accountable for our career and worldly recognition is assigned a seemingly minor part of the body. Yet, the knees are quite important when it comes to supporting the body's weight!

Illnesses and disease: Injuries to the knees, knee cap dislocation or replacement, arthritis and degenerative knee-joint diseases, patellar tendonitis, ligament tears, cysts on the back of the knees, infections involving the knees, knock-knees and walking abnormalities (scissors gait, spastic gait, addling gait, bow leggedness and leg length inequality).

9B: thighs & buttocks
10B: knees
11B: calves & ankles
12B: feet

11B and Aquarius

The 11B is specific to the lower part of the legs and includes the muscles (gastrocnemius, soleus, tibialis anterior, Achilles tendon), bones (fibula, tibia), arteries and veins (tibial artery, peroneal artery, tibial vein), nerves (lower sciatic) and ankles. However, as mentioned previously, all bhavas from the 9B through the 12B should be considered when assessing the overall health of the legs and feet.

The 3B represents hearing in general and is specific to the right ear, while the 11B is specific to the left ear. In a similar manner, the 3B is the arms and hands of the Kalapurusha and is specific to the right arm and hand, while the 11B is specific to the left arm and hand.

Illnesses and disease: Broken or sprained ankles, varicose or spider veins, Achilles tendon rupture, leg cramps ("Charley horse"), spasms and twitching, bow-leggedness, peroneal nerve dysfunction, fractured calf bone, hearing disorders of the left ear, ear infections and diseases of the left ear.

12B and Pisces

The 12B represents the feet and toes of the Kalapurusha. The feet are complex mechanical structures containing several dozen bones and joints and over a hundred muscles, tendons and ligaments.

Illness and disease: Athlete's foot, arthritis of the foot or gout, foot injuries, bunions, ingrown toenails, ganglion cysts, plantar warts, ulcers on the foot and genetic disorders, such as club foot or flat feet. As the bhava of sleep, it also shows sleep disorders (insomnia) hyperpnoea syndrome, night terror, sleep apnea and sleep walking.

Chapter 9: Identifying Khavaigunyas

Introduction

In a chart that indicates a healthy constitution and the ability to adhere to supportive daily routines, an aggravated dosha in the early stages of samprapti is soon arrested through corrective measures. Should curative measures not be taken, a vitiated dosha eventually spills over from its site and enters into the general circulation. For example, in the case of kapha vikruti, its gunas of cold, heavy, dull, dense, cloudy and hard produce kapha-type signs and symptoms such as head congestion, sinus blockage, water retention or a sense of heaviness.

The aggravated dosha seeks out tissues that are predisposed to morbidity (khavaigunyas) and creates qualitative disturbances. As the disease progresses, it can be identified by more specific signs and symptoms. If aggravated kapha dosha lodges in the rakta dhatu (red blood tissue), morbid conditions can include edema, high blood pressure or high cholesterol. If, instead, it lodges in the majja dhatu (nerve tissue), hypersomnia (excess sleep), depression or lethargy may be observed.

In the final stage of disease, affected tissues are damaged or destroyed. In our example, what began as a mild case of aggravated kapha dosha restricted to its site of origin now mutates into a chronic and complicated disease. Tumors, hardening of tissues, hypoglycemia, severe edema and diabetes are examples of vitiated kapha dosha in its final stage of disease manifestation. Diseases that reach this phase often trigger additional health complications. Tissues that are inherently strong resist this doshic infiltration, but those that are weak are more vulnerable to it.

In this chapter, we employ the Jyotisha notion of Kalapurusha to identify inherently weak tissues as shown by the birth chart. We can strengthen these vulnerable tissues using various Ayurvedic and Jyotisha remedial measures. Because Kalapurusha is bhava-specific, rashi confluence and chart rotation techniques help us confirm our birth chart findings.

Khavaigunyas and the Birth Chart

Using our Kalapurusha significations, we can identify khavaigunyas in the birth chart by applying our familiar bhava-bhavesha condition methodology.

Figure 6: Bhava-Bhavesha Condition Spectrum

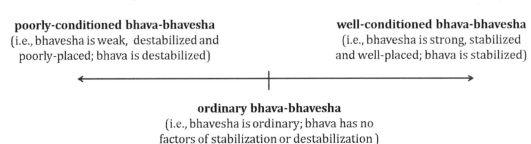

The further to the left on our condition spectrum that the bhava-bhavesha fall, the more likely that their Kalapurusha significations denote khavaigunya sites. We are also concerned with any bhavas or bhaveshas that are destabilized by weak or strong trik-dusthana bhaveshas.

Once we identify khavaigunyas in the birth chart, we should corroborate these using standard chart confluence techniques. In the following section, we examine the birth charts of Katrina and Johnathan for khavaigunyas and apply chart rotation and rashi confluence techniques to confirm and refine our interpretations.[1]

Later in Section III, we will see that each graha (except Rahu and Ketu) serves as the primary karaka for one of the seven dhatus and its related srotas. With this new information, we return to our client chart illustrations in this chapter and confirm our khavaigunya findings using dhatu-vaha srotas graha karakas.

Be sure to interpret your birth chart findings within the context of the client's overall constitutional strength, disease proneness and age.

Client Case Illustration: Katrina

Let us begin with Katrina and her birth chart. Earlier, we concluded that 58-year old Katrina has a vata prakruti.[2]

How would you describe Katrina's overall constitutional health? Recall that we determine this by looking at the condition of the Lagna-Lagnesha, yogas for health and ill-health, and Surya, the graha karaka for constitutional strength and vitality.[3]

Katrina: Taurus Lagna

In Katrina's Taurus-ruled Lagna chart, the Lagnesha (Shukra) is of mixed condition (sva rashi and combust). The Lagna *and* Lagnesha are destabilized by two factors: an aspect from strong (dig bala and retrograde) Shani *and* flanking by papa grahas—the latter forming papa kartari yoga. Other yogas for health and sickness are not present.[4] Based on these indicators, the Lagna-Lagnesha fall to the left of center on our condition spectrum.

Does graha karaka Surya support this conclusion? Surya is of mixed condition (exalted and rashi sandhi), mixed stabilization (influenced by Budha, Chandra and Guru as well as Ketu) and poorly-placed in the trik-dusthana 12B. This lends confluence to our initial findings.

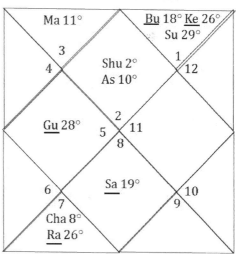

---

[1] Surya Lagna and Chandra Lagna are additional confluence techniques that can be applied. These techniques are demonstrated in *Your Healing Stars: Volume I*.
[2] Refer Chapter 3: "Dosha Prakruti".
[3] Refer to Chapter 5: "Constitutional Strength and Vitality".
[4] Because Shukra is of mixed condition, we do not have shubha yoga.

Next, we need to note those bhavas-bhaveshas that fall closest to the extreme left on our condition spectrum and consider the unique impact of the trik-dusthanas. Recall that the trik-dusthanas function just like other bhavas in that each represents particular Kalapurusha body parts and organs. But, unlike other bhavas, the trik-dusthanas are also places of acute health conditions (6B), chronic illness and disease (8B) and slow wasting of bodily tissues and organs (12B).[5]

Let us begin our assessment of khavaigunyas with the Lagna and its Lagnesha. Since we have established that the Lagna-Lagnesha fall to the left on our condition spectrum, it means that the head, brain and/or skull are potential khavaigunya sites. Is there rashi confluence? Mangala (planetary ruler of Aries, the natural rashi of the Lagna) is ordinary, but the Aries-ruled 12B is of mixed stabilization, including occupation by two papa grahas. Hence, rashi confluence lends some support that the head, brain or skull may represent a khavaigunya site.

We identified the Lagnesha (Shukra) as being of mixed condition and with two factors of destabilization. This alerts us to potential health issues involving the 6B, the other bhava ruled by Shukra. Notice that the 6B is of mixed stabilization (occupied by Rahu and Chandra and aspected by Surya and Budha). Because Chandra and Surya line up with the nodes of the moon, we would want to check whether a lunar eclipse occurred on the day of Katrina's birth. According to NASA, a lunar eclipse was visible from Katrina's birth location 36 hours *after* Katrina's birth. Hence, Chandra was not eclipsed on the day of Katrina's birth.[6] Still, the condition of the 6B-6B bhavesha raise concerns over its associated khavaigunya sites: kidneys, small intestine and most of the large intestine.

Now let us see if there is confluence for our 6B findings. Using chart rotation, notice that the 6B bhavesha (Shukra) is placed eight (chronic conditions) away from its own bhava. What about rashi confluence? Budha (planetary ruler of Virgo, the natural 6B rashi) is strong, but of mixed stabilization and placed in the trik-dusthana 12B, a bhava eight away from its own 5B. Further, the 5B is destabilized by an aspect from Mangala. Both chart rotation and rashi confluence confirm the potential for 6B Kalapurusha health concerns.

Next consider the unique trik-dusthana function of the 6B. We learned earlier that this bhava and its bhavesha are the primary indicators for vikruti health conditions that are characterized by sudden onset and of finite duration. Let us apply the trik-dusthana principles presented in Chapter 6: "Vikruti and the Trik-Dusthanas" to Katrina's chart.

A papa graha (that is not also weak) occupying the upachaya 6B helps us to overcome the acute health issues of this bhava, although it harms its Kalapurusha significations. When that graha is Rahu, it is a mixed bag because, as a node of the moon, Rahu can also cause health conditions to go undetected or to be misdiagnosed. What about Chandra and its placement in the 6B? Stabilization of the trik-dusthanas by shubha grahas is optimal for health when it occurs through aspect rather than bhava occupation. Chandra stabilizes the 6B, yet this gentle graha that represents the emotional mind is challenged by its dusthana nature *and* its association with Rahu. This harms Katrina's emotional steadiness.

---

[5] Refer to Chapter 6: "Vikruti and the Trik-Dusthanas".
[6] See *Your Healing Stars: Volume I* for a discussion of solar and lunar eclipses.

What about the 6B bhavesha? Since, for a Taurus-ruled Lagna, Shukra is both the Lagnesha and trik-dusthana 6B bhavesha, its placement in the Lagna is not detrimental to health. Indeed, such placement adds strength to the Lagnesha (because the Lagnesha is sva rashi).[7] However, we earlier determined that Shukra is of mixed condition and greatly destabilized. Based on our 6B-6B bhavesha evaluation, we can expect Katrina to experience frequent bouts of doshic imbalance that result in acute illnesses.

What do we notice about Katrina's dietary habits, as indicated by the 2B-2B bhavesha? The 2B bhavesha (Budha) is parivartana with the trik-dusthana 12B bhavesha (Mangala). This suggests possible concerns regarding Katrina's food choices.

Are there other bhaveshas that fall to the left on our condition spectrum? All other bhaveshas are ordinary or strong. So, we would next consider any greatly destabilized bhavas or bhaveshas and those that are influenced by strong or weak trik-dusthana bhaveshas.

The 7B is destabilized by the strongly conditioned (dig bala and exalted) Shani, and the 7B bhavesha (Mangala) is placed eight away from its own bhava. Using rashi confluence, we just noted the condition of the Libra-ruled 6B and its bhavesha (Shukra) and that Shukra is also eight away from its own 6B. Hence, chart rotation and rashi confluence confirm our 7B findings. Potential 7B khavaigunyas include the female reproductive organs, pelvic cavity, hip bones, sacrum, lower urinary system (bladder, lower ureters, urethra) and lower intestinal tract (descending colon, sigmoid colon).

Any bhava-bhavesha that implicate khavaigunyas also alert us to a problematic area of life in general. Based on our assessment of the 7B-7B bhavesha, we can expect Katrina to have challenges in the marriage and perhaps even separation for a period of time or divorce (7B bhavesha placed eight away, and its bhava is occupied by strong Shani, a separating graha). In cases like Katrina's, 7B health issues often go hand-in-hand with marital tension.

What about the 12B and its bhavesha? We noted earlier that the 12B is destabilized by two papa grahas (Surya and Ketu). Importantly, the 12B bhavesha (Mangala) is parivartana with the 2B bhavesha (Budha). Parivartana closely unites the trik-dusthana nature of the 12B with the affairs of the 2B. Moreover, the 12B bhavesha (Mangala) and Surya and Ketu form papa kartari yoga. We can use Kalapurusa bhava significations to interpret the potential impact of this yoga. The 12B-12B bhavesha represent the left eye, feet and/or chronic sleep issues; the 2B is the face, including the oral cavity and nose, vision in general, and the right eye. Health issues concerning one or more of these areas can stress the body and reduce Katrina's constitutional strength.

Now apply rashi confluence, first to the 12B and then to the 2B. Guru is placed six away (acute health conditions) from its own Pisces-ruled 11B and destabilized by strongly conditioned Shani. Shukra-ruled Taurus is the rashi of the 2B in the natural zodiac and the Lagna in Katrina's chart. We noted our concern about Shukra's mixed strength and two factors of destabilization. Thus, rashi confluence affirms our 2B and 12B findings.

---

[7] Refer to Chapter 6: "Vikruti and the Trik-Dusthanas" for a discussion of preferred bhava placement of trik-dusthana bhaveshas.

Since the 12B is a trik-dusthana, we would also apply our trik-dusthana principles. The 12B bhavesha (Mangala) is ordinary and does not influence the Lagna or Lagnesha. Still, along with Surya, it does form papa kartari yoga. The health consequences of its placement and yoga participation are noted above. In addition to the 12B bhavesha (Mangala) participating in papa kartari yoga, the 12B is greatly destabilized. Within the contexts of a problematic Lagna-Lagnesha, these factors suggest the possibility of a prolonged bedrest and/or gradual wasting of one or more organs or tissues.

Because Surya is of mixed condition (exalted and sandhi), poorly-placed and forming one part of the papa kartari yoga, we should evaluate the Leo-ruled 4B. The 4B is of mixed condition (stabilized by Guru and destabilized by Shani). Importantly, Guru is the 8B bhavesha, and its strength exceeds that of the Lagnesha, i.e., Guru is retrograde. Recall that a trik-dusthana bhavesha should not possess greater strength than the Lagnesha, and optimally not occupy a kendra. Furthermore, because of its abnormal back-and-forth motion, a retrograde trik-dusthana graha requires careful monitoring, particularly in sensitive areas such as health.[8] Therefore, we might expect health issues related to 4B Kalapurusha significations: breasts, chest and lower respiratory system.

The condition of the 4B-4B bhavesha also suggests that Katrina's relationship with her mother is problematic. Notice that the 8B bhavesha influences both the 4B and its bhavesha. Alternatively (or in addition), Katrina's mother may have had many ups and downs in life (strong 8B bhavesha placed in the 4B) or was literally or figuratively not available for Katrina (4B bhavesha poorly-placed in the 12B of loss).

Due to the special considerations afforded the trik-dusthanas, it is fortunate for Katrina that the 8B bhavesha (Guru) does not influence the Lagna or Lagnesha.

Based on our above evaluation, the Kalapurusha significations associated with the following bhavas are potential khavaigunya sites: Lagna, 2B, 4B, 6B, 7B and 12B.

Ideally, we would want to prioritize our findings, focusing on the 2 to 3 most troublesome khavaigunyas. However, given Katrina's generally weak constitution, we can expect health issues involving one or more Kalapurusha significations associated with each of the above bhavas.

Katrina's health history
During our consultation, Katrina shared the following health history.

1. Vision (2B and 12B): Katrina was born with a congenital eye defect she inherited from her father's side of the family. At the age of three, she had cosmetic surgery on her left eye, which had been turned since birth. Her vision progressively worsened over the years. At the age of 45, Katrina was told by her physicians that, absent the discovery of a new cure, she will lose complete vision over the next 10-12 years.

---

[8] Refer to *Your Healing Stars: Volume I, Fundamental Principles of Vedic Astrology* for a discussion on retrograde grahas.

2. Reproductive issues (7B): Throughout her thirties, Katrina attempted to get pregnant. During this time, her husband underwent two surgeries for the treatment of reproductive tract obstruction. As she approached her forties, Katrina opted for in vitro fertilization (IVF). This required Katrina to receive repeated hormone injections, which caused a very severe and painful condition known as ovarian hyperstimulation syndrome (OHSS). Ultimately, Katrina conceived three fetuses concurrently. One of these was lost during the late stage of pregnancy, but Katrina gave birth to two healthy twin boys.

3. Kidney stones (6B): Katrina has had multiple bouts of kidney stones.

4. Other significant health issues include the following. Periodic cases of insomnia (12B), unrelenting stress and emotional anxiety (Chandra in the 6B and in association with Rahu) and frequent and debilitating migraines (Lagna greatly destabilized and flanked by papa grahas).

When queried about potential health issues involving the breasts/chest or lower respiratory system, Katrina indicated that she had not experienced any to date. Yet, interestingly, the 4B-4B bhavesha represents the womb when pregnant with child.[9] So, this bhava-bhavesha is implicated in cases of miscarriages, abortions or the premature loss of a fetus. Further, as explained in the Section IV, the 4B-4B bhavesha represents a person's happiness and peace of mind. Katrina repeatedly mentioned that she is easily stressed by challenges in the marriage as well as her relationship with her mother.

In Chapter 11, we return to Katrina's chart to assess the health of each dhatu in relation to the above reported conditions.

Client Case Illustration: Jonathan

Our next client is Jonathan. We have not worked with Johnathan's Capricorn-ruled birth chart previously.

Firstly, Jonathan has a vata-pitta prakruti. Strongly conditioned (retrograde) Shani (a vata graha) aspects the Lagna and strongly conditioned (exalted) Surya (a pitta graha) occupies a kendra.[10] Notice that Shukra (a kapha graha) is also strongly conditioned and aspects the Lagnesha, but its impact is secondary.[11]

Johnathan: Capricorn Lagna

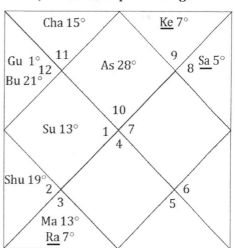

---

[9] Refer to Chapter 8: "The Kalapurusha of the Birth Chart".
[10] Since kapha graha Guru is of mixed condition (sva rashi and rashi sandhi), we cannot include its influence on the Lagnesha (Shani).
[11] Strongly conditioned grahas influencing the Lagna or occupying the kendras take priority over strongly conditioned grahas influencing the Lagnesha. See Chapter 3: "Dosha Prakruti" for the primary and secondary dosha factors.

What about Jonathan's overall constitutional? The presence of chamara yoga indicates a strong and vital constitution: the Lagnesha (Shani) is strong (retrograde), stabilized by Shukra and well-placed in the 11B. This places the Lagna-Lagnesha to the right in our condition spectrum. Johnathan's overall health is confirmed by a strong (exalted) and well-placed Surya.

Noteworthy is the difference between Johnathan's constitution and that of Katrina's, as graphically illustrated in the condition spectrum below. This means that health issues indicated in Johnathan's birth chart are likely to be less severe or more readily overcome, occur much later in life and/or implicate others in Johnathan's life, rather than himself.

Never underestimate the importance of a well-conditioned Lagna-Lagnesha supported by positive yogas including, in Johnathan's case, chamara yoga.[12] The auspicious effects of a well-conditioned Lagna-Lagnesha that also participate in multiple auspicious yogas will play out in all areas of Johnathan's life.

Even in the case of a well-conditioned Lagna-Lagnesha, we must assess the birth chart for potential khavaigunyas because, sooner or later, troublesome dashas, transits or the natural aging process will trigger disease-sensitive areas of the body.

Three bhavas and their bhaveshas stand out in Jonathan's chart: the 3B-3B bhavesha, 4B-4B bhavesha and 6B-6B bhavesha.

The 3B bhavesha (Guru) is of mixed condition (sva rashi and rashi sandhi). Guru, who is also the trik-dusthana 12B bhavesha, and Budha, the debilitated trik-dusthana 6B bhavesha (Budha), occupy the 3B. Applying rashi confluence, the Gemini-ruled 6B is destabilized by Rahu and Mangala, and we just noted that its bhavesha (Budha) is debilitated. This indicates potential 3B khavaigunyas: the arms, hands-fingers and upper respiratory system. We might also suspect that Johnathan's relationship with one or more siblings (3B) is troublesome and/or the sibling suffers from health conditions.

Next, notice that the 4B is destabilized by strongly conditioned (exalted) Surya, who is also the trik-dusthana 8B bhavesha. Its bhavesha (Mangala) is ordinary, destabilized by Rahu and placed in the trik-dusthana 6B. Is there rashi confluence for 4B potential khavaigunyas? The

---

[12] There are also two raj yogas: sambandha between the Lagnesha (Shani) and the 5B and 10B bhavesha (Shukra). This same planetary configuration forms two dhana yoga: sambandha between the 2B bhavesha (Shani) and 5B bhavesha (Shukra) and the 2B bhavesha (Shani) placed in the 11B. Here is a perfect example of auspicious yogas formed by the same planetary configuration. Refer to *Your Healing Stars: Volume I, Fundamental Principles of Vedic Astrology* for a discussion on raj and dhana yogas.

Chapter 9: Identifying Khavaigunyas

bhavesha (Chandra) of the Cancer-ruled 7B is placed eight away from its own bhava. As with chart rotation, any bhavesha placed six, eight or twelve away from its bhava is adversely impacted by its trik-dusthana bhava placement.

Thus, 4B Kalapurusha significations can represent defective spaces in the body: chest/breast, rib cage and lower respiratory system. We can also expect challenges relative to other 4B affairs, such as Johnathan's home life or early education. Sensitive areas like his relationship with his mother are likewise greatly impacted. Perhaps Johnathan's mother is domineering (exalted Surya) and/or the relationship is fraught with argumentation and combativeness (4B bhavesha placed in the 6B).

We noted earlier that the Gemini-ruled 6B is destabilized by Rahu and Mangala and that its bhavesha (Budha) is weak (debilitated) and associates with Guru, who is of mixed condition (sva rashi and rashi sandhi). Budha is also the bhavesha of the Virgo-ruled 9B. Hence, rashi confluence adds to our concern about 6B health matters.[13] Potential 6B khavaigunyas include the small intestine, most of the large intestine and the kidneys.

Lastly, we need to assess the trik-dusthanas and their unique ability to create vikruti or doshic imbalance.

As noted above, the condition of the 6B bhavesha (Budha) is problematic. However, from its 3B placement, it does not influence the Lagna or Lagnesha (Shani). According to our general rule, papa grahas placed in the 6B that are not weak provide the required resilience to overcome acute health conditions. Of course, the papa nature of Rahu and Mangala harm the Kalapurusha significations of this bhava, as noted above.

When considering the special health features of the 6B-6B bhavesha, it is a good idea to also evaluate the 2B-2B bhavesha for dietary habits that can contribute to vikruti. The 2B bhavesha (Shani) is strong (retrograde) and well-placed in the positive 11B and stabilized by Shukra, the bhavesha for the positive 5B and 10B. The 2B is stabilized by Chandra, the bhavesha for the positive 7B. This indicates that Johnathan generally adheres to a good diet.

Now let us take a look at the 8B of chronic disease. The 8B bhavesha (Surya) is strong (exalted) and placed in a kendra. Fortunately, in Johnathan's birth chart, its strength does not exceed that of the Lagnesha (Shani), nor does it influence the Lagna or Lagnesha. Of course, a powerful trik-dusthana bhavesha can still harm the Kalapurusha aspects associated with its bhava placement. No grahas occupy the 8B, but the bhava is destabilized by an aspect from Shani. However, given the strength of the 8B bhavesha (Surya), this is not particularly concerning.

Lastly is the trik-dusthana 12B. Noted previously, the condition of the 12B bhavesha (Guru) is problematic. In addition to its mixed condition, this bhavesha is destabilized by debilitated Budha, the 6B bhavesha. Moreover, from the 3B, Guru aspects the Lagnesha (Shani). The 12B is destabilized by Ketu and Mangala and the nodes of the moon line up on the 6B and 12B axis of ill-health and disease. This suggests the possibility of a health condition that will

---

[13] Budha aspects its own 9B, but because of its weak condition, this does not stabilize the 9B. Likewise, since Guru is of mixed stabilization, its aspect on the 9B is not particularly stabilizing.

require extended bedrest or prolonged hospital stay. We should also consider the feet (indicated by the 12B) as potential areas of khavaigunya. Notice that this is confirmed by rashi confluence (Pisces-ruled 3B).

In summary, the Kalapurusha significations associated with the following bhavas represent potential khavaigunya sites: 3B, 4B, 6B and 12B. Considering Johnathan's overall robust constitution, we would expect most health concerns to be deferred until later in life and/or implicate others in his life.

Jonathan's health history

Jonathan reported having had excellent health most of his life and has never missed a work day due to sickness. In fact, even at the age of 90, Johnathan cannot remember the last time he had a cold or flu. He continues to drive, cook all his own meals and travels extensively. Johnathan is an advent day-trader, an interest he undertook in his early sixties to keep his mind active.

Despite such stellar health, Johnathan did incur a serious health condition in his early seventies (see #1 below). Several other less significant issues were also reported.

1. Breast cancer (4B): In his early seventies, Jonathan noticed a lump in his breast tissue that grew in size over the pursuant twelve months. Urged by his wife to have the lump examined, Jonathan eventually sought medical advice. It was diagnosed as malignant and had spread to the local lymph glands. (Breast cancer is rare for men, accounting for less than 1% of all breast cancers.) Jonathan refused surgical removal of the lump and chemotherapy, electing alternative therapy that included a strict dietary regime and intensive vitamin and mineral supplementation. Today, nearly two decades later, Jonathan remains cancer-free.

   The association of Rahu (an unorthodox graha) with the 4B bhavesha (Budha) and its placement in the 6B (a bhava of health regimens) suggests alternative approaches to healing. That Johnathan deferred medical diagnosis for over a year after first discovering the lump is also attributable to Rahu's placement in the 6B and its association with the 4B bhavesha (Mangala).

2. Essential tremors (hands) (3B): Jonathan suffers from essential tremors of the wrist and hands. These symptoms first appeared in his mid-sixties.

3. Intestinal hernia (6B): When querying Jonathan about 6B health issues, he recalled having an intestinal hernia in his early thirties that required minor surgical treatment.

4. Foot infection (12B): During his early fifties, Jonathan contracted a bacterium in his left foot. Unable to find a cure, the doctors warned Jonathan that it might require the amputation of his foot. True to the trik-dusthana nature of the 12B, Jonathan remained in the hospital for nearly two weeks while the doctors tried different antibiotics. Fortunately, an effective antibiotic was discovered in time.

In Johnathan's case, we see that major health issues did not manifest until much later in life. What is more, even at the age of 90, Johnathan remains active and vibrant. This validates the importance of a well-conditioned Lagna-Lagnesha that also forms chamara yoga.

Chapter 9: Identifying Khavaigunyas

Chapter 10: Dhatus-Srotamsi and the Grahas[1]

Introduction

There are seven basic tissues or dhatus that maintain and nourish the body: rasa dhatu (blood plasma, including white blood cells and lymph fluids), rakta dhatu (red blood cells), mamsa dhatu (muscle tissue), meda dhatu (adipose tissue), asthi dhatu (bone tissue), majja dhatu (nerve tissue) and shukra and artava dhatus (male and female reproductive tissue, respectively).

Srotamsi (pathways) circulate bodily substances, including the three doshas and seven dhatus, throughout the body. Named according to the substances they carry and their functions in the body, srotamsi are somewhat comparable to the Western notion of systems, such as the digestive, circulatory or respiratory systems. Each dhatu is aligned with a particular srotas (singular for srotamsi). For example, the pathway or channel for rasa dhatu is called rasa vaha srotas.

Each graha (except Rahu and Ketu) serves as the primary karaka for one of the seven dhatus and its related srotas. Graha assignment is based on the qualities (*gunas*), dosha and psychological attributes of the graha and those of the dhatu and its srotas ("dhatu vaha srotas").

Take for example, kapha-dominated meda dhatu vaha srotas (adipose tissue and pathway), which has the gunas of heavy, slow, cold, oily, dense and soft. Its psychological attributes include compassion, forgiveness, love and understanding. These gunas and psychological attributes of meda dhatu vaha srotas align with kapha graha Guru. Hence, Guru is the karaka for this dhatu vaha srotas.

Table 3: Graha Karakas for the Dhatus

Dhatu	Tissue	Primary Graha	Secondary Graha
Rasa	plasma tissue	Chandra	Shukra
Rakta	red blood cells	Mangala	Surya
Mamsa	muscle tissue	Shani	Mangala
Meda	adipose tissue	Guru	Chandra
Asthi	bone tissue	Surya	Shani
Majja	nerve tissue	Budha	Shani
Shukra and Artava	male-female reproductive tissue	Shukra	Chandra

Since a dhatu and its pathway consist of multiple organs and involve a complex array of physiological processes, one or more secondary grahas also serve as karakas. For instance,

---

[1] Srotamsi pictures in this chapter are reprinted with the permission of the Ayurvedic Institute: Lad, B.A.M.S., M.A.Sc, Vasant D. The *Textbook of Ayurveda: Fundamental Principles of Ayurveda*, Volume One. 2002.

mamsa dhatu vaha srotas (muscle tissue and its pathway) is responsible for covering and protecting the bones with muscle tissue, thereby providing strength and mobility to the body. Vata initiates muscle movement and assists in muscle coordination. Hence, Shani, the major vata graha, is the primary karaka for this dhatu vaha srotas. The flow of blood is also essential for muscle movement. This makes Mangala, the signifcator for red blood cells, an important secondary karaka. The psychological attributes of mamsa dhatu vaha srotas are those of Shani: fortitude, ambition, determination and the ability to shoulder responsibility *and* Mangala: ambition, willpower and the courage to move forward in life.

The graha karakas of the seven dhatus and their related srotamsi are discussed in the following sections.[2] In addition to seven dhatus and srotamsi, there are three channels for nourishment: *anna vaha srotas* (channel for food), *prana vaha srotas* (channel for prana) and *ambu vaha srotas* (channel for water). There are also three channels for elimination: *purisha vaha srotas* (channel for feces), *mutra vaha srotas* (channel for urine) and *sveda vaha srotas* (channel for sweat). The graha karakas for these channels are included under the appropriate graha section below. For a more detailed discussion, see Appendix F: "Channels of Nourishment and Elimination".

Rasa Dhatu Vaha Srotas & Chandra

Having the gunas of slow, oily, slimy, soft, liquid and cloudy, rasa dhatu vaha srotas is governed by kapha dosha. Its function of *prinana* (nourishment and gratification) is to nourish the cells, tissues and organs of the body. The word prinana also expresses its psychological attributes of satiation, love, care and tenderness. Rasa dhatu vaha srotas shares these attributes with Chandra, making Chandra its primary karaka.

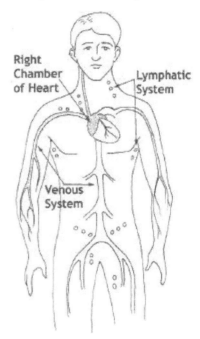

Rasa dhatu vaha srotas includes the lymphatic system and spleen (a secondary lymph system rich in lymphoid tissue, lymph nodes and lymphocytes), white blood cells and plasma and menstrual flow.[3] Chandra also represents chyle, a milky white substance formed in the digestive system that is rich in lymph fluid. The general function of lymph tissue is to bathe the cells with water and nutrients and to nourish all bodily tissues.

Rasa dhatu vaha srotas includes the endocrine system. Shukra is the general karaka for this system and thus, a secondary karaka for the rasa dhatu vaha srotas. However, each endocrine gland has its own karaka: Surya is karaka for the pituitary gland, Chandra, pineal gland, Mangala, adrenals, Budha, thyroid gland, Shani, thymus gland, Guru, pancreas gland, and Shukra, ovaries and testes.

---

[2] See Appendix G: "Ayurvedic Significations of the Grahas" for a by-graha summary, including the qualities, mental guna and rasa (taste) of each graha.
[3] Mangala, graha karaka for red blood cells, also plays a role in menses.

The venous system forms part of the rasa dhatu vaha srotas. Venous blood is dark red as a result of a lower content of oxygen and flows from the organs to the right chamber of the heart. Mangala is the karaka for the venous system and veins.

Chandra as graha karaka for other dhatus and srotamsi: sweat glands (meda), womb when pregnant with child (artava), mucosa lining of the lungs (prana) and gastro-intestinal tract (anna), phlegm (prana), lacteal system, including the breasts and breast milk (artava) and bladder (mutra and ambu).

Sundry other medical significations: white matter of the brain (responsible for memory), left side of the body, left eye.

Rakta Dhatu Vaha Srotas & Mangala

Rakta dhatu vaha srotas is the channel for the production, distribution and storage of red blood cells and bile. Its gunas of hot, sharp, light, liquid and spreading are also those of pitta dosha. *Jivana* (life giving), the provision of oxygenation and vigor to the body by way of the blood, is the function of rakta dhatu. Mangala (primary) and Surya (secondary) serve as its graha karakas.

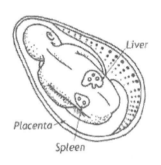

Mangala is the karaka for the production of red blood cells and bone marrow, where red blood cells are produced. It also governs the liver functions of filtering blood and removing old red blood cells, and the spleen's job of storing red blood cells. As explained elsewhere, although Mangala is the primary karaka for red blood cells and rakta dhatu vaha srotas, it is the secondary karaka for the liver and spleen. The primary graha karaka for the liver and its function of fat metabolism is Guru and for the spleen and its lymphatic functions, Chandra.

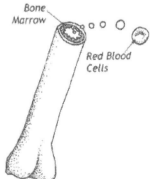

Mangala governs bile and the organs associated with its production (liver) and storage (gallbladder). Bile has a bitter taste and its gunas are hot, sharp and penetrating. Mangala shares this taste and these qualities. Along with bile, Mangala is the karaka for the sharp, hot and penetrating digestive enzymes, which are part of anna vaha srotas.[4] Digestive enzymes and bile are transformative agents of pitta dosha.

The psychological attributes of rakta dhatu vaha srotas include competitiveness, enthusiasm, ambition, courage, drive, passion and a willingness to take risks. These attributes are common to Mangala.

A major function of this dhatu vaha srotas is to distribute oxygenated blood through the circulatory system, which includes the arterial system. Surya represents these systems and the heart. Thus, Surya is an important secondary karaka for rakta dhatu vaha srotas.

---

[4] Refer to Appendix F: "Channels of Nourishment and Elimination".

Mangala as graha karaka for other dhatus and srotamsi: adrenal glands, venous system and veins (rasa), red blood that circulates through the muscles (mamsa), digestive enzyme and bile (anna).

Sundry other medical significations: head, forehead, neck, arms.

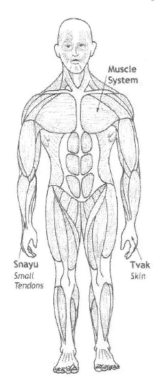

Mamsa Dhatu Vaha Srotas & Shani

Mamsa dhatu vaha srotas carries muscle tissue. Its function is *lepana* (plastering), the plastering of the bones by muscle tissue, which gives strength and mobility to the body. This dhatu vaha srotas includes the tendons (which bind muscle to bone) and ligaments (which bind bones together).

Vata initiates movement in the mamsa dhatu by stimulating muscle contraction. It also assists in muscle coordination. Shani, the major vata graha, is the karaka for this dhatu vaha srotas. Shani also represents the legs, which contain the longest muscles in the body, and the knees, where the longest tendons are located.

Good blood flow is essential for muscle movement. Thus, Mangala is a secondary karaka for mamsa dhatu vaha srotas. The integumentary system (skin), closely linked to mamsa dhatu, is also associated with this srotas. It is governed by Budha.

Healthy mamsa dhatu gives psychological attributes related to Shani: fortitude, ambition, determination and the ability to shoulder responsibility, and Mangala: ambition, will-power and the courage to move forward in life.

Shani as graha karaka for other dhatus and srotamsi: porous nature of the bones, the pelvic girdle, nails and teeth (asthi), CNS, joints and open spaces in the body (majja) and the large intestine, sigmoid colon, rectum and anal orifice (purisha).

Sundry other medical significations: legs, knees and kneecaps.

Meda Dhatu Vaha Srotas & Guru

The gunas of heavy, slow, cold, oily, dense and soft are those of kapha dosha and meda dhatu vaha srotas. This srotas includes subcutaneous fat, omentum and the sweat glands. Its function of *snehana* (literally love and affection) lubricates and insulates the body.

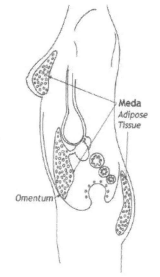

Kapha graha Guru is the primary karaka for this dhatu vaha srotas. The psychological attributes of meda dhatu are compassion, forgiveness, love and understanding. These correspond to the attributes of Guru.

The sweat glands, which secrete a salty-watery substance, are represented by Chandra (a watery graha with a salty rasa).

Guru as graha karaka for other dhatus and srotamsi: endocrine function of pancreas (rasa), sebaceous glands (sveda).

Sundry other medical significations: thighs, buttocks, vocal cords.

Asthi Dhatu Vaha Srotas & Surya

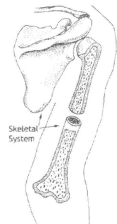

Skeletal System

The function of asthi dhatu and its srotas is *dharana* (to bear or support), to provide a solid structure for the body and protect vital internal organs. The metabolic function of bone tissue (as a reservoir for minerals) is a pitta function, making Surya the primary karaka. The psychological attributes of asthi dhatu are stability, consistency and firmness in our truth. Surya has these same qualities.

The bones themselves contain the qualities of vata, for they are hard, dry and contain space. Thus, Shani is an important secondary karaka of this srotas as well as the graha karaka for the pelvic girdle, nails and teeth, which are associated with this dhatu.

Surya as graha karaka for other dhatus and srotamsi: pituitary gland (rasa), circulatory system, arterial system and arteries and heart (rakta), stomach and its digestive fire (anna vaha srotas).

Sundry other medical significations: grey matter of the brain (responsible for comprehension), right side of the body, right eye.

Majja Dhatu Vaha Srotas & Budha

Having the qualities of subtle, mobile and lightweight, majja dhatu vaha srotas has an affinity for vata dosha. This srotas facilitates communication throughout the body. It includes the central nervous system (CNS), brain, spinal cord, bone marrow, joints and synaptic space. Its function of *purana* fills the empty spaces within the body.

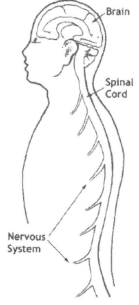

Brain
Spinal Cord
Nervous System

Budha is the karaka for nerve impulses, intercellular communication, synaptic space and the neuro-muscular junction. The brain receives and interprets nerve impulses from the body and dispatches nerve impulses, enabling actions. Budha facilitates this two-way communication. The psychological attributes of majja dhatu are common attributes of Budha: curiosity, intelligence, calmness, open-mindedness and clarity.

Shani is an important secondary karaka for this srotas, representing the central nervous system (CNS), spinal cord and joints. Shani also represents the space in the open cavities of the body.

Budha as graha karaka for other dhatus and srotamsi: thyroid gland (rasa), skin (mamsa), respiratory tract (including the nose and sense of smell), bronchial tree and trachea (prana) and small intestine (anna).

Sundry other medical significations: throat, all tube-like structures in the body (esophagus, ureters, urethra, bile ducts) and hands and fingers.

Shukra and Artava Dhatus Srotamsi & Shukra

Shukra dhatu vaha srotas relates to the male reproductive tissues and artava vaha srotas, to the female reproductive tissues. The gunas of these dhatus are oily, slimy, cloudy and liquid.[5]

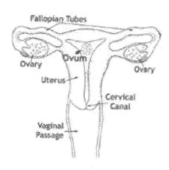

The reproductive fluids are the most refined substances in the body. This explains why the graha of refinement, Shukra (translated as semen), is the primary graha karaka for both dhatus and their related srotamsi. The psychological attributes of shukra and artava dhatus include love, sensuality, charisma and devotion. These are also the attributes of Shukra.

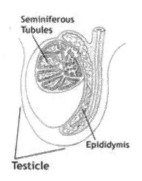

Chandra is a secondary karaka for artava vaha srotas and represents the breasts and the womb when pregnant with child. (Note that for men, the breast area (i.e., the chest) is represented by Mangala.)

Shukra as graha karaka for other dhatus and srotamsi: hormonal system in general and ovaries and testis specifically (rasa), kidneys (mutra).

Sundry other medical significations: appendix.

---

[5] Shukra dhatu is considered cool, while artava dhatu is hot.

Chapter 11: Evaluating Dhatus using Graha Karakas

Graha Karaka Confluence for Dhatus

As emphasized throughout this book, we need multiple confluence factors to make accurate birth chart predictions. Mantreswara cautions us that this is especially true when predicting disease: "A particular disease may be predicted (*only*) if the same disease happens to be indicated by two, three or more independent planetary configurations."[1] The sage provides an illustrious example: "If the 3rd bhava and 11th bhava and Guru are associated with or aspected by papa grahas Mangala or Shani, the native will suffer from diseases of the ears."[2] Notice in Mantreswara's illustration, that *both* bhavas representing the ears (3B and 11B) *as well as* Guru (graha karaka for the ears and hearing) must be influenced by Mangala or Shani. The greater the number of confluence factors, the more certain we can be about our birth chart predictions.

Since each graha is a karaka for one or more dhatus and their related channels, we can employ graha karaka confluence to confirm and prioritize the khavaigunyas discovered through a Kalapurusha-based assessment. At times, the use of graha karakas is the only technique available, as certain aspects of dhatus and their srotamsi are not bhava-specific. Take for example, the rakta dhatu (red blood cells) and rasa dhatu (white blood cells and plasma), whose tissues are represented by all 12 bhavas. In this case, we can't use the notion of Kalapurusha and our standard by-bhava confluence methodologies of rashi and chart rotation confluence to identify khavaigunyas.

Graha karaka confluence is also helpful for specifying khavaigunyas when multiple bhava organs are involved. To illustrate, assume the 5B-5B bhavesha are poorly-conditioned. To more precisely identify the organ at risk, we would evaluate the karakas that represent 5B Kalapurusha significations: Surya indicates the heart and stomach; Guru, the liver and fat metabolism; Mangala, the blood filtration function of the liver, gallbladder, digestive enzymes and bile, and so on.

Graha karaka confluence requires the familiar technique of evaluating the condition of a graha. We are concerned not only with poorly-conditioned grahas, but also with grahas that are destabilized by weak or strong papa grahas and/or weak or strong trik-dusthana bhaveshas.

Client Case Illustration: Katrina

In Chapter 9, we used Katrina's chart to demonstrate how to identify and confirm a number of bhavas and their bhaveshas whose Kalapurusha significations represent khavaigunyas. We then compared our list of birth chart findings with Katrina's self-reported health conditions: severe vision problems, OHSS (ovarian hyperstimulation syndrome), kidney stones, insomnia and migraines. We will now apply graha karaka confluence to evaluate the

---

[1] *Mantreswara's Phala Deepika*, S.S. Sareen (translator), Chapter 14.1. Sagar Publications.
[2] Ibid., Chapter 14.10.

Katrina: Taurus Lagna

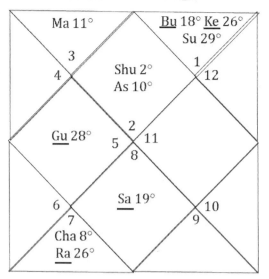

dhatu vaha srotas that corresponds to each health condition.

The Shukra-governed artava dhatu vaha srotas and mutra vaha srotas are implicated in Katrina's health conditions of OHSS and kidney stones, respectively. Noted in Chapter 9, Shukra is of mixed condition (sva rashi and combust) and greatly destabilized.

This is a good example of how a single problematic graha can cause multiple health conditions. In this case, Shukra is also the all-important Lagnesha, which further jeopardizes Katrina's health.

Budha is the karaka for the majja dhatu vaha srotas, which is the source of Katrina's insomnia and migraines. This graha is strong (retrograde) but associates with Ketu and is poorly-placed in the trik-dusthana 12B.

Also associated with the majja dhatu vaha srotas is vision. In this case, all four grahas, Budha (majja dhatu vaha srotas), Shukra (vision in general), Surya (right eye) and Chandra (left eye), are problematic, and all but Shukra associate with the nodes of the moon along the 6B and 12B axis of disease and illness.

Using graha confluence, we are able to quickly verify concerns with the dhatu vaha srotas related to each health concern Katrina reports.

Client Case Illustration: Jonathan

During Jonathan's health evaluation, we identified and confirmed two main health issues: essential tremors and breast cancer.

Budha is the primary karaka for the majja dhatu vaha srotas, implicated in Johnathan's essential tremors, and the only weak (debilitated) graha without strength. Its condition affirms the likelihood of issues with the majja dhatu vaha srotas.

However, Jonathan's most serious health issue was breast cancer. Shukra is the karaka for the artava-shukra srotamsi, but Chandra is specific to breast tissue. In Jonathan's chart, Chandra is ordinary, receives no graha influences and is placed in the neutral 2B. Hence, we do not have graha karaka confluence specific to the breast tissue as a khavaigunya.

Johnathan: Capricorn Lagna

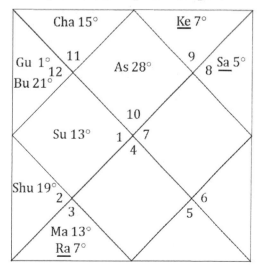

Still, recall that rashi confluence supports the possibility of 4B-related health issues. Also of importance, Chandra occupies Shatabhishak, one of a handful of nakshatras reputed for its ability to produce severe disease and illness. This topic is addressed in Chapter 28: "Health Aspects of the Nakshatras". Another confluence technique is Nakshatra Purusha, a topic also discussed in Chapter 28. According to Nakshatra Purusha, each nakshatra represents a body part of Lord Vishnu. A strong or weak papa graha or weak shubha graha harms the Nakshatra Purusha body part associated with its nakshatra placement. In Jonathan's chart, strongly conditioned (retrograde) papa graha Shani occupies Anuradha, which represents the breasts of Nakshatra Purusha.

Breast cancer is extremely rare in men, but a family history increases the odds of having it, even for males. Three of Johnathan's maternal aunts died of breast cancer. (Maternal aunts are represented by the 6B, which is third (siblings) from the 4B of mother. Noted earlier, the 6B-6B bhavesha is troublesome.) In Johnathan's chart, the strong (exalted) 8B bhavesha (Surya) occupies the 4B, a bhava of hereditary disease.[3] This does not mean that everyone whose natal birth chart has the 8B bhavesha placed in the 4B will experience some type of hereditary disease. As in Johnathan's case, we need to determine if other birth chart factors and actual family history support such conditions.[4]

Conclusion

As Jyotishis we must never forget the prudent advice of Mantreswara: "A particular disease may be predicted (*only*) if the same disease happens to be indicated by two, three or more independent planetary configurations." Jyotisha offers us numerous ways to confirm health findings, many which are illustrated in this book. These include: by-bhava Kalapurusha, Nakshatra Purusha, rashi confluence, chart rotation and Surya and Chandra Lagna.

Several methodologies incorporate well-known Ayurveda concepts and principles, such as dhatu vaha srota graha karakas. The dosha prakruti of a graha can also assist us in identifying or confirming vikruti-specific disease patterns. This technique is demonstrated in the next section.

Rarely is the karma involving a particular health issue so fixed that all confluence methods point to the same conclusion. So, don't be surprised if three or four techniques confirm a particular finding, but several others do not.

Lastly, more advanced tools, such as the use of *vargas* (sub-charts) and different timing systems, are not included in this book. Once you master the concepts and techniques in *Your Healing Stars: Volume II*, you can undertake these more advanced topics.

Graha Combinations

You can supplement your chart interpretation techniques by combining your knowledge of dhatu graha karakas and the doshic nature of grahas. For example, what planetary

---

[3] Refer to Chapter 8: "The Kalapurusha of the Birth Chart".
[4] Interestingly, Katrina has this same configuration: a strongly conditioned 8B bhavesha placed in the 4B. Katrina inherited an eye disease that severely affects her vision. This was confirmed by other configurations in her birth chart.

combinations might suggest the tendency towards facial acne, a pitta disorder? In addition to our standard birth chart factors, see if Budha (graha karaka for the integumentary system, part of the mamsa dhatu vaha srotas) associates with Mangala, Ketu or Surya, the three pitta grahas. If Ketu is involved, the skin condition is typically more severe or unusual in nature. What type of skin condition is indicated by an association between Budha and Rahu (a vata graha)? We could expect skin concerns characterized by excessive dryness, itching and/or pain and throbbing.

Graha combinations are particularly useful for identifying diseases that are not bhava-specific. Take for example anemia, which is defined as insufficient red blood cells and hemoglobin. Since Mangala is the karaka for rakta dhatu (red blood cells function), its affliction by Shani or Rahu or combustion with the sun, could indicate anemia.

Or, consider health issues involving the asthi dhatu (bone tissue). Using our by-bhava Kalapurusha technique, we could identify likely skeletal areas more susceptible to disease: the skull (Lagna), facial bones (2B), clavicles and bones in the arm and hands (3B), etc. We can also look for specific graha combinations that suggest general susceptibility to osteoporosis, arthritis, osteomyelitis and other asthi dhatu disorders.

How might osteoporosis, a vata condition, show in the birth chart? Surya is the primary karaka for the asthi vaha srotas. Thus, often osteoporosis is indicated by an association between Surya and Rahu (a vata graha) or Surya and Shani (a vata graha), particularly if Surya is weak or Shani is combust the sun. Using this same methodology, what graha combinations might indicate inflamed arthritis, a pitta-related condition? This could be shown by an association between Surya and Ketu (a pitta graha) or Surya and Mangala (a pitta graha), particularly if Surya is weak or Mangala is combust the sun.

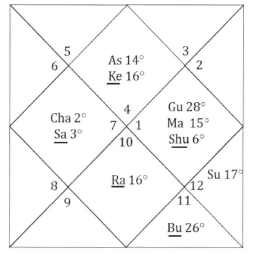

Terrance: Cancer Lagna

Let us look at a few more examples using this same technique. How might kidney stones show in the birth chart? Kidney stones form due to the crystallization of chemicals and minerals present in the urine. In addition to evaluating the 6B-6B bhavesha (the kidneys of the Kalapurusha), we would look at influences on Shukra, karaka for the mutra vaha srotas and the kidneys. Calcification or crystallization of matter in the body is often indicated by Shani. So, certain Shani-Shukra combinations, such as planetary war, association or aspect, can indicate kidney stones.

In Terrance's chart (first introduced in Chapter 3), Shukra is aspected by retrograde, exalted Shani and so is the 6B bhavesha (Guru). This provides confluence for possible kidney stones. Terrance has suffered from kidney stones for the last 25 years.

Another common health issue is gallstones, which form in the gallbladder or bile duct. The most common type of gallstones is cholesterol stones, caused by excess cholesterol in the bile. Recall that Mangala governs bile and the organs associated with its production (liver) and storage (gallbladder).⁵ Mangala's association with kapha graha Guru can be a mark for cholesterol gallstones. Should Shani, the karaka for removal of organs, also be implicated in this planetary combination, the person may have his or her gallbladder removed. Returning to Terrance's chart, notice that Mangala associates with Guru and both are aspected by strongly conditioned Shani. For a Cancer-ruled Lagna, Mangala is also the 5B bhavesha that represents the liver and gallbladder. Terrance had his gallbladder removed in his late twenties.

In this way, leverage your knowledge of the grahas and their doshic nature to identify disease-specific graha combinations. Where possible, apply confluence techniques for confirmation.

Proforma for Disease-Specific Conditions

The concepts and techniques presented in Section II and III are organized in a manner that allows us to easily evaluate multiple indications for a particular disease. To illustrate, assume you are concerned about the health of the liver. The liver is part of the rakta dhatu vaha srotas, with Guru (primary) and Mangala (secondary) as its graha karakas. In this case, we would check the following birth chart factors.

   5B-5B bhavesha (bhava-bhavesha for the liver)
   Guru (primary karaka for the liver)
   Mangala (secondary karaka for the liver)
   Leo-ruled bhava-bhavesha (rashi confluence)
   Placement of the 5B bhavesha six, eight or twelve away from its own bhava (chart rotation)
   5B-5B bhavesha from the Surya Lagna and Chandra Lagna

Alternatively, suppose your client has symptoms of adrenal fatigue. The endocrine system is part of the rasa dhatu vaha srotas, and Mangala is specific to the adrenal glands. In this case, examine the following birth chart factors.

   6B-6B bhavesha (bhava-bhavesha for the adrenal glands)
   Mangala (graha karaka for the adrenal glands)
   Virgo-ruled bhava-bhavesha (rashi confluence)
   Placement of the 6B bhavesha six, eight or twelve away from its own bhava (chart rotation)
   6B-6B bhavesha from the Surya Lagna and Chandra Lagna

Or consider the example of IBS (irritable bowel syndrome). IBS is a syndrome involving inflammation of the large intestine, part of the purisha vaha srotas.

   6B-6B bhavesha (bhava-bhavesha for the ascending and traversing large colon) and 7B-7B bhavesha (bhava for the descending large colon)
   Shani (karaka for the purisha vaha srotas)
   Virgo-ruled bhava-bhavesha and Libra-ruled bhava-bhavesha (rashi confluence)

---

⁵ Refer to Chapter 10: "Dhatus-Srotamsi and the Grahas".

Placement of the 6B bhavesha or 7B bhavesha six, eight or twelve away from its own bhava (chart rotation)

6B-6B bhavesha and 7B-7B bhavesha from the Surya Lagna and Chandra Lagna

Following these principles, we can confirm in the birth chart specific issues that we discover during an Ayurvedic examination.

Summary

When you first look at a birth chart, it is natural to become fixated on stand-out bhavas and graha combinations. In every chart, there is something that immediately grabs your attention. Perhaps Guru occupies the Lagna, Mangala and Rahu are in association or Surya is eclipsed by Rahu. I have seen inexperienced *and* experienced Jyotishis fall into the trap of making "quick and dirty" conclusions based on such eye-popping configurations. The concepts and methodology presented in Section II and III will prevent you from falling into this same trap.

You now have the tools and techniques necessary to evaluate the dosha prakruti and constitutional strength of your client. You can also assess the health of the dhatus and identify specific khavaigunyas.

In the next section, our health evaluation process is broadened to include the mental and emotional health of the client and his or her susceptibility to health conditions related to *mano vaha srotas* (channel of the mind).

Introduction to Section IV

The one who is established in the Self, who has balanced doshas, balanced agni, properly formed dhatus, proper elimination of malas, properly functioning bodily processes, and whose mind, soul and senses are pure is called a healthy person. (Sushruta Samhita, 15.10)

The channel of the mind is the *mano vaha srotas*. Its functions include thinking, feeling, desire, memory and discrimination. Its origin (*mula*) is the subtle heart center (represented by the cardiac plexus)[1] and its opening (*mukha*) is the sense organs: ears, skin, eyes, tongue and nose. The pathway (*marga*) of this vaha srotas is the entire body. That the mind originates in the space of the heart and that consciousness flows throughout the body is in contrast to the Western notion that the mind and awareness is located in the brain.

As a holistic science, Ayurveda recognizes that body and mind work together in human beings. The affinity between the channel of the mind and that of the nervous system (majja vaha srotas), the physical structure by which the mind acts in the body, exemplifies this notion.

This same interconnectedness of body and mind is evidenced by the interplay of doshas and gunas. The doshas are elemental compositions responsible for the physiological functioning of the brain, nervous system and hormonal secretions of the body—activities that influence a person's personality and mental make-up. The gunas are subtle energies that influence the mind, shaping our mental-emotional orientation and spiritual nature. Gunas give rise to subtle thinking and behavioral patterns that form over lifetimes, and cause us to act and react in predictable ways. The doshas and gunas intimately intertwine—each impacts and shapes the other—making differentiation of cause and effect near impossible.

This dynamic interaction of the doshas and gunas with the mano and majja srotamsi delineates the psychosomatic nature of a person. Considered broadly, it may be labeled as "personality". A comprehensive perspective on personality is presented by the authors of *Comparative Study of Personality with Ayurvedic Prakriti*:

> Personality can be defined as a dynamic and organized set of characteristics possessed by a person that uniquely influences his or her cognitions, motivations and behaviors in various situations. Personality also refers to the pattern of thoughts, feelings, social adjustments and behaviors consistently exhibited over time that strongly influences one's expectations, self-perceptions, values and attitudes. It also predicts human reactions to other people, problems and stress.[2]

In Section IV, we journey deeper into the yantra of the birth chart to understand the unique make-up of the individual. We will examine the interaction of the subtle gunas of sattva, rajas and tamas with the doshas and learn how the birth chart can give insight into a person's

---

[1] The *mula* (root) of the mano vaha srotas includes the ten sensory pathways located in this same area. There is one pair of channels for each sense faculty: hearing, touch, vision, taste and smell.
[2] *Comparative Study of Personality with Ayurvedic Prakriti*, pg. 125.

emotional and mental construct.

SECTION IV: Manas Prakruti and Mental-Emotional Health

Chapter 12: The Interplay of the Trigunas and Tridoshas

Sankhya System of Tattvas

Sankhya is a philosophical system well-known to the Ayurvedic practitioner. It forms the foundation of many important aspects of Ayurveda. Much of its perspective and terminology has been adopted by Jyotisha. In Section IV: "Manas Prakruti and Mental-Emotional Health", the tattvas identified by Sankhya philosophy are frequently referenced. Thus, we begin with a brief overview of the Sankhya school of thought.

Figure 7: Journey of Consciousness into Matter[1]

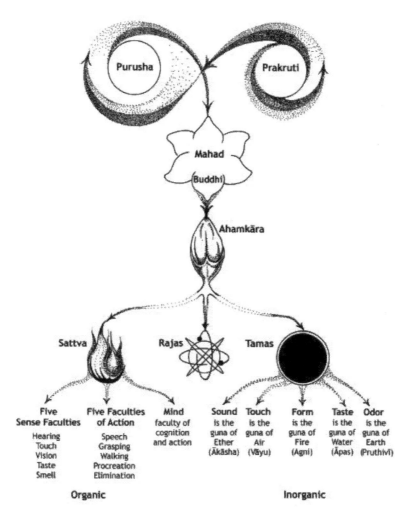

---

[1] Lad, B.A.M.S., B.A.Sc., Vasant D. *The Textbook of Ayurveda: Fundamental Principles of Ayurveda, Volume One.* 2002, Journey of Consciousness into Matter, p.7.

Sankhya evolved over many hundreds, perhaps even thousands, of years. Kapila, the sage most recognized for his contribution to Sankhya, identifies 25 tattvas (or building blocks of material reality), beginning with Purusha (individual souls).[2] Patanjali and other great Indian philosophers and spiritual leaders have used the Sankhya classification system as the foundation for a comprehensive theological and/or spiritual construct.

Sankhya discerns the principles (*tattvas*) of the universe in a successive manner, beginning most broadly with consciousness (Purusha) and reducing to five elements (*maha bhutas*): ether, air, fire, water and earth. According to this system of classification, some tattvas precipitate subsequent tattvas and some are products only; that is, they do not give rise to a subsequent tattva. The successive appearance of the tattvas depicts the journey of consciousness into matter, as illustrated in the above figure.

During the journey of consciousness into matter, each tattva manifests as a particular blend of matter and consciousness which resonates at a unique frequency. Compare the subtle vibration of refined perception to the dense vibration of consciousness embodied within the earth element.

Pure consciousness is Purusha, or the soul nature of human beings. Prakruti is the Creatrix of the universe. As choiceless, passive awareness, Purusha sits as spectator to Prakruti, as she dances her dance of creation. With eternal desire for her beloved Purusha, Prakruti manifests a universe that reflects his light, just as the moon reflects the light of the sun as it moves across the night sky.

The first expression of Prakruti is *mahat*, the cosmic intelligence that sustains the order of the universe and the arrangement of intelligence into orderly and constructive action. As Prakruti continues her dance of creation, *ahamkara* (I-maker) forms. Ahamkara is the ego principle that allows us to function as individuals in the mundane world. It is our sense of independence and the source of our will-power. The moment we identify ourselves as separate individuals (via ahamkara), *mahat* (universal intelligence) becomes individualized intelligence, or *buddhi*.

Because of ahamkara, we experience the effects of the gunas (sattva, rajas and tamas) on our minds. All three gunas are required for proper action. For example, sleeping requires the tamasic qualities of dullness and inertia. An excessive amount of rajasic energy at night-time creates insomnia, but some rajasic energy is needed in order to stimulate wakefulness. The sattvic quality of clarity is needed for meditation. If an excess of rajasic energy is present, the mind wanders in many directions. Likewise, if there is too much tamasic energy during mediation, sleep soon overcomes us. In these same ways, all grahas are required for optimal functioning, each in its proper place and proportion.

The three gunas interact to create the organic and inorganic universe. Sattva predominates in the realm of sensory perception, made up of *manas* (mind), the 5 *jnanendriyas* (sensory pathways: hearing, touch, vision, taste and smell) and 5 *karmendriyas* (motor pathways: speech, grasping, walking, procreation and elimination). Manas is the faculty of cognition and

---

[2] In the Sankhya system, the state of the universe prior to the manifestation of individual souls is called *avyakta* (not manifest) or *mula prakruti* (root of origin).

includes the sensory mind, the recipient of input from the jnanendriyas.

The inorganic universe consists of the 5 *maha bhutas* (great elements) and the 5 *tanmatras*. Tanmatras are the subtle, essential qualities of the elements. The tanmantra of sound is the essential (and only) quality of ether, just as touch is the most prominent quality of wind. The tanmantra of form is the quality of fire; that of taste, water, and that of odor, earth.

The 25 tattvas of Sankhya are reflected in the Vedic birth chart. The position of the grahas at the time of birth shows the unique expression of consciousness that characterizes the individual in this lifetime. As such, the Vedic birth chart reflects the distinct way in which creation and consciousness dance in an individual.

Sattva, Rajas and Tamas

Although minds come from sattva (and hence all minds are inherently sattvic), a person's *manas prakruti* or mental nature is influenced by experiences and related samskaras (conditioning) that may be sattvic, rajasic or tamasic. These samskaras become deeply crystalized in all levels of our being and, according to the Jyotisha worldview, even follow us from one incarnation to the next. Thus, a person's mind is typically a mix of sattvic, rajasic and tamasic impressions, with one guna predominant.

Sattva is the principle of truth, balance and intelligence in creation. It has the qualities of clarity, joy, compassion, harmony and love. It supports spiritual evolution and inclines a person towards spiritual values and ethics. Rajas is the essence of desire and passion. It gives us the drive to act and react, and promotes change and movement. Tamas has the characteristics of resistance, inertia, cohesion and attachment. These qualities give slowness of mind and incline one toward inaction.

Rajas and tamas play important roles, but they should operate under the jurisdiction of sattva, which brings order and balance to their functions. When rajas or tamas override sattva, the result is stress, imbalance or mental dis-ease. The gunas have an affinity for the mano vaha srotas, carrier of our impressions, emotions, thoughts and ideas, and they strongly affect its functioning.[3]

Ayurveda acknowledges a relationship between the doshas and gunas. For example, when tamas is increased in a predominantly kapha person, there is stubbornness, attachment, living in the past, hoarding and cloudy or slow thinking. When rajas predominates in this same person, it shows as emotional vacillation, sentimentality, living in the future, excessive worry about others, and so on. Kapha can also become a channel for sattva qualities. In that case, we see qualities like emotional stability, conviction, commitment and compassion.

In contrast, consider how pitta dosha expresses in combination with the three gunas. Tamas with pitta shows as hostility, dominance, intolerance of others and even violence; rajas, as passion, lust, ambition for power and position, criticism, pride and sense of superiority; and sattva, as comprehension, self-reliance, excellence, courage, enterprise and motivation.

Lastly, each guna finds expression through vata dosha in the following ways. Tamas displays

---

[3] For a discussion of mano vaha srotas, see "Introduction to Section IV".

as loneliness, mental confusion, fear, panic or reclusiveness. Nervousness, hyperactivity, racing mind, changeable nature and hypersensitivity are indications of rajas working through vata dosha. Sattva expressed through this same dosha shows as curiosity, mental alertness, subtlety, creativity, enthusiasm and quick comprehension. In these ways, we can see how the bodily doshas interact with the mental gunas.

The classical texts of Ayurveda define 9 types of dosha prakruti. Acknowledging the subtle influence of the gunas, these same texts identify 19 mental-emotional temperaments. Eight of these temperaments are sattvic, and these eight are aptly named after a divine godhead. For example, the mental qualities of a Brahma (the Creator God) temperament are purity, self-control, love for truth, sophisticated self-expression, freedom from passion and anger and the tendency to care for all creatures.

Aindra (having the traits of Indra, the fierce protector of the Gods) is another sattvic temperament, but it has attributes associated with Lord Indra's courageous manner and royal command: authoritative speech, bravery, magnanimity, strength and splendor, far-sightedness and self-sufficiency. There is also Gandharva (celestial musician) temperament, another sattvic mindset. One with a Gandharva temperament is relaxed and happy-go-lucky. He is expert in dance, song and music, proficient in story-telling, versed in poetry and ballads and knowledgeable in the great stories and the history of his culture.

Charaka Samhita also illumines the different mental temperaments in which rajas or tamas overtake sattva guna. The former types are named after various demonic forces, like Asura (ghostly demon), Rakshasa (evil demon) and Sakuna (bird-like demon). For instance, the Sakuna temperament is unsteady, passionate, preoccupied with sexual gratification, fickle, undisciplined. He lives for the moment, and constantly indulges in food.[4]

In contrast, tamas mentalities are named after lower life forms, such as Pasava (sharing the traits of an animal) and Matsya (sharing the traits of a fish). Illustrative of the tamas mindset is Vanaspatya (sharing the traits of vegetable life) which is indolent, devoid of intellectual faculties, idle and dependent on others.

This Ayurvedic perspective has its parallel in Jyotisha. Although each graha has an inherent guna, various planetary conditions and influences as well as yogas can bring sattva, rajas or tamas to its expression. Therefore, we can distinguish 21 (7 grahas and 3 gunas) mental-emotional temperaments, compared to Ayurveda's 19 dispositions. These 21 mental inclinations are described in Chapter 4: "Graha Archetypes".

The Gunas of the Grahas and Rashis

Just as each graha has a dominant dosha prakruti, it also has a prominent guna. Surya, Chandra and Guru are sattvic, for their life-force is one of harmony, balance, virtue and clarity. Budha and Shukra are naturally rajasic, making these grahas active, mobile and change-oriented. Mangala, Shani, Rahu and Ketu tend toward tamasic actions that are often self-centered, self-destructive or contrary to societal norms.

---

[4] Sakuna is an ancient atmospheric demon who wanders aimlessly in the mid-space, has a mouth of iron, sharp bird-like beak and embellished with countless adornments.

Table 4: Gunas and Grahas

Graha	Guna
Surya	sattva
Chandra	sattva
Mangala	tamas
Budha	rajas
Guru	sattva
Shukra	rajas
Shani	tamas
Rahu	tamas
Ketu	tamas

Similarly, each rashi has a manas prakruti based on the guna of its ruling planet. Surya-ruled Leo, Chandra-ruled Cancer and Guru-ruled Sagittarius and Pisces are sattvic rashis. Rajasic Budha and Shukra rule Gemini and Virgo and Taurus and Libra, respectively. These rashis display rajas guna. The remaining rashis are ruled by tamasic Mangala, e.g., Aries and Scorpio, and Shani, e.g., Capricorn and Aquarius, and are of the tamas guna.

Table 5: Gunas and Rashis

Lagna	Guna	Lagna	Guna
Aries	tamas	Libra	rajas
Taurus	rajas	Scorpio	tamas
Gemini	rajas	Sagittarius	sattva
Cancer	sattva	Capricorn	tamas
Leo	sattva	Aquarius	tamas
Virgo	rajas	Pisces	sattva

Manas Prakruti as Shown in the Birth Chart

In Chapter 3: "Dosha Prakruti", the Lagna and Lagnesha are shown to be the basis for evaluating dosha prakruti, because they represent the physicality and constitutional make-up of the individual. Since Chandra is the indicator for our mental-emotional construct, we assess a person's manas prakruti using the Chandra Lagna.

Our basic rule is: the manas prakruti of the individual is that of the rashi that rules the Chandra Lagna (primary) and that of its Lagnesha (secondarily). For example, if Chandra occupies Virgo and its Lagnesha (Budha) is placed in Aries, the manas prakruti is rajas (Virgo-ruled Chandra Lagna) and, secondarily, tamas (the Lagnesha placed in Aries).

However, this basic principle must be refined to incorporate birth chart-specific graha placements and conditions, just as we do when evaluating dosha prakruti. When assessing which gunas are predominant in a person's manas prakruti, give priority to those grahas that meet the following criteria.

1. Strongly conditioned grahas that influence the Chandra Lagna (primary) or its Lagnesha (secondary), or that occupy the kendras from this lagna (primary).

   We saw in Chapter 3 that strong grahas influencing the Lagna or Lagnesha or occupying the kendras from the Udaya Lagna powerfully imprint their doshic nature and physical attributes on the individual. Likewise, grahas meeting these same requirements from the Chandra Lagna strongly impart their mental gunas on the individual.

   For example, assume that Chandra is ordinary in condition and sva rashi Guru (a sattva graha) aspects the Chandra Lagna and/or occupies a kendra. This indicates a sattvic mental disposition. Should an exalted Shani (a tamasic graha) also influence the Chandra Lagna and/or occupy a kendra from the Chandra Lagna, then one's temperament has qualities of sattva *and* tamas.

   Of course, from Chandra Lagna, Chandra itself occupies the lagna. Hence, when strong (e.g., bright moon, sva rashi, exalted moon), it contributes towards a sattvic temperament.

   Importantly, do not consider the guna of any graha that is of mixed condition.

2. If #1 above does not apply, give priority to grahas of ordinary condition that influence the Lagna (primarily) or its Lagnesha (secondarily) from the Chandra Lagna.

   For instance, when Shukra (a rajasic graha) influences the Chandra Lagna and is ordinary in condition, the manas prakruti is rajas. If, as well, Mangala (a tamasic graha) is ordinary in condition and also influences the Chandra Lagna, then the manas prakruti is a mix of rajas and tamas.

Should this second principle also not apply, we are left with our fundamental rule: the manas prakruti of the individual is that of the rashi that rules the Chandra Lagna (primary) and that of its Lagnesha (secondarily).

Client Birth Chart Illustrations

Let us return to several client charts presented in Chapter 3, beginning with Frank, who has a Taurus-ruled Chandra Lagna.

Applying the first principle, we notice that Chandra (a sattva graha) has two factors of strength: it is bright and exalted. There are no other strongly conditioned grahas that influence the Chandra Lagna or its Lagnesha (Shukra) or that occupy a kendra from this lagna. This shows a sattvic mindset. Recall that Frank has a kapha dosha prakruti, hence, we can expect sattva to express itself in Frank's life as devotion, compassion and sensitivity to the needs of others.

Chapter 12: The Trigunas and their Interplay with the Doshas

Frank: Chandra Lagna

Terrance: Chandra Lagna

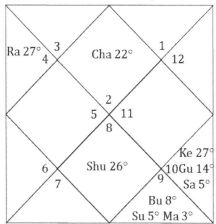

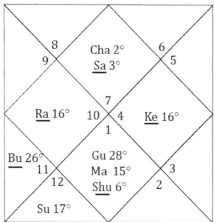

From Terrance's Libra-ruled Chandra Lagna, what could you surmise about his manas prakruti? Shani (a tamasic graha) is the only graha that has two factors of strength (exalted and retrograde) and it influences the Chandra Lagna and its Lagnesha (Shukra). Sva rashi Mangala (also a tamasic graha) also influences this Lagna and its Lagnesha, adding another factor of tamas manas prakruti. But, notice that two strong sattva grahas, Chandra (a bright moon) and Shukra (retrograde), influence the Chandra Lagna. In this case, tamas is the predominant guna, and sattva is secondary.

Given Terrance's vata-pitta prakruti, how might tamas guna manifest? Terrance may feel burdened by a heavy sense of responsibility to others in his life, such as his wife and family. He might experience frequent bouts of moodiness or depression, or come across as being obstinate and set in his ways.

For our next example, let us evaluate Sandra's Virgo-ruled Chandra birth chart. No strongly conditioned grahas influence the Chandra Lagna or its Lagnesha (Budha), nor are there any strongly conditioned grahas placed in a kendra from this lagna. So we need to look at influences from ordinary grahas. In Sandra's case, Mangala is ordinary and influences the Chandra Lagna (primary) from its 7B position. Thus, Sandra has tamas as her primary mental guna. Since we determined earlier that Sandra has a pitta dosha prakruti, she is likely to express signs of tamas through pitta dosha. For example, she may be critical and domineering, or show frequent signs of anger.

For our final client example, we have the birth chart of Alexandra, a Scorpio-ruled Chandra Lagna. We assessed Alexandra's prakruti as vata dosha in Chapter 3. What is her dominant mental guna? The Chandra Lagna is influenced by a strongly conditioned (retrograde) Shani. This gives Alexandra a tamas-dominated mental prakruti.[5] Tamas expressed through vata dosha shows as mental confusion, a sense of being burdened with responsibilities, feelings of isolation, fears, etc.

---

[5] Chandra is a full moon but, since a lunar eclipse occurred on the day Alexandra was born, its light was not visible. Therefore, we do not consider an eclipsed moon as strongly-conditioned.

Chapter 12: The Trigunas and their Interplay with the Doshas

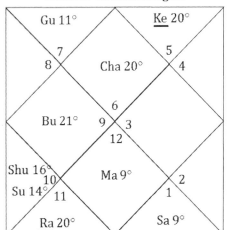
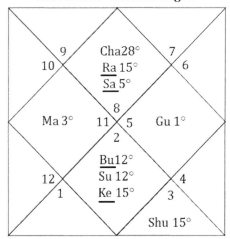

Be sure to corroborate your Jyotisha findings with the results you obtain from pulse diagnosis or the questionnaire in Appendix D.

Manas Vikruti

Manas prakruti, that is, the fundamental samskaras that influence a person's primary or default responses and behavior, may change over the course of a lifetime, but this is surprisingly rare. Still, because of the subtle nature of thoughts and emotions, a person's superficial mental state (manas vikruti) can change daily, hourly, or even moment-to-moment. Perhaps you take a jog on the beach, engage in a peaceful mediation, have a hectic day at work or argue with your spouse. Each action has the ability to influence the quality of your mind and emotions.

When we consistently practice life-promoting regimes, such as following a good daily routine (dinacharya), we support the expression of sattva. The longer we practice any habit, the more likely it is to become a predominant pattern (part of our manas prakruti). Rajas or tamas prevail in our mindset when we make inappropriate lifestyle choices, have lack of clarity in our relationships, experience unresolved mental-emotional stress or suppress our emotions. Since rajas and tamas also promote these poor choices (cause becoming effect and effect becoming cause), it can become a vicious cycle.

Just as long-term doshic imbalances result in a buildup of physical toxins (*ama*), a long-term excess of rajas and tamas produces mental ama, the basis for mental illness and disease. Because of the close connection between gunas and doshas, if the imbalance is left unaddressed, it eventually disturbs tissues and organs, causing physical disease.

Jyotisha recognizes that each natal graha is subject to a stream of dynamic influences, including planetary transits and changing dashas and bhuktis. A person may be generally inclined towards sattvic thoughts and actions, but challenging dashas, grueling transits or the triggering of daridra or arishta-like yogas can alter his or her mental and emotional state.[6]

---
[6] Daridra yogas are covered in *Your Healing Stars: Volume I, Fundamental Principles of Vedic Astrology*.

For instance, a person may have a sattvic disposition, but when tamasic Shani transits natal Chandra, it often causes emotional moodiness, grief and sorrow, a sense of loneliness or mental dullness. Alternatively, a transit of rajasic Budha over natal Chandra may express as emotional vacillation, excessive sentimentality, and so on. The effect of these shifts on a short and long-term basis depends on the relative strength and weakness of the grahas involved.[7]

Importantly, be proactive in identifying upcoming changes in a person's mental perspective by using the Jyotisha timing techniques presented in *Your Healing Stars: Volume I*. This can buy a client time to implement supportive daily practices that enhance favorable modifications and minimize the anguish and anxiety associated with unfavorable ones.

Summary

A healthy and productive life is more likely when the body is free from disease, the mind is calm and lucid and the spirit is uplifted. Ayurveda promotes practices that cultivate a sattvic state of mind and promote mental clarity, intelligence and balance.

The interplay of the doshas and gunas gives opportunity for a multitude of therapeutic and restorative measures that address issues from both cognitive and somatic perspectives. These include diet, herbs and clinical therapies on the physical level; yoga asanas, pranayama and color therapy on the mental-emotional level and mediation, rituals and devata worship on the spiritual level.

Similarly, in Section VI: "Healing through the Grahas", sundry Jyotisha upayas are recommended, such as planetary aromatherapy, mantras, gemstone usage and nakshatra rasayana. These Jyotisha remedial measures are suggested for grahas that are causing excessive rajas or tamas.

---

[7] Be sure to review Chapter 4: "Graha Archetypes" for the sattva, rajas and tamasic mental inclinations of each graha.

Chapter 13: Emotional Health and Wellbeing

Introduction
Submerged in the subconscious field of manas are samskaras, mental-emotional tendencies arising from repetitive or powerfully influential experiences over countless lifetimes. These samskaras help determine the way we react to our present-time experiences. Samskaras condition the mind and body by creating ingrained habits and behavior responses. Less ingrained than these deep, subconscious samskaras are our memories from current lifetime experiences, many of which are readily recoverable. Our present-time memories and subconscious samskaras percolate to the surface of the sensory mind as emotions and feelings. Taken as a whole, samskaras, memories and emotions are associated with Chandra. This is why Jyotisha considers Chandra as the most important graha. Natal Chandra's condition, planetary associations and yogas define our unique perspective on life.

Our primary interaction with the material world is through the lens of the sensory mind, which receives input from the jnanendriyas (sense organs). Shukra is the graha of carnal pleasures that allows us to experience the beauty of the world through the sense organs of hearing, touch, vision, taste and smell.

Chandra and Shukra operate on the vital realm of feelings and sensations. They are responsible for our desires, passions and attractions and repulsions, be that wishing for fame, longing for an intimate relationship or craving for particular foods. Much of our life is spent in the pursuit of sense gratifications. As one urge is satiated, another soon arises . . . and then another, and another and another. The stilling of our emotions and putting at bay petty desires, likes and dislikes is an important step on the spiritual path. This topic is addressed in Section V: "Spiritual Welfare & Dharma".

If we allow our obsessions, attractions and aversions to overcome us, disease manifests as emotional anxiety, fear, depression and even violence. In the realm of psychosomatic illness, it has long been established that emotional imbalance can exacerbate disequilibrium (doshic imbalance) on the physical level, or even cause it.

In this chapter, we examine the emotional and desire nature of the client, as shown by natal grahas Chandra and Shukra, lunar yogas and the 4B-4B bhavesha and 7B-7B bhavesha and their yogas.

Other critical aspects of the mind include its capacity for discrimination and the mental functions of organizing, prioritizing and interpreting information. These functions are performed by the rational mind. Far vaster than the rational mind is buddhi, our individual access to mahat and the source of universal wisdom and revelation.[1] The rational mind and buddhi are topics addressed in the next chapter.

Fruits of the Moon
Surya's queen, Chandra, with its glowing white light, radiates nurturance, familial love,

---
[1] For an explanation of the Sankhya tattvas and mahat and buddhi, see Chapter 12: "The Interplay of the Tridoshas and Trigunas".

emotional security and connectedness. Lording over the rasa dhatu, whose function is to bathe and nourish the cells of the body, Chandra has prinana, 'the act of pleasing, delighting or satisfying', as its function.

Astrologer Sphujidhvaja, author of *Yavanajataka*, describes the courteous ways of this night-time luminary, who in the ancient scriptures is considered masculine:[2] "The Moon is white, shining and handsome, with an appearance like that of smooth waters ... He is wise, patient and fond of courtesy, controlling himself in accordance with the laws of Manu. Speaking kindly and clothed in spotless garments, the playful Moon with pleasing eyes laughs softly and sweetly."[3]

The sensitive and intuitive deer is Chandra's celestial animal. These gentle animals are constantly on the move, just like Chandra. Deer prefer to roam in small family-units, the elders tending to the care of newborns. In this same way, sensitive and nurturing Chandra is all about family and imparts a strong sense of community. These aspects of our life provide deep contentment and peace of mind.

The birth chart condition of Chandra reveals the circumstances of one's early upbringing, including the extent to which one felt loved and nurtured and, related to that, one's ability to love and nurture others. Most outer displays of nurturing, be that cooking, caretaking, home-making or gardening (i.e., nurturing Mother Earth), are represented by Chandra.

When Chandra is well-conditioned and participating in positive yogas,[4] the person more likely perceives choice and learns from life's adversities. As well, there is a sense of unconditional acceptance and unwavering support by family members, and the person easily forms lasting bonds with others. A well-conditioned Chandra creates fertile ground that nourishes the blossoming of auspicious yogas in the birth chart. Indeed, scripture reminds us that natal Chandra is the seed from which all things flower and flourish.

When Chandra is poorly-conditioned and involved in challenging yogas,[5] a sense of limitation sets in and a person may feel trapped. Familial support can seem unavailable and the person struggles to connect with others. In this case, even if there are auspicious yogas in the birth chart, the person often lacks the emotional foundation required to make the most of them.

For these reasons, the condition of natal Chandra is critical for assessing emotional health and inner peace of mind. Determine where on the graha condition spectrum natal Chandra falls.

---

[2] In the older astrological scriptures, the grahas are considered masculine and the lunar nakshatras are feminine.
[3] *Yavanajataka of Sphujidhvaja*, D. Pingree (translator), pg. 8. Harvard University Press, 1978.
[4] Positive yogas include yogas for health, raj yogas, dhana yogas, yogas of intelligence, auspicious bhava yogas and lunar yogas. Lunar yogas are presented in this chapter.
[5] These yogas include daridra yogas, arishta-like yogas for ill-health and inauspicious bhava yogas.

Papa graha influences

Chandra is the most sensitive of the nine grahas. When influenced by papa grahas, it greatly impacts the person's state of mind and emotional orientation. Beginning with Shani, let us consider the results of various papa graha influences.

When Shani influences Chandra, it can indicate an emotionally-sensitive individual, particularly if Shani is strong, while Chandra is weak. Moreover, Shani imparts a heavy sense of responsibility, often accompanied by the fear of not satisfying basic needs in life. Alternatively (or additionally), there can be an intense feeling of withdrawal from the world that stems from an inability to connect with others at a deep level. Deep-seated emotional blockages and loneliness are other potential results of this planetary combination.

Interestingly, Shani's influence on natal Chandra is a prerequisite for certain spiritual yogas. When Chandra is influenced by this graha of detachment, it can strengthen a person's ability to witness. As well, this combination promotes ascetic disciplines such as prolonged fasting and meditative contemplation. Add to this an influence from papa graha Mangala and you have the makings for *sanyasa* (renunciation) *yoga*. (Sanyasa yogas are presented in Chapter 18: "Yogas for Spiritual Growth".)

Another challenging lunar combination is an association with one of the nodes of the moon. Rahu-Chandra can be an explosive combination, indicating emotional volatility, impulsiveness or impatience. These attributes can be extreme when Rahu is weak (debilitated) or strong (exalted),[6] or when Chandra is a new moon or eclipsed by Rahu. Yet, if Rahu occupies a benefic rashi (i.e., one ruled by a shubha graha) and Chandra is bright on the day of birth (or possesses other factors of strength), this same combination provides farsightedness (Rahu) and gives one the vision to perceive future (Rahu) needs of the masses (Chandra). These are positive traits for a politician or business person.

Chandra-Ketu combinations create a very different emotional profile. When in association with Chandra, moksha graha Ketu can lead one down the path of enlightenment. Still, it often does so as a result of lifelong emotional distance in relationships or a frequent sense of being invisible to others. Whereas Chandra-Rahu creates psychic vulnerability (possession by spirits), Chandra-Ketu is more prone towards psychic sensitivity (ability to connect with "helpers" on the other side). As with Chandra-Rahu, the condition of natal Chandra and Ketu determine more precisely the impact of this planetary duo.

Multiple papa graha influences on Chandra, especially when Chandra is weak, suggests a troubled childhood, perhaps from family violence, emotional abandonment or the absence of nurturing parents. Since Chandra represents the mother as well as the family unit, such difficulties may revolve around the mother. Often, such early childhood experiences seem to lead to a spiritual orientation later in life. Hence, what may appear in the birth chart as a deep psychological disturbance may be an important part of the tapestry in which a spiritual life is woven.

---

[6] Note that Chandra is debilitated in Scorpio, the exaltation rashi of Rahu and Ketu, and Rahu and Ketu are debilitated in Taurus, the exaltation rashi of Chandra. This illustrates the inherent incompatibility of Chandra and the nodes of the moon.

Shukra, graha karaka for happiness

Shukra is an important subset of the manas, for it represents the sense mind through which we derive enjoyment from the external world, be that a stunning sunset, a delectable meal or the sweet scent of flowers in full bloom. As the rashi ruler of Taurus (the natural 2B rashi), Shukra shows our sense gratification derived from the appearance (eyes), taste (mouth) and smell (nose) of objects (2B affairs).

Shukra is also the karaka for sensuality and responsible for the pleasure gained from intimate relationships with others. An elegant white horse is its celestial animal, for the rarity of a pure white horse is symbolic of this graha's unusual beauty.

White is also the color of fertility. Since antiquity, Shukra has been associated with fertility and credited for beautiful offspring. Shukra is the rashi ruler of Libra (the natural 7B rashi) and the graha karaka for love, marriage and sexual intimacy. Artava (female reproductive tissues) and shukra (male reproductive tissues) srotamsi, and their psychological attributes of affection, sensuality, charisma and devotion, are represented by Shukra and the 7B.

Mantreswara describes sense-oriented Shukra in the following way: "From Venus should be sought the information regarding . . . the three branches of dance, drama and music, wife, pleasure, flowers, sexual union . . . sex and women, lustfulness, ministership, politeness, marriage and festivity."[7]

Determine where on the graha condition spectrum natal Shukra falls. When Shukra is well-conditioned, relationships are harmonious due to mutual respect and cooperation. The person approaches each acquaintance with kindness and thoughtful consideration. When it comes to intimacy, there is ease in expressing love and an understanding of the partner's human frailties. The wonders of nature inspire the person and creativity and visual acumen find expression in the home, through hobbies and at work.

When Shukra is poorly-conditioned, intimate relationships are anything but smooth sailing. Perhaps, a person feels that the grass is always greener on the other side, or compares potential partners to a predetermined checklist of required attributes rather than approaching people from the heart. One may also be consumed by sensual pleasures. None of these scenarios bode well for a loving, sustainable marriage. Other consequences can include a sense of vulnerability and insecurity when engaging in social situations with people one does not know. Or, one may struggle to uncover his unique creative expression, causing him to doubt his inner worth.

Lunar yogas

There are three lunar yogas that indicate emotional wellbeing. These yogas are called: *sunapha, anapha* and *duradhara yoga*.[8] They require graha occupation of the second and/or

---

[7] *Mantreswara's Phala Deepika*, S.S. Sareen (translator), Chapter 2.6. Sagar Publications, 2001.
[8] Note that for these yogas, it is helpful to view the birth chart from the Chandra Lagna.

twelfth bhava from natal Chandra. Because Surya's occupation in either bhava (or the same bhava as Chandra) indicates a dark moon, such a position disqualifies these yogas. (Rahu and Ketu, the mathematical points in the sky where lunar eclipses occur, do not qualify as participants in lunar yogas.)

Sunapha yoga forms when a graha occupies the second bhava from natal Chandra. According to the principle of bhavat bhavam (bhava from bhava), the bhava that is second from any other bhava represents the resources that a person acquires to fulfill that bhava's affairs. Thus, a graha 2 away from natal Chandra serves as a support for the manas and a resource for expanding the person's consciousness.

For example, if Budha is second from natal Chandra, then curiosity, intelligence and reasoning are the means by which a person enhances their perception of the world. If Shani is second from natal Chandra, then the person uses structure, focus and discipline for that purpose. In sunapha yoga, a person actively seeks the mental-emotional and/or intellectual qualities of those grahas that are second from natal Chandra.

Anapha yoga forms when a graha occupies the twelfth bhava from natal Chandra. Grahas 12 away from Chandra behave very differently than the acquisitive nature of grahas 2 away. When a graha is 12 away from Chandra, the person receives emotional satisfaction and the manas is nourished by the giving away to others or sharing the qualities of twelfth bhava grahas.

To illustrate, when Guru is twelfth from Chandra, a person establishes emotional connections through sharing spiritual wisdom. Alternately, when Shukra is twelfth from Chandra, the person seeks emotional fulfillment through acts of kindness and friendships. In these ways, grahas that are situated 12 bhavas away from natal Chandra support and nourish the manas.

Lastly, when grahas occupy the bhava on *both* sides of Chandra (i.e., when they flank Chandra), duradhara (invincible) yoga forms. This is a combination of sunapha and anapha yoga and promotes Chandra's acquiring *and* giving nature.

Importantly, grahas participating in lunar yogas should not be weak. As might be imagined, when Chandra itself is weak, the karma phala of these yogas are greatly reduced or absent. When multiple grahas form sunapha, anapha or duradhara yoga, look to the strongest graha, for its qualities are the ones the person will inculcate.

4B-4B Bhavesha

The acquisition of learning, the welfare of the mother, happiness, sweet-smelling substances, kin relations, emotional attributes, royal vehicles, lands and houses arise from the 4th house, say the sapient astrologers.[9]

The 4B is the nadir of the birth chart, representing the part of the sky hidden from view at the time of birth. As such, it represents our inner being—the emotional part of us that was shaped during early childhood by our mother, family life and social environment. The 4B

---

[9] *Vaidyanatha Dikshita's Jataka Parijata*, V. Subramanya Sastri (translator), Vol. III, Chapter XII.59. Rajan Publications, 2004.

indicates the love and nurturing we experienced during childhood, and our ability to form loving relationships with others. These are important indicators of emotional health.

This bhava is also one of the four kendras (places of action) that support our material existence. It represents our desire to raise a family and, more broadly, to contribute to our community.[10] Hence, this *sukha sthana* (place of happiness) is the window into our emotional wellbeing. It offers tremendous insight into the mental-emotional state of the individual.

In Chapter 5: "Constitutional Strength and Vitality", we presented two bhava yogas that are formed by the Lagna and its Lagnesha. These are called chamara and ava yoga. Similarly, there are two bhava yogas formed by the 4B and its bhavesha: *jaladhi* (water) and *kuhu* (new moon) *yoga*. As indicated below, these two yogas have similar requirements.

When the 4B bhavesha is strongly conditioned and well-placed *and* the 4B *or* 4B bhavesha is stabilized by the influence of a shubha graha, the auspicious jaladhi yoga forms. Mantreswara cites the karma phala of this yoga: "Person will have wealth via property and agriculture and own a large home. He will be *blessed with steady and lasting happiness* and have plenty of elephants and earnestly engages himself in the service of the Brahmins and the gods."[11]

In contrast, kuhu yoga forms when the 4B bhavesha is weakly conditioned and poorly-placed *and* the 4B *or* 4B bhavesha is destabilized by the influence of a papa graha. Using the notion of artha veda, Mantreswara declares the karma phala of kuhu yoga: "Person is *bereft of mother*, vehicles, friends, *happiness*, and without a house."[12]

Determine where along the continuum of well-conditioned to poorly-conditioned the 4B-4B bhavesha fall and whether jaladhi or kuhu yoga is present.

7B-7B Bhavesha

Marriage, loose sex life, victory in love or passion . . . deviation from the right or proper path . . . semen, husband's or wife's purity . . . sexual union, adopted son,[13] sex affairs . . ."[14]

The 7B *yuti sthana* (place of union) connects us with others for the mutual fulfillment of kama (desires), including sexual intimacy, common business goals and shared hopes and dreams. Relationship-specific mental tendencies (samskaras), behavioral patterns and outcomes are 7B territory. Thus, our interactions with *all* others and the joy we receive from them are seen from this bhava. At the root of most 7B problems are improper choices in partners, attraction to the "wrong" people, over dependence on others and/or poor relationship skills.

Two bhava yogas involving the 7B-7B bhavesha are *kama* (desire or passion) and *dushkriti*

---

[10] Early childhood-to-teenage socialization mechanisms are represented by the 4B-4B bhavesha. Thus, in addition to one's immediate community, this bhava-bhavesha represents the socialization process imparted from one's school environment.
[11] *Mantreswara's Phala Deepika*, S.S. Sareen (translator), Chapter 6.48. Sagar Publications, 2001.
[12] Ibid., Chapter 6.51.
[13] In earlier times, it was customary for the sister or brother of a deceased parent to marry the surviving spouse and adopt the child as their own. The 7B is the fifth (children) from the 3B of siblings.
[14] *Uttara Kalamrita*, Kalidasa, pg 118. Ranjan Publications, 1996.

(acting disrespectful) *yoga*. As stipulated below, the requirements for these yogas are the same as that of other bhava yogas presented.

When the 7B bhavesha is strongly conditioned and well-placed *and* the 7B or 7B bhavesha is stabilized by the influence of a shubha graha, kama yoga forms. Mantreswara cites the karma phala of this yoga: "The person with kama yoga in his birth chart does not cast evil looks at the wives of others as he himself is blessed with a charming wife, children and relatives. He surpasses his father by his noble qualities and attains great prosperity."[15]

In contrast, dushkriti yoga forms when the 7B bhavesha is weakly conditioned and poorly-placed *and* the 7B or 7B bhavesha is destabilized by the influence of a papa graha. Mantreswara declares the karma phala of dushkriti yoga: "The man born with this yoga in his birth chart suffers separation from his own wife and is inclined towards those of others. He wanders on the road unperceived and suffers from venereal diseases,[16] wrath from the sovereign, condemnation by his own relatives; all which causes a miserable life."[17]

Determine where on our bhava-bhavesha spectrum the 4B-4B bhavesha fall and whether kama or dushkriti yoga is present.

Client Case Illustration: Linda

To illustrate several principles described in this chapter, let us return to Linda's Cancer-ruled Lagna birth chart and look specifically at the following items: the condition and yogas of the 4B-4B bhavesha, condition of natal Chandra and the presence of lunar yogas.[18] (The reader is encouraged to evaluate the condition of natal Shukra and the condition and yogas of the 7B-7B bhavesha in Linda's birth chart.)

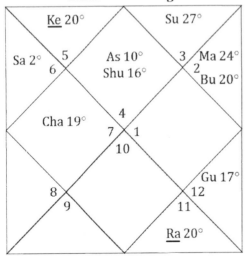

Linda: Cancer Lagna

Earlier, we determined Linda's dosha prakruti as kapha.[19] Her manas prakruti is sattva: from the Chandra Lagna, strongly conditioned (sva rashi) Guru (a sattva graha) aspects the Lagnesha (Shukra) of this lagna.

Now let us evaluate aspects of emotional health and stability as shown in Linda's birth chart, beginning with the 4B-4B bhavesha.

The 4B is stabilized by strongly conditioned (dig bala) Chandra. The 4B bhavesha (Shukra) is ordinary in condition, of mixed stabilization (aspected by Guru and papa graha flanking) and well-placed in the Lagna. Hence, we would place

---

[15] *Mantreswara's Phala Deepika*, S.S. Sareen (translator), Chapter 6.48. Sagar Publications, 2001.
[16] In accordance with Kalapurusha 7B significations (i.e., reproductive organs) and related diseases, the 7B is the bhava of venereal disease.
[17] *Mantreswara's Phala Deepika*, S.S. Sareen (translator), Chapter 6.64. Sagar Publications, 2001.
[18] Linda's chart is first presented in Chapter 5: "Constitutional Strength and Vitality".
[19] Ibid.

the 4B-4B bhavesha to the right of center on the bhava-bhavesha condition spectrum. Because the 4B bhavesha (Shukra) is not strongly conditioned, we do not have jaladhi yoga.

Importantly, notice that the Lagnesha (Chandra) is parivartana with the 4B bhavesha (Shukra). This closely unites Linda's sense of self-worth and direction (Lagna) with 4B affairs. Linda is likely to be maternal, emotionally-oriented and strongly influenced by her environment. Furthermore, home and family life are essential to her happiness. Linda's relationship with her mother is also intimately connected with her emotional wellbeing. Chart rotation (Libra-ruled 4B becomes the Lagna) and rashi confluence (Cancer rashi) confirms our initial 4B findings.

For a Cancer-ruled Lagna, the Lagnesha is also the karaka for manas. This makes Chandra's condition doubly important in Linda's chart. We noted above that Chandra is strong and well-placed in the 4B. Hence, it appears that Linda's emotional mind is stable, and that she has a satisfying home life and close bond with her mother.

Are there lunar yogas in Linda's chart? Shani's placement in the bhava twelfth from natal Chandra forms anapha yoga. Since Shani is the graha of seva (service), we would expect that Linda derives happiness by reaching out to others in need. Shani is as well the 7B bhavesha, so her emotional satisfaction would also come from providing for the needs of her husband.

Client Case Illustration: Alexandra

Next, let us take a look at Alexandra's birth chart to evaluate the same factors as examined in Linda's chart. (Once again, the reader is encouraged to evaluate the condition of natal Shukra and the condition and yogas of the 7B-7B bhavesha in Linda's birth chart.) We had earlier determined that Alexandra has a vata prakruti and rajas manas prakruti.[20]

Both the 4B and its bhavesha (Mangala) are stabilized by an aspect from Guru, although Guru is the bhavesha for the dusthana 3B and 12B. The 4B bhavesha (Mangala) is of ordinary condition and placed in the neutral 2B. Based on this assessment, we would place the 4B-4B bhavesha somewhere around the center on our bhava-bhavesha condition spectrum.

Notice that the 4B bhavesha (Mangala) is parivartana with the 11B bhavesha (Shani). This links Alexandra's emotional happiness with worldly goals and achievements. Further, chart rotation (Aries-ruled 4B becomes the Lagna) shows a similar 11B connection, i.e., Mangala is placed in the 11B.

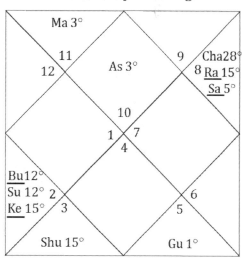

Alexandra: Capricorn Lagna

What is particularly unusual about Alexandra's birth chart is the condition of natal Chandra.

---

[20] Refer to Chapter 3 "Dosha Prakruti" and Chapter 12: "The Interplay of the Doshas and Gunas", respectively.

Chandra is not only debilitated, but also eclipsed by an exalted Rahu.[21] On the day Alexandra was born, a lunar eclipse was visible from her birth location. Moreover, natal Chandra is greatly destabilized by strongly conditioned (retrograde) Shani.

Although the 4B-4B bhavesha fall near the medium of our bhava-bhavesha condition continuum, our evaluation of natal Chandra is problematic for Alexandra's peace of mind. It suggests that Alexandra is likely to experience frequent bouts of emotional instability and/or mental stress and anxiety.

In Alexandra's case, signs of emotional volatility developed during her forties. She had entered into partnership with her husband (Chandra is the 7B bhavesha) and, together, they set ambitious financial goals (parivartana between 2B bhavesha and 11B bhavesha). They embarked on a joint real estate venture that involved owning and managing low-income rental properties. (Shani and Mangala, the graha karakas for real estate and property management, are parivartana.) The business partnership caused a great deal of anxiety for Alexandra, which in turn, stressed the marriage.

Notice that there are no lunar yogas in Alexandra's birth chart.

Summary

In summary, after determining the manas prakruti of your client, the next step in the mental-emotional health evaluation process is a methodical assessment of the client's emotional stability and soundness. For this purpose, consider the following.

1. Condition of Chandra (karaka for the manas), including difficult graha influences
2. Condition of Shukra (karaka for happiness and marital bliss)
3. Presence of lunar yogas
4. Condition of the 4B-4B bhavesha, including the presence of jaladhi or kuhu yoga
5. Condition of the 7B-7B bhavesha, including the presence of kama and dushkriti yoga

---

[21] Although an eclipsed moon is also a full moon, its light is not visible. Therefore, we do not consider an eclipsed moon as strongly-conditioned.

Chapter 14: Intelligence and Discernment

Introduction

Over 6,000 years ago, the enlightened seers of the *Rigveda* queried as to who really knows the purpose and end result of the human race? Who shall proclaim it? They conjure that even the gods may not know, for they came *after* the beginning of time. Still, the sages take refuge in their realization that an organized process of evolving universal intelligence guides the outcome. This is the notion of *ritam*, or dynamic truth: universal intelligence actively unfolding through a structured process of self-reflection and self-learning.

Douglas Brooks elegantly illustrates this underlying force in the universe: "As we peer out into the universe, we see gaseous bundles of stars that appear inchoate; nothing but an enormous collection of matter and gases. Given a few tens of millions of years, what appears as disorganized bundles of matter, mass and energy turns into beautiful spiral, spinning forms of orderly galaxies."[1]

In the Sankhya paradigm, the first expression of Prakruti is mahat, the cosmic intelligence that sustains the order of the universe. Guru, the graha responsible for the arrangement of intelligence into righteous action, encompasses this cosmic intelligence and its dynamism (ritam). At the individual level, mahat manifests as the higher, discerning mind, which is the gateway for profound spiritual insights, flashes of inspiration and revelations of truth. A sattvic graha, Guru allows us to perceive the commonality in all things; the unity and harmony of all life forms.

During the Vedic period, Guru is also known as Brahmanaspati. Sri Aurobindo, the renowned Indian spiritual sage, comments that Brahmanaspati is from the Sanskrit verb root *"brih"*, as in *brahman.* He further explains that *"brahman"* implies an expression of the heart or soul, as distinguished from an expression of thought in the mind.[2] Aurobindo describes *brahman* as "luminous intelligence" and wisdom "fashioned by the heart".[3] Others define the term as "the craving and fullness of the soul and striving towards the gods".[4] This is the notion that the ancient Vedic seers intended when they gave Guru the epithet Brahmanaspati.[5] Indeed, this graha of wisdom "fashioned by the heart" is none other than the inner guru that resides deep within our subtle heart region, the origin (mula) of the mano vaha srotas (channel of the mind).

In contrast is the rational mind, which allows us to see particularities in commonly shared features; to distinguish between things by way of their differences. This is an oak tree; that is not an oak tree. This is my home; that is not my home. The capacity of the mind to analyze and distinguish is an important function, one represented by Buddha. Like the rational mind, Budha is a quick moving planet, second only to Chandra. Its quickness supports intellectual

---

[1] *An Introduction to the History and Practice of Yoga*, a lecture by Douglas Brooks.
[2] *Secret of the Veda*, Sri Aurobindo, p. 271. Twin Lakes: Lotus Press, 1995.
[3] Ibid.
[4] *Traividyam = Traividyam: Vedic Studies in memory of Durgamohan Bhattacharyya*, p. 130.
[5] See *The Divine Forces of the Lunar Nakshatras*, written by the author, for the legends and myths of Brahmanaspati.

dexterity and mental fluidity.

In this chapter, we examine the higher mind and the intellect, as shown by natal grahas Guru and Budha, the 5B-5B bhavesha and 3B-3B bhavesha and their yogas, and yogas for intelligence and mental dexterity.

Grahas of Discernment and Ingenuity
Guru and the Higher Mind

Guru is the epitome of cosmic wisdom and divine grace. His Sanskrit name means 'dispeller of darkness', for Guru pierces the veil of ignorance with his brilliant light of truth. As well, this graha imparts curiosity about the meaning of life and interest in all things sacred. Its life-force is one of generosity, upliftment, optimism and hope.

According to Mantreswara: "From Jupiter the learned should seek information about knowledge, noble qualities, sons, minister, good behavior, teaching profession, magnanimity, knowledge of the Vedas and Puranas, progress and beatitude, reverence to gods and brahmins, yajana, worship, religious faith, treasure, wisdom, control over passions, honor and compassion . . . "[6]

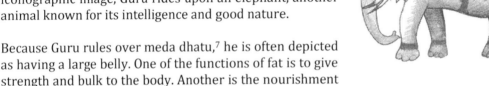

Guru is often associated with the sacred hamsa, a mystical swan. When offered milk mixed with water, the hamsa siphons only the milk. This sacred bird symbolizes the power of Guru's refined discrimination. In his iconographic image, Guru rides upon an elephant, another animal known for its intelligence and good nature.

Because Guru rules over meda dhatu,[7] he is often depicted as having a large belly. One of the functions of fat is to give strength and bulk to the body. Another is the nourishment and lubrication of the cells. In Ayurveda, this function is called *snehana*, meaning both 'lubrication' and 'affection'. Healthy fat tissue also nourishes the mental-emotional and spiritual body by providing a sense of wellbeing, faith, compassion and hope—qualities associated with Guru.

More than any other graha, Guru expands our awareness of the world. He does this in many ways—inspiring us towards higher education, overseas travel and foreign studies, to name a few. This consciousness-broadening graha also graces us with gurus and encourages us to live life in accordance with values, morals and beliefs that support our higher selves.

Determine where on the graha condition spectrum Guru falls. When Guru is well-conditioned, life flows in accordance with righteous morals and spiritual ideals. A person places importance on living a spiritual and dharmic life. Radiating with optimism and full of faith, the person envisions a better tomorrow. One can feel Guru's expansive and uplifting nature even in troubled times. The person discovers opportunities and blessings around every corner and feels deep gratitude for all that comes his or her way.

---

[6] *Mantreswara's Phala Deepika*, S.S. Sareen (translator), Chapter 2.5. Sagar Publications, 2001.
[7] See Chapter 10: "Seven Dhatus and the Grahas".

When Guru is poorly-conditioned, one may become excessively orthodox in his beliefs, adhering to outdated values and principles. Humble and broad-minded intelligence turns to narrow-mindedness or dogmatism. The faith-inspired energy inherent to Guru may dissipate into spiritual skepticism, causing criticism of others who are more spiritually oriented. Lacking faith and failing to find purpose, one may struggle to make sense of the world.

Budha and the rational, linear mind

Despite their shared wisdom-path, Guru's faith-inspired nature and abstract intellect is juxtaposed to Budha's rational perspective and practical approach. The broad values and philosophical-ethical principles that preoccupy Guru are outside of Budha's domain. Instead, Budha instructs on mundane subjects like accounting, mathematics, journalism and commerce.

Budha provides intellectual acumen and gives us the capacity to evaluate multiple vantage points of a situation in an objective compare-and-contrast manner. It is precisely this neutrality that allows us to manage things with clarity. Budha also indicates our ability to efficiently work with an endless array of facts, figures and information. This graha gives adeptness in managing the countless details of our life—planning, prioritizing and scheduling an infinite assortment of tasks. Budha's versatility, intellectual curiosity and manual dexterity provide an ever-expanding array of mundane interests and talents.

According to Mantreswara: "Mercury denotes learning, eloquence, fine arts, skill, recognition from scholarly pursuits, oratory, application of intelligence to learning . . ."[8] Sphujidhvaja adds: "Mercury's intellect is full and pure . . . He is pre-eminent in the composition of poetry, in craftsmanship and in the arts, and so charming because of his gracefulness, laughter and so forth. His speech is clear and cheerful . . ."[9]

Budha is the karaka for majja dhatu vaha srotas, carrying nerve impulses and enabling intercellular communication. As such, this graha represents the communication between the brain and the rest of the body. Recall that this srotas has the psychological attributes of curiosity, intelligence, calmness, open-mindedness and clarity, all qualities common to Budha.[10]

Whereas Jyotisha scripture assigns Guru the celestial cabinet post of *purohita* (priest) and spiritual counselor to King Surya, it is interesting to note that Budha is acclaimed the crown prince of this cosmic cabinet. Only Budha is qualified to fill the exalted shoes of his father, Surya. Hence, the worth of this graha is not to be judged by its small size.

A lion with the head of an elephant is Budha's celestial animal. This mythological animal symbolizes Budha's chameleon-like nature, which explains Budha's ability to assume the

---

[8] *Mantreswara's Phala Deepika*, S.S. Sareen (translator), Chapter 2.4. Sagar Publications, 2001.
[9] *Yavanajataka of Sphujidhvaja*, D. Pingree (translator), pg. 8. Harvard University Press, 1978.
[10] Refer to Chapter 10: "Seven Dhatus and the Grahas".

attributes and qualities of any graha next to it in the birth chart. For example, when Budha associates with wise Guru, the person's left-brain functions (Budha) are complemented by a holistic perspective and the ability for intuiting symbols and images (Guru). When with flowery and artistic Shukra, he takes to poetry and other forms of creative verbal expression, and so on.

Evaluate where on the condition spectrum natal Budha falls. When Budha is well-conditioned, one's intellect is sharp and his communications with others are clear and objective. One plans and prioritizes daily activities in advance. Comfortable with change, the person is at home even in transitional times and environments.

When Budha is poorly-conditioned, one of two extremes can surface. One extreme is apathy towards learning and a lack of interest in experimentation. Struggling to go with the flow, the person resists change every step of the way. The other extreme results when flexibility and fluidity make it difficult for a person to stick with a decision and/or have resolve. Pursuing an endless variety of interests and hobbies, one is jack of all trades, but master of none. Or perhaps, the person fritters his time away in cyber-world, texting, tweeting and face talking, or getting consumed by trivial news, game shows and video games.

5B-5B Bhavesha

It is from the 5th house that an astrologer should think about a person's tutelary deity (ishta devata), children, intelligence, power of discrimination and religious merit.[11]

The 5B *dhi sthana* (place of wisdom) represents our higher knowing and inborn creative adeptness. Guru is the karaka for these 5B affairs. The significance of the 5B is best exemplified by a bhavat bhavam comparison between it and the 3B, one that has Budha for its karaka.

Like the rational mind of the 3B, the 5B *viveka sthana* (place of discrimination) (third from the 3B), is also a bhava of intelligence, but of a very different nature. For example, the 3B represents our thoughts, reasoning, communications, talents and rote learning skills. The 5B of innate wisdom imbues all types of 3B activities with creative inspiration, uniqueness and originality. Hence, the communication skills of the 3B are elevated to the status of advice-giving and ambassadorship. Whereas the 3B shows our mental dexterity, the 5B is our strategic acumen.

In a similar manner, 3B-related activities of routine writing and publishing endeavors (short-stories, technical publications, newspaper articles) are transformed into distinguished literary authorship, be it a screenplay, play script, song, novel or poetry. Further, 3B interests and hobbies take the form of exceptional creative expression in the fields of classical arts (visual art, music, literature, architecture) and performing arts (dance, theatre, opera). Hence, the 5B outshines the 3B in terms of inborn wisdom and creativity.

Being second (further fulfillment, resources) from the 4B (education), the 5B shows the pursuits of the higher mind, including the subject matter of one's post-graduate education.

---

[11] *Vaidyanatha Diskshita's Jataka Parijata*, V. Subramanya Sastri (translator), Vol. III, Chapter XIII.1. Rajan Publications, 2004.

Being ninth (longer-term pursuits) from the 9B (higher learning), it as well represents the intellectual discernment we gain from long-term educational and/or spiritual pursuits that refine and mature the mind. Hence, this *dhi sthana* (place of wisdom) allows for discernment, right judgment and proper discrimination.

Once again, shastra stipulates two bhava yogas, this time formed by the 5B and its bhavesha: *chatra* (royal umbrella) and *pamara* (idiot) *yoga*. The requirements are equivalent to those of other bhava yogas presented.

Chatra yoga forms when the 5B bhavesha is strongly conditioned and well-placed *and* the 5B bhavesha *or* 5B is stabilized by an influence from a shubha graha. Chatra yoga gives discernment and the capacity for right action. Shastra results include: "The person lives in the abode of Goddess Lakshmi, possess immense wealth, renowned, soft spoken and learned. He rises to be a minister to a ruler, sharp witted and respected by others."[12]

In contrast, pamara yoga forms when the 5B bhavesha is weakly conditioned and poorly-placed *and* the 5B *or* 5B bhavesha is destabilized by an influence from a papa graha. In the case of pamara yoga, the person is less inclined to follow the high path and/or may lack discernment between right and wrong thought and action. Although exaggerated, shastra cited results include: "One born under such a yoga leads a miserable life, cannot discriminate and is a liar and a cheat".[13]

As with any yoga, the condition of the Lagna and its Lagnesha are crucial. When the Lagna-Lagnesha are poorly-conditioned, the auspicious results of chatra yoga may fructify only partially or not at all. On the other hand, when the Lagna-Lagnesha are well-conditioned, the results of pamara yoga are far less detrimental, particularly if other indications of intelligence are shown in the birth chart, such as a well-conditioned Guru, Budha Aditya yoga or Saraswati yoga.

3B-3B Bhavesha

From the 3rd house, the welfare of the brothers (i.e. siblings), enterprise, daring, tone of voice,[14] hearing, select ornaments,[15] steadiness, valor and strength(are read).[16]

A *parakrama sthana* (place of enterprise and initiative), the 3B is our inquisitiveness, enterprising nature and intellectual and physical dexterity. It represents our sense of adventure and includes mental competitiveness and initiative. Having Budha as one of its two graha karakas (the other is Mangala), the 3B is the rational mind that is good with details and the logical ordering of information. Hence, this bhava shows our ability to plan, execute

---

[12] *Mantreswara's Phala Deepika*, S.S. Sareen (translator), Chapter 6.49. Sagar Publications, 2001.
[13] Ibid, Chapter 6.62.
[14] The 2B is a bhava of words and our choice of words (i.e., speech) and the 3B is our adeptness in using words to communicate (e.g., writing, texting, journaling) and for the purpose of entertainment (acting, singing, authorship) or persuasion (selling).
[15] "Select ornaments" is in reference to earrings, as the 3B represents the ears in general and the right ear specifically.
[16] *Vaidyanatha Diskshita's Jataka Parijata*, V. Subramanya Sastri (translator), Vol. III, Chapter XII.1. Rajan Publications, 2004.

and administer the many daily details of our personal and professional life. As the linear, left-brain mind, it gives adeptness in sciences such as physics and engineering.

Gemini is the natural zodiac ruler of the 3B, where fluidity, change, movement and mobility are inherent characteristics. Hence, the 3B indicates one's ability to go with the flow amidst ever-changing external environments. It represents one's mental tolerance for change and uncertainty.

The two bhava yogas involving the 3B and its bhavesha are called *saurya* (valor or prowess) and *mriti* (death) *yoga*. Below are the familiar requirements for bhava yogas.

When the 3B bhavesha is strongly conditioned and well-placed *and* the 3B *or* 3B bhavesha is stabilized by the influence of a shubha graha, saurya yoga forms. Mantreswara cites the karma phala of this yoga: "The person born in saurya yoga shines like Shri Rama. He is fully involved in the state affairs, praised by his younger brothers who themselves are glorious and endowed with such valor as commands admiration from all. He is loved by one and all and becomes exceedingly celebrated."[17]

In contrast, mriti yoga forms when the 3B bhavesha is weakly conditioned and poorly-placed *and* the 3B *or* 3B bhavesha is destabilized by the influence of a papa graha. Mantreswara declares the karma phala of this yoga: "The person born under this yoga is vanquished by his enemies, is without brothers, is shameless, weak and poor. He suffers from loss of power due to improper acts; gets easily excited; work causes disappointment."[18]

Yogas for Wisdom and Intelligence
Budha Aditya yoga

Budha Aditya yoga is formed by an association between Budha and Surya, whose Sanskrit name is Aditya (of Aditi). In the ancient Vedas, Aditi is the birth mother of Surya. Budha-ruled Gemini and Surya-ruled Leo are the natural rashis of the 3B (rational mind, intellectual skill set) and 5B (wisdom, inspired creativity). An association between these two grahas unites the rational intellect with the higher mind, making Budha Aditya yoga a signature for high intelligence.

Since Budha is never more than 45° away from the sun in the sky, Budha Aditya yoga occurs in roughly one third of all birth charts. Thus, further qualification of this yoga is required.

Firstly, it is important that Budha Aditya yoga influence the personality (via the Lagna or Lagnesha) and/or the discerning mind (via the 5B or 5B bhavesha). This requirement is met in a variety of ways. For example, Budha Aditya yoga can take place in the Lagna or 5B, in the 7B or 11B (from where it aspects the Lagna or 5B, respectively) or in any other bhava when it is in association with the Lagnesha or 5B bhavesha.

As is true for most yogas, graha condition matters. It is preferable that neither Surya nor Budha is weakly conditioned. (Note that for this yoga, Budha's combustion does not

---

[17] *Mantreswara's Phala Deepika*, S.S. Sareen (translator), Chapter 6.47. Sagar Publications, 2001.
[18] Ibid, Chapter 6.60.

disqualify the yoga.) However, even in this case, Budha Aditya can bear fruit as long as the other graha is strongly conditioned.

The bhava placement of this yoga shows where the person uses his skills, intelligence, and discernment to advance in life.

In our Gemini-ruled Lagna chart example, Budha and Surya are in association in the 7B and both are ordinary in condition. Importantly, Budha is the Lagnesha *and* Budha Aditya yoga aspects the Lagna. Furthermore, the 5B bhavesha (Shukra), which represents innate intelligence, participates in this yoga. Thus, for our Gemini-ruled Lagna, Budha Aditya yoga qualifies several times over. This individual will develop meaningful and influential relationships (7B placement) as a result of his communication skills, intelligence and discernment.

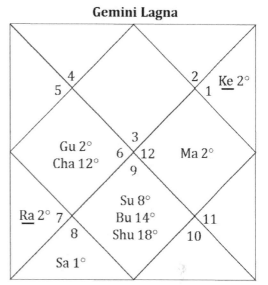

Sarasvati yoga

Shri Sarasvati is the goddess of refined judgement and spirituality. In her iconographic form, she holds a rosary of crystal beads (used for recitation of mantras) and the ancient Vedic texts, symbols for spiritual wisdom, in two of her hands. Sarasvati is also the goddess of creativity, as illustrated by the vina (a string instrument) that she plays with her other two hands.

Sarasvati yoga is well known to students of Jyotisha. This yoga of intelligence blesses the individual with an appreciation for higher knowledge and spiritual wisdom. It is often the mark of a teacher, advisor or instructor.

Sarasvati yoga forms when Budha, Shukra and Guru (the three learning grahas) occupy one or more of the kendras, trikonas and/or the 2B (oral traditions). In addition to its graha placement, at least one of the grahas must be strongly conditioned, unless other indications of intelligence are present in the birth chart, such as Budha Aditya yoga or chatra yoga.

To illustrate the required graha bhava positions, if Guru occupies the 2B and Budha and Shukra occupy the 5B, Sarasvati yoga is formed. Alternatively, if Guru occupies the 10B, while Budha occupies the 4B and Shukra, the 7B, Sarasvati yoga likewise forms.

In our Gemini-ruled Lagna chart example, Budha, Shukra and Guru each occupy kendras and are ordinary in condition. At least one of these grahas must be strongly conditioned. However, since Budha Aditya yoga is present, this configuration qualifies as Sarasvati yoga. Furthermore, two of the three grahas (Budha and Shukra) forming Sarasvati yoga are implicated in the Budha Aditya yoga.

Yoga-like configurations for higher intelligence

Several additional indicators of a refined or cultivated mindset are "yoga-like". These include: parivartana between the Lagnesha and 5B-bhavesha, the placement of Guru in the

Lagna (where it receives dig bala) and the placement of the Lagnesha in the 5B (bhava of discernment).

Lastly, should Mangala influence any of these yoga or yoga-like configurations, or the 5B or its bhavesha, its sharp and piercing nature stimulates the intellect. Notice in our Gemini-ruled Lagna chart example that Mangala aspects Guru, one of the three grahas forming Sarasvati yoga.

Client Case Illustration: Maria

Maria, who has a Scorpio-ruled Lagna, recently turned 40 (see below chart). Applying the concepts presented in this chapter, what can we conclude about Maria's level of intelligence and capacity for discernment?

Right away, we see that chatra yoga is present: the 5B bhavesha (Guru) is strongly conditioned and well-placed in its own 5B, which stabilizes the bhava.

Furthermore, for a Scorpio-ruled Lagna, Guru is a double indicator of innate intelligence, for it is the 5B bhavesha *and* graha karaka for discernment. Noted above, Guru is strongly conditioned and well-placed.

Are there yogas or yoga-like configurations for discernment in Maria's chart? Guru's placement in the 5B is a yoga-like configuration for proper judgement. What about Budha Aditya yoga? Surya and Budha are in association, but their bhava position and bhava rulerships disqualify this graha configuration as an indicator for Maria's intelligence. However, since these grahas are placed in the 3B, we could conclude that Linda will acquire many useful mental skills during her life and that one or more of her siblings possess intelligence and mental dexterity.

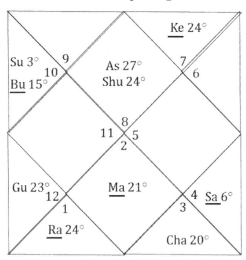

Maria: Scorpio Lagna

Does chart rotation (Pisces-ruled 5B becomes the lagna) or rashi confluence (Leo rashi) reinforce our findings? Rotating the chart, we see that the 5B bhavesha (and graha karaka Guru) receives an added factor of strength, i.e., Guru is dig bala. What do we notice when applying rashi confluence to Maria's birth chart? Mangala aspects the Leo-ruled 10B, stimulating the higher intellect, and Surya, planetary ruler of Leo, is in association with Budha, forming Budha Aditya yoga.

In Maria's chart, most indicators for intelligence are present *and* confirmed by chart rotation or rashi confluence. What additional information is given by the 3B-3B bhavesha and Budha, graha karaka for the rational mind?

Summary

After assessing the emotional health of your client, evaluative the birth chart for indications of higher powers of discernment and a rational mindset. For this purpose, consider the following.

1. Condition of Guru (karaka for higher intelligence)
2. Condition of Budha (karaka for the rational, objective mind)
3. Condition of the 5B-5B bhavesha, including the presence of chatra or pamara yoga
4. Condition of the 3B-3B bhavesha, including the presence of saurya or mriti yoga
5. Yogas for intelligence

Chapter 15: Life Factors and Timing Considerations

Introduction

Ayurveda approaches health and healing in the context of the whole person, so health professionals need to be familiar with many aspects of the client's life. Financial security, marital happiness, domestic harmony and satisfaction at work are integral to one's physical, mental-emotional and spiritual wellbeing.

The chart interpretation methodology presented in *Your Healing Stars: Volume I* is given below.[1] Apply this template to methodically identify those areas in the birth chart that promise positive life experiences, thereby supporting the physical health and mental-emotional well-being. As well, detect scenarios that are more challenging and have the potential to create poor physical health and mental-emotional stress.

Identifying Important Life Factors

To interpret a particular area of life, follow the methodology outlined below.

Step 1: Lagna-Lagnesha

Begin by evaluating the condition of the Lagna and its Lagnesha, for they represent the person's health, vitality and self-esteem. When the Lagna-Lagnesha are well-conditioned, the person is confident in his ability to accomplish his goals. Furthermore, he leverages the positive karma reflected in the birth chart, and finds the strength to overcome adverse circumstances.

On the other hand, when the Lagna-Lagnesha are poorly-conditioned, there are likely self-esteem issues and the person may feel that his aspirations are unattainable. Small hurdles and setbacks hinder him, and he may even be unable to leverage the good karma embedded in the birth chart.

Determine where on the condition spectrum the Lagna-Lagnesha fall. The strength of the Lagnesha is always more important than its stabilization and bhava placement.

Step 2: Bhavas-bhaveshas

Next, identify the bhava-bhavesha that are accountable for delivering on the particular area of interest (i.e., for marriage, assess the 7B-7B bhavesha, schooling, the 4B-4B bhavesha, and so on).

Determine if the bhava is stabilized or destabilized by graha occupation, aspect or flanking. Recall the exception regarding papa graha influences: a papa graha that owns the bhava it aspects or occupies fortifies the affairs of its. Still, the subtle and sensitive aspects of the bhava are adversely impacted. This includes the happiness that one gains from matters represented by the bhava as well as its associated personal relationships and health aspects.

---

[1] For an illustration of this methodology applied to a particular area of life, refer to *Your Healing Stars: Volume I, Fundamental Principles of Vedic Astrology*.

In the case of graha occupation or aspect, find out if the graha is the bhavesha for one or two dusthana bhavas. This further harms the affairs of the bhava, even when such bhavesha is a shubha graha.

Next, see which bhava the bhavesha occupies. A bhavesha manifests the affairs of its bhava through its bhava placement *and* in a manner consistent with its inherent nature and rashi placement. Most importantly, assess its condition (strength, stabilization and bhava placement). This determines whether the bhavesha is empowered to deliver on the affairs of its bhava or will struggle to do so. Lastly, consider any influences from a dusthana bhavesha, particularly if the bhavesha rules two dusthana bhavas.

When a bhava-bhavesha are well-conditioned, the affairs of the bhava manifest with greater certainty and ease. In contrast, when the bhava-bhavesha are poorly-conditioned, it will take more time, effort, and focus to manifest its bhava affairs. Determine where on the condition spectrum the bhava-bhavesha fall. The strength of the bhavesha is always more important than its stabilization and bhava placement.

Step 3: Yogas
Yogas are powerful indicators of fixed karma and can even override our by-bhava results. For example, if the 2B-2B bhavesha are ordinary in condition, but dhana yogas are shown in the chart, then money and financial security are present in the person's life.

Step 4: Confluence factors
After summarizing your by-bhava findings and identifying all yogas, apply confluence techniques such as chart rotation, rashi confluence and Surya and Chandra Lagna to help confirm and refine your initial interpretations. The more factors that confirm your initial findings, the more fixed the karma and hence, the greater the chance of such event occurring.

Timing Triggers
How to predict the timing of events using the Vimshottari system and planetary transits are presented in *Your Healing Stars: Volume I*. These basic rules can be applied when assessing the most likely "at-risk" periods for sickness and major illnesses.

The condition of the Lagna and its Lagnesha is paramount in assessing how devastating a dasha, bhukti or transit may or may not be. When the Lagna-Lagnesha are well-conditioned and participating in positive yogas for heath, then during the planetary period of a dasha lord implicated in ill-health, such conditions will not impact the person's health as adversely, if they manifest at all. Instead, the sickness and health disorders shown in the birth chart may relate to others in the person's life, such as the mother, spouse, child or sister. Contrast this scenario to a birth chart in which the Lagna-Lagnesha are poorly-conditioned and involved in inauspicious yogas for health. In this case, ill-health is more certain to occur during difficult transits and/or problematic dashas-bhuktis.

Chhidra grahas were defined in Chapter 6: "Vikruti and the Trik-Dusthanas" as those grahas that rule or occupy the trik-dusthanas. Meaning 'defect or blemish', chhidra denotes grahas that represent the challenges and struggles associated with these inauspicious bhavas. For a chart that indicates a weak or compromised constitution, back-to-back dashas of two chhidra grahas can be detrimental to health. For example, in a Cancer-ruled Lagna, Guru is the bhavesha for the trik-dusthana 6B and Shani rules the trik-dusthana 8B. Since the dashas of Guru (16 years) and Shani (19 years) run back-to-back, under the right chart conditions, these dashas can represent an extended period of ill-health. If, instead, only Guru is implicated in ill-health, then Shani dasha may become a dasha of recovery from any ill-health triggered during Guru dasha.

Also take note when the dasha and bhukti of two chhidra grahas run, particularly if one or both grahas are poorly-conditioned and are involved in daridra or aristha-like yogas.

When difficult planetary health configurations are activated in the birth chart, certain non-health-related factors are often the trigger for disease or illness. For example, assume that the dasha of the 7B bhavesha runs in a chart where the 7B-7B bhavesha are poorly-conditioned. In this case, the pressure and responsibility associated with marriage, troubles from the partner, or the partner's ill-health may create a high level of mental and emotional stress. This stress will affect the kidneys, colon or reproductive organs (i.e., 7B Kalapurusha significations). Or consider the dasha of a weak 10B bhavesha placed in the 5B. As eighth from the 10B of career, the 5B can indicate a fall in status or loss of a job. Perhaps troubling circumstances at work are the cause of stomach ulcers or heart conditions (i.e., 5B Kalapurusha significations).

Chart-Side Etiquette

A person's birth chart is an intimate portrayal of his innermost being and the blueprint of his karma for this lifetime. For this reason, before requesting a client's birth information, explain to him the purpose and value of Jyotisha and the sacredness of the birth chart. I have seen too many instances where an intrigued individual eagerly relinquishes private birth information without an appreciation of Jyotisha or an understanding of how the birth chart will be used.

It is important to ask the client for permission to share your findings with him. Boundaries are often blindly overstepped when a Jyotishi assumes that the client wants to know everything and anything shown in his chart. To this day, I vividly recall my first birth chart reading. Without asking what I may or may not be interested in, the astrologer opened our session matter-of-factly with: "You will end this life at the age of xx." This greatly disturbed me, as I did not feel it was his position to convey such an event—nor I was interested in knowing this information.

This personal experience drove home the significance of beginning the Jyotisha consultation on a positive and empowering note. There is plenty of light in each birth chart that we can share with a client. When we begin with challenging or adverse circumstances, it sets the ambiance for the entire consultation. Remember that a person is likely to lock onto a negative opening comment, never to hear more uplifting and positive subsequent comments. Point in fact; the only thing I remember from my hour-long session with the above astrologer is his opening statement!

This is not to say that we should ignore difficult life circumstances we glean from the chart. Although it might seem easier to focus on indications of happiness and success, we have a responsibility as Jyotishis to also address less desirable areas (assuming that we have received permission from the client to do so). Chances are that the client is already intimately aware of these areas and/or events and feelings, and if we ignore them, we might seem to invalidate the client's experiences.

Use your professional consultation skills to provide guidance toward potential solutions. The operative word is "guidance", rather than "directive". It is important for the client to assume responsibility for his life by making his own decisions.

Lastly, where necessary, leverage your referral network to recommend professional counseling in difficult areas.

Introduction to Section V

Within the region of the heart is *hridaya guhayam*, the 'hidden space of the soul'. Its essence is brilliant light (consciousness) enveloped in the sattvic qualities of pure love and eternal bliss. From this subtle region, the channel of the mind (mano vaha srotas) originates. The gateway to the soul is the emotional heart, also located in this same region. This is described in *Charaka Samhita*, where the physical heart, emotional heart, mind and soul are seen as being united at the root of the mano vaha srotas.

> The heart region is the root of ten vessels of great significance.[1] The words 'mahat' (great), 'artha' (serving all purposes) and 'hridaya' (soul) are synonymous (*with this region*). The body with its six divisions, the intellect, sense organs (*eyes, skin, ears, tongue and nose*), sense objects (*hearing, touch, vision, taste and smell*), self (soul) together with its qualities and mind along with its gunas (*sattva, rajas, tamas*) are located in the heart. (*Charaka Samhita*, Sutrasthana, Chapter 30.3-4)

Vedanta describes the various gross and subtle bodies as *koshas* (sheaths). They are the *annamaya kosha* (food sheath), *pranamaya kosha* (prana sheath), *manomaya kosha* (mind sheath), *vijnanamaya kosha* (wisdom sheath) and *anandamaya kosha* (bliss sheath). Beginning with the anandamaya kosha, each sheath encompasses and permeates the subsequent grosser one.

Figure 8: The Koshas of the Body

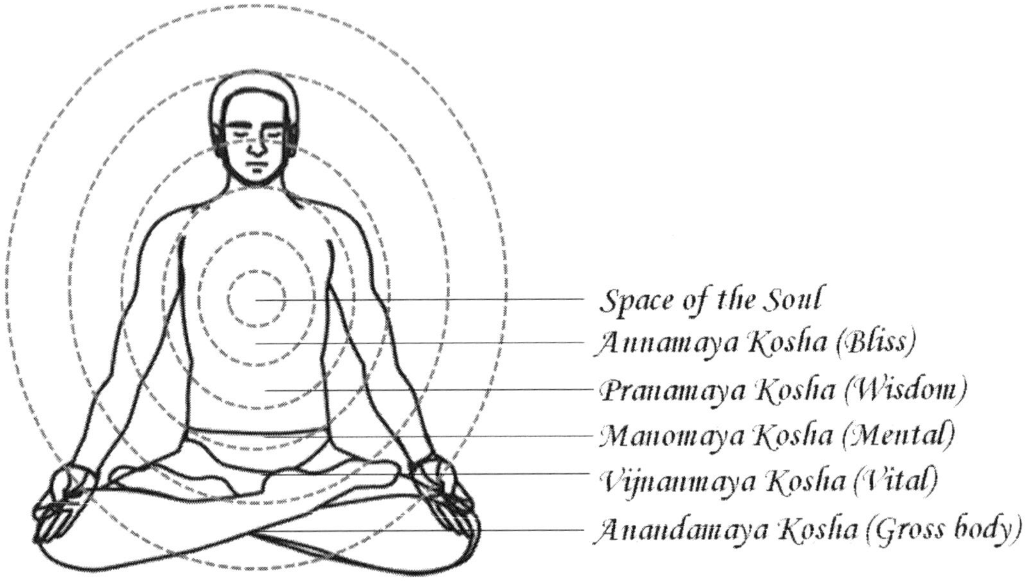

- Space of the Soul
- Annamaya Kosha (Bliss)
- Pranamaya Kosha (Wisdom)
- Manomaya Kosha (Mental)
- Vijnanmaya Kosha (Vital)
- Anandamaya Kosha (Gross body)

---

[1] These ten vessels in the heart region relate to specific aspects of blood circulation. However, in this same region, there are 10 subtle channels relating to the jnanendriyas. These subtle channels function on a mental, emotional and spiritual level.

The annamaya kosha (sheath of food) is the gross physical body made up of bones, muscles, organs and the other bodily tissues. It is composed of the mahabhutas of ether, air, fire, water and earth, and it houses the three doshas that arise from those elements. The annamaya kosha relies on the organs of action (vocal cords, hands, feet, reproductive organs and anus) and their corresponding functions (speech, grasping, walking, procreation and elimination) to experience and act in the world. Food is its source of nourishment and vitality. The health of this sheath is important for spiritual development, for the annamaya kosha houses all the others and serves as the dwelling place of the soul.

The pranamaya kosha (sheath of prana) is the sheath of the vital life force that unites all koshas. It supports the annamaya kosha with its five vayus (*prana, apana, vyana, udana* and *samana*) which are responsible for initiating physiological functions such as respiration, oxygenation and circulation. It is also the force behind the sense organs (eyes, skin, ears, tongue and nose) and their corresponding functions (*sight, touch, hearing, taste and smell*).

Closely associated with the majja vaha srotas (nervous system), the pranamaya kosha is the mediator between the physical body (annamaya kosha) and the mental body (manomaya kosha). Comprised of prana, this kosha carries life and consciousness to all sheaths.

The manomaya kosha (sheath of mind) is the mental sheath and the recipient of all impressions coming from the sense organs and transported by the pranamaya kosha. Thoughts and the emotional drives they stimulate (fear, desire, ambition, attachment, and so on) constitute the manomaya kosha. The mind and its faculties of reason, logic, ideas and concepts are part of this kosha.

Whereas the manomaya kosha is adept at seeing the particulars of the world (the many in one), the vijnanamaya kosha (sheath of wisdom) is proficient at synthesis and perceives commonalities (the one in many). This kosha is the sheath of wisdom and creative insight. It is the source of higher forms of expression, such as inspired poetry, deeply moving music and brilliant writing.

In Sankhya terms, the vijnanamaya kosha is the realm of mahat; our higher-knowing self. The vijnanamaya kosha is beyond the primal needs of the physical body, the sensations of the prana body and the dualistic framework of the mental body. It is the realm of revelation, intuition and inspiration. Through the lens of the vijnanamaya kosha, the truth of the cosmos is revealed.

Lastly is the anandamaya kosha (sheath of bliss). This is the innermost kosha that envelopes the soul in a sheath of bliss and love (*ananda*). Beyond the realm of time and space, the anandamaya kosha is vast and eternal.

The *Gita* illumines three gateways into the anandamaya kosha. The first is *karma yoga*, the yoga of actions. Karma yoga is described as acting without being attached to the results of our actions. A karma yogin has no preference for particular actions, realizing that we are but agents of Spirit. The second path is *jnana yoga*, the yoga of wisdom beyond the limitations of the mind. Jnana yoga leads to higher knowledge and self-realization—the discovery of our true nature. Last is *bhakti yoga*, the yoga of devotion and unconditional love. Bhakti yoga moves us beyond the feelings, sensations, attractions and repulsions of the emotional heart and connects us with unconditional, all-embracing Divinity.

The Vedantic concept of koshas gives an important philosophical and spiritual component to Ayurveda. It readily accommodates the notion of chakras, energy vortices related to nerve plexuses along the spinal column.

Figure 9: Koshas and Charkas

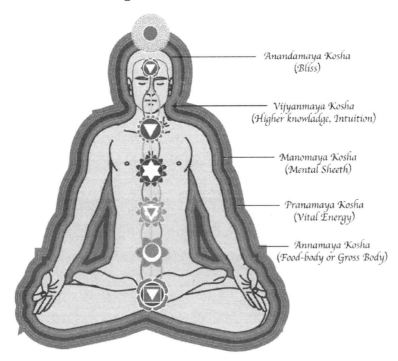

In Tantra Yoga, the chakras are emphasized as part of the path of enlightenment. Descriptions of these energy portals are as ancient as the six thousand year-old *Rigveda*. In the devotional hymns of this Indian scripture, the seers mystically reveal their knowledge of the seven major chakras when referring to the seven flowing sister-rivers, the seven enlightened rishis, the seven sacred Rigvedic meters and the seven flaming tongues of Lord Agni.

In Section V, we journey deeper into understanding the energetic construct of the individual by evaluating each chakra through the birth chart.

But first, we address the question most frequently asked of Jyotishis: What is my purpose or dharma? Dharma is one of the four *purusharthas*, or aims in life. We will consider how best to guide the client through this very important query by examining the dharmic bhavas and their bhaveshas in the natal birth chart.

Other topics include yogas for spirituality and the person's spiritual inclinations and path as denoted by prominent birth chart configurations.

SECTION V: Spiritual Welfare & Dharma

Chapter 16: Purusharthas and the Birth Chart

Introduction

The *purusharthas* (goals of human existence), commonly referred to as the four aims of life, is an important foundational concept of Jyotisha and Ayurveda. According to it, we are born for the purpose of fulfilling four aims in life.

dharma (right action) fulfilling our purpose and duty
artha (resources) gathering and accumulating necessary resources
kama (desires) enjoying the pleasures of the world
moksha (liberation) pursing a spiritual path

Each purushartha is aligned with a set of trinal bhavas in the birth chart: dharma (Lagna, 5B, 9B), artha (2B, 6B, 10B), kama (3B, 7B, 11B) and moksha (4B, 8B, 12B), and each bhava supports its aim in a unique way.

Figure 10: Purusharthas and the Birth Chart

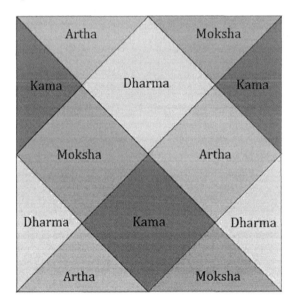

Purushartha Bhavas

Dharma sthanas

The Lagna, 5B and 9B of the birth chart show one's dharmic purpose and duty in life. The Lagna is known as the *sva sthana* (place of self). Each person has a duty to discover and embrace his or her uniqueness and fully develop his or her potential. That unique purpose and direction are primarily shown by the Lagna and its Lagnesha. It is in this manner that we cultivate a sense of purpose and find our direction in life. The specific aspect of dharma that the Lagna shows is that of our everyday life activities that keep us connected to our higher purpose. It is the only bhava where action (a kendra) and divine grace (a trikona) unite.

The trikona 5B is a *purva punya sthana*. It shows past life credits, the result of good deeds that have been carried forward into this lifetime and that we can benefit from. This includes our creative, inborn intelligence—something that we develop over many lifetimes. It is our dharmic duty to accumulate additional good karma in this lifetime through proper discernment, moral integrity and spiritual worship (5B affairs). The 5B is an extension of the Lagna's purpose, for it requires that we birth and foster our distinct gifts, be that an inborn artistic aptitude, intellectual proficiency or even birthing a child. In this manner, the 5B deepens our sense of having a unique contribution to make, and propels our destiny forward.

Referred to as the *sukrita sthana* (place of virtue), the dharmic 9B includes upholding societal laws and ethics and living life by a set of higher values, morals and philosophical principles. Fifth from the 5B of inborn intelligence, the 9B broadens our consciousness through the pursuit of sacred studies and higher education. This *ahcarya sthana* (place of preceptor) graces us with enlightened gurus who help us on our spiritual journey. A reflection of the 3B (neighbors), it also represents our broader neighborhood, i.e., the society we live in. Thus, the 9B instills in us the desire to give back to society. It completes the circle of dharma: embracing who we are and cultivating a sense of purpose (Lagna), fostering our inborn talents (5B) and furthering society by helping others (9B).

When dharma is the primary goal of life, a person feels strongly driven to find his or her purpose and give back to society.

Artha sthanas

The 2B, 6B and 10B are bhavas of material pursuit. They represent resources we acquire to support and maintain our daily life. First of the artha bhavas, the 2B *vitta sthana* (place of money) includes the personal resources one has available for satisfying basic needs, such as food, clothing and money. This bhava shows one's motivation to take responsibility for his own needs and those of his family. It also indicates our sense of financial and material security, resourcefulness and self-sufficiency. 2B personal resources include non-financial means of support. For instance, as the *vidya sthana* (place of oral traditions), it is knowledge gained through oral transmission, such as Jyotisha, Ayurveda and the Vedic scriptures.

The 6B *ahva sthana* (place of challenge) requires us to work hard, endure adversities and face our competitors in order to overcome the challenges and setbacks of everyday life. It is an extension of the 2B of self-support, for the 6B is connected with financial resources obtained through short-term borrowing (credit card debt, lines of credit, bridge loans) and the stress of satisfying these obligations.

Twice the size of other bhavas, the kendras (Lagna, 4B, 7B, 10B) are Vishnu sthanas—powerful places of action and manifestation. They represent the four cardinal directions (east, north, west, south, respectively) and the pivotal turning points of the sun in the course of a day: rising, mid-day, setting and mid-night. As the last of the four kendras and the most visible region of the sky, the 10B is particularly noteworthy for mundane manifestation.

The 10B indicates the manner in which one is involved in the world. It is a bhava of public life, as opposed to the hidden, private life of the 4B, which it reflects. It shows our ability to carry our weight in the world and to act with strength, resilience and purpose—to walk the talk. The last of the artha bhavas, this bhava represents our material livelihood and professional status, prestige and reputation, i.e., the outward display of our ability to be self-

Chapter 16: Purusharthas and the Birth Chart

sufficient (2B) and our willingness to work hard to improve our daily lot (6B).

When artha is the primary purushartha, themes of resource acquisition, pursuit of income and outer, worldly actions are dominant in the person's life.

Kama sthanas

The kama bhavas reflect our desires in life and our pursuit to satisfy them. The 3B shows our immediate personal wants as expressed through hobbies, interests and curiosities. It also speaks to the courage and impulsiveness with which we pursue these shorter-term interests.

The 7B represents our yearning to unite with others for the mutual fulfillment of desires, be that as committed lovers, business partners or two individuals sharing common hopes and dreams. As one of the four kendras, the 7B powerfully draws us into to various kinds of relationships that hold the promise for personal satisfaction and gain. Our relationship skills and ability to sustain healthy partnerships with others through respect, diplomacy and honoring agreements is also read from the 7B.

Ninth (higher purpose) from the 3B (short-term personal desires) and the last of the kama sthanas, the 11B shows our longer-term, more purposeful aspirations. It is imbued with ambition and self-will directed toward achieving these grand goals. With its intense desire nature, the 11B also represents one's social kama—the longing to belong, and to elevate one's position in the world through acquaintances and organizations such as clubs, corporations or associations with others. Through these connections, we gain access to the higher echelons of society and connect with those who can help us achieve our mundane aspirations. The modus operandi of the 11B is: "It's not what you know, but who you know."

The risk of the 11B is its powerful kama nature that can entangle us in a web of neverending aspirations and mundane goals. Yet, as the bhava of influential groups and high society, it holds the promise of giving broad social influence and having a wide-ranging worldly impact.

When kama is the primary purushartha, then the pursuit of personal interests, relationships with others and lofty, worldly aspirations are pivotal aspects of life.

If we visually connect the kama sthanas of the birth chart, a downward-pointing triangle is formed. This triangle encompasses the delight of our physical existence: personal pursuits (3B), relationships with others (7B) and worldly gains (11B). Overlapping is an upward pointing triangle shaped by the dharma sthanas. The dharma triangle shows the quality of consciousness behind our every action and thought: right behavior (Lagna), right discernment (5B) and right purpose (9B). When the kama sthana bhaveshas come under the influence of the dharma sthana bhaveshas in the birth chart, our desire nature is guided by a moral and ethical sense.

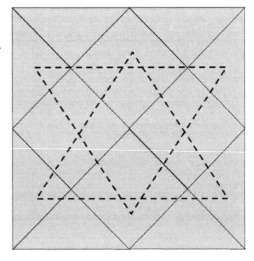

Moksha sthanas

Lastly, the places of spiritual development and growth are the moksha sthanas, the 4B, 8B, and 12B. The 4B represents the inner peace and emotional stability that serves as the foundation for a spiritual life. It also denotes our ability to stay heart-centered in thought and action. As the nadir of the birth chart, it is that area of the sky that is completely concealed at the time of birth. Hence, the 4B is a place of privacy, introversion and all things that are hidden from view, including our deepest sentiments. Being the eighth (upheavals) from the 9B (higher purpose), it represents the emotional turmoil that results when our dharma is not aligned with our true feelings. At the root of these innermost sentiments are the circumstances of our early upbringing, including the extent to which we felt loved and nurtured (another 4B affair).

The 4B moksha sthana represents our ability to quiet our emotions and experience stillness. These skills are important for spiritual practices. In contrast, the moksha sthana 8B triggers spiritual transformation through earth-shattering events, spiritual awakenings and profound psychological healing. Whereas the 4B represents the doorway to the subconscious mind, the 8B is the path into deeper states of the unconscious. It brings fascination with altered states of consciousness and out-of-body or near-death experiences. Having Scorpio for its natural rashi ruler, the 8B has a built-in fascination with all things deep and mysterious.

The last of the moksha sthanas, the 12B represents our final liberation from the material world, as we merge with the infinite, all-pervading Spirit. Thus, the 12B is a separating bhava, for it has the capacity to literally or figuratively estrange us from the world as we know it. The reclusive nature of the 12B is the reason that it represents spiritual pilgrimages. This moksha sthana is capable of giving immensely on the spiritual level. Twelfth from the Lagna, it is our ability to detach from a self-centered perspective on life. Thus, the 12B gives birth to renunciants, seekers and spiritual aspirants. For this same reason, the 12B is one of *seva*, acts of charity and non-for-profit endeavors of all kinds.

Of the three moksha sthanas, the 4B is our ability to quiet our emotions and connect with our hearts in preparation for spiritual practices. In this state, access to the subconscious mind is gained. The 8B is the gateway into altered states of consciousness and radical transformations that hold the key to spiritual awakenings. The 12B, the final moksha sthana, is our capacity to tap into the supramental realm where we can perceive truth directly and experience transcendence.

When moksha is the main aim of a person's life, the importance of a spiritual life can override more worldly or mundane goals.

Purusharthas and the Birth Chart

The natal birth chart indicates the relative significance of each purushartha and hence, which goal or aim of life is most important to the individual.

Let us take a look at our Leo Lagna birth chart to see which purushartha stands out. For this exercise, two different techniques are presented. As with any chart reading, when we find confluence between varying techniques, it increases the certainty of our interpretation.

Chapter 16: Purusharthas and the Birth Chart

Methodology 1: The Lagnesha is the most important graha in the birth chart, for it represents the person. Which purushartha bhava does the Lagnesha occupy in this chart? Notice that the Lagnesha (Surya) is placed in the 10B, an artha bhava.

Methodology 2: Now determine the primary aim in life based on graha occupation. How many grahas occupy each set of dharma, artha, kama and moksha bhavas? In our example chart, 3 grahas occupy the dharma sthanas (Lagna, 5B, 9B); 4 grahas, the artha sthanas (2B, 6B, 10B); 0 grahas, the kama sthanas (3B, 7B, 11B), and 2 grahas occupy the moksha sthanas (4B, 8B, 12B).

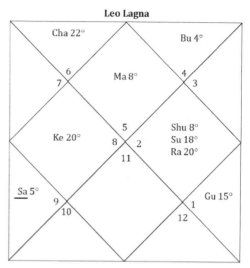

This second methodology lends confluence to the importance of artha as a goal in life. As well, it suggests that dharma and moksha are key aims.

As with our Leo Lagna client, two or more aims are typically prominent in the birth chart. Different dashas and transits also serve as triggers, causing us to shift away from one goal in life and focus on another.

In Chapter 17: "Uncovering Your Dharma", a methodology is introduced to help us provide added insight and depth concerning a person's primary aim in life.

Chapter 17: Uncovering Your Dharma

One's own dharma, performed imperfectly, is better than another's dharma well performed. Destruction in one's own dharma is better, for to perform another's dharma leads to danger. (Bhagavad-Gita, 3.35)

Introduction

Although artha, kama or moksha may be most prominent in the natal birth chart, each of us searches for this higher purpose. Indeed, one of the most frequently asked questions of a Jyotishi is: What is my dharma? As you might imagine, this seemingly straight-forward question is anything but simple. Yet, offering insight and guidance in this area is an important part of the Jyotisha consultation, so in this chapter, a methodology is presented that helps us address it. The process described here is the loom on which the tapestry of dharma is made visible.[1]

As with everything in life, dharma rarely remains static. It shifts and deepens as we mature and gain a broader perspective on the world and ourselves. Planetary periods (dashas) and transits activate new aspects of dharma—or an entirely new dharma altogether—and bring others to a close.

Dharma as Revealed by the Birth Chart

Each facet of the dharma bhavas reveals an important part of the person's purpose and duty. Hence, most often there is no single outstanding chart feature that displays the totality of a person's dharmic aim. Instead, we must integrate multiple birth chart factors, connecting shades and shadows until images take shape. As we will see, a person's path often involves certain aspects of artha, kama and moksha.

Lagna and its Lagnesha

The Lagna and Lagnesha is *always* the place to begin when reading any aspect of the birth chart. The all-important Lagna determines the rashi and ruling graha for each area of life, including those of the dharma bhavas.

The Lagna and Lagnesha represent our personal path and the daily conduct that supports it. As such, it is the cloth upon which our dharma is to be woven. When the Lagna-Lagnesha are well-conditioned, the person is more apt to have the confidence, determination and health to fully develop his or her potential. Moreover, a well-conditioned Lagna-Lagnesha provides a strong sense of purpose, which gives direction and motivation in life.

After evaluating the condition of the Lagna-Lagnesha, ascertain if any grahas influence the Lagna. The characteristics and indications of these grahas are to be

---

[1] Note that this same methodology may be applied to other purusharthas, illuminating important aspects of artha, kama or moksha. Simply substitute the dharma bhavas-bhaveshas with those relating to another aim in life.

cultivated and incorporated into everyday activities. For example, should Budha occupy the Lagna, intellectual curiosity and learning are unique aspects of the personality. What if Mangala aspects the Lagna? Then, instead, courage, passion and enterprise are crucial components. Should multiple grahas influence the Lagna, the strongest graha will have the most impact.

Add depth and color to this initial analysis by weaving in the meaning of bhava rulerships. If Mangala is the bhavesha for the 10B, then the person's courageous manner and pioneering ways (Mangala) are to be directed towards outer-world actions or one's professional life (10B). Alternatively, if Mangala is the 2B bhavesha, then this same courage and innovation should be channeled towards financial independence and providing for the family. In both cases, artha is part of the person's dharma, for these two bhavas have artha as the primary aim.

In this same manner, continue to weave the story by incorporating the meaning of graha influences on the Lagnesha. Once again, should multiple grahas be involved, look to the strongest graha, as its significations will dominate.

Now, consider the bhava placement of the Lagnesha, as it represents the area of life and purushartha in which the person's daily path and duty unfolds. For instance, when the Lagnesha is placed in the 4B, then the home life and family are central. Emotional stability and inner contentment (the moksha aspects of the 4B) are other important aspects of the person's path.

Lastly, determine if the Lagna and Lagnesha are implicated in yogas and, if so, which ones? Suppose raj yoga forms in the Lagna. In this case, receiving recognition and honor for one's actions promotes self-confidence and provide a sense of purpose. Alternatively, if the Lagnesha participates in daridra or arishta-like yogas, the person is meant to develop his self-esteem and confidence though certain hardships in life.

5B and 5B bhavesha

The 5B represents our innate wisdom (the result of past life learning) and moral integrity. Central to any dharmic path is right thought and action, which is the product of a refined mind. When evaluating the 5B-5B bhavesha, leverage your findings from Chapter 14: "Intelligence and Discernment".

Evaluate the 5B and its bhavesha using the same process stipulated above: (1) the condition of the 5B and 5B bhavesha and any graha influences, (2) yogas that implicate the 5B and/or 5B bhavesha and (3) the bhava placement (and its related purushartha) of the 5B bhavesha. Insights gleaned from the 5B and its bhavesha add texture and color to our understanding of a person's dharma.

Recall that unique to the 5B is its representation of purva punya, or past life virtues—the merits and gifts that have been carried forward from previous lifetimes into the current one. An essential component of a person's dharmic duty is to foster these inborn talents. When evaluating the 5B-5B bhavesha, see if you can provide your client with some suggestions as to what his or her talents may entail. Use graha and bhava significations to help identify these. For example, if the 5B bhavesha is placed in the 2B, the person's gift might involve oral teachings (2B of sampradayas) or advising (5B) others on proper nutrition and diet (2B). Music, writing or athleticism could be interpreted by the 5B bhavesha placed in the 3B.

In this same way, evaluate grahas occupying the 5B. Should Guru occupy the 5B, counselling others becomes important. If Guru is also the 6B bhavesha, then perhaps the person's dharma includes instructing on health issues or teaching yoga.[2] Be sure to identify yogas involving the 5B or its bhavesha. For example, if Budha Aditya yoga forms in the 5B, this highlights one's capacity for great discernment, and this gift should be developed.

Spiritual worship and one's *ishta devata* (personal deity) are additional 5B dharmic affairs. (See section: "Your Ishta Devata" at the end of this chapter.)

9B and 9B bhavesha

The 9B represents our higher purpose, including the need to give back to society. Along with the Lagna and 5B, it shows our ability to live with integrity. The 9B indicates our willingness to adhere to societal values and morals and live by a set of philosophical and spiritual principles that support our dharmic path.

Once again, use the same methodology that we used for the Lagna-Lagnesha and 5B-5B bhavesha to evaluate the 9B-9B bhavesha.

The combined condition of the 9B-9B bhavesha serves as a critical gauge for a person's moral receptivity to the traditions and conventions set by society. When the 9B-9B bhavesha are well-conditioned, our spiritual and philosophical belief system promotes exemplary conduct and furthers the culture we live in. Should the 9B-9B bhavesha be weakly conditioned, the person may unknowingly (or knowingly) display eccentric, scandalous or other unacceptable behavior that veils and/or interferes with his or her sense of higher purpose.

Does a graha influence the 9B and, if so, what is the nature of the graha? Which bhavas does it rule? Its nature and bhava rulership reveals important aspects of the person's calling. For example, if Shani occupies the 9B, the person's dharma might be colored by a sense of social responsibility (Shani is the graha of duty and the 9B, our social dharma). Or, perhaps, the person is here to learn important but difficult life lessons (Shani) through the relationship with the father (9B). If Shani is also the 12B bhavesha (as happens in a birth chart with a Pisces or Aquarius Lagna), seva and charitable activities (12B affairs) will be essential components of dharma. When multiple grahas influence the 9B, always put more importance on those that are strongly conditioned.

---

[2] For an in-depth analysis of the affairs of each of the 12 bhavas, see *Your Healing Stars: Volume I, Fundamentals of Vedic Astrology.*

Chapter 17: Uncovering Your Dharma

What bhava does the 9B bhavesha occupy? The affairs of this bhava will be emphasized in the person's dharma. Look also at the purushartha (dharma, artha, kama or moksha) of the bhava. If the 9B bhavesha is placed in the 7B, then the calling involves kama; in this case, through developing good and meaningful relationships with others.

The auspicious raj and dhana yogas form when the 9B bhavesha (or another trikona bhavesha) is in sambandha (mutual relationship) with a kendra (Lagna, 4B, 7B, 10B) or money bhavesha (2B, 11B), respectively.[3] Such yogas closely unite success in the material world with the person's higher calling.

With insights gained from the above process, further texture is given to the storyline. As you interweave your 9B-9B bhavesha findings with those of the other dharma bhavas-bhaveshas, behold the scene that takes shape on the tapestry of dharma. Don't be surprised if a variety of images appear.

Lastly, in certain charts, the 5B or 5B bhavesha and/or 9B or 9B bhavesha are linked together or linked with the Lagna or Lagnesha by way of bhava occupation or sambandha. This adds confluence that dharma is an important aim in life. Hence, when one or more of these planetary configurations appear in the birth chart, the person typically perceives his dharma more clearly and, thus, actively pursues it.

An Important Note

Remember that there is no such thing as a superior or inferior path—only the path that is right for the individual. If the dharma bhavas-bhaveshas are poorly-conditioned, the person may not recognize his path or may repeatedly veer off course. In this case, look to the strongest part of the chart, for this can serve as a starting point for revealing one's dharma. For instance, if Sarasvati yoga shows in the birth chart, then the mind will be a pathway to dharma. If, instead, dhana yogas are prominent, the pursuit of money becomes a channel for discovering one's dharma.

Your Ishta Devata

The term ishta devata (most desired divine being) denotes the beloved godhead that an individual worships throughout his lifetime. The nature and attributes of the ishta devata support a devotee's spiritual growth and expansion of consciousness. Importantly, revering an ishta devata does not preclude the worship or honoring of other godheads.

We evaluate one's ishta devata by looking at either the Udaya Lagna or Chandra Lagna, whichever is more powerful and auspicious. To determine this, compare and contrast from both lagnas the condition of the Lagna and its Lagnesha and the presence of auspicious birth chart yogas, such as Sarasvati yoga, Budha Aditya

---

[3] Refer to *Your Healing Stars: Volume I, Fundamentals of Vedic Astrology* for a description of raj and dhana yogas.

Chapter 17: Uncovering Your Dharma

yoga, raj yogas and dhana yogas.

The 5B and its bhavesha show the type of worship and devotional expression (mantra, affirmation, prayer, meditation, ritual, puja) that a person is drawn to as well as the ishta devata. After determining which lagna (Udaya Lagna or Chandra Lagna) to work with, next identify grahas that occupy the 5B and that graha serving as the 5B bhavesha. The strongest of these grahas denotes the person's ishta devata.

Table 6: Ishta Devatas

Graha	Godhead	Alternative Godheads
Surya	Lord Agni (Fire God)	Shri Rama
Chandra	Gauri (Mother Earth)	Shri Krishna
Mangala	Hanuman	Lord Skanda (Shiva's son)
Budha	Shri Sarasvati	Lord Vishnu
Guru	Guru (the inner Guru)	Lord Indra
Sukra	Shri Lakshmi	Kamadeva (lord of love)
Shani	Lord Shiva	Goddess Kali
Rahu	Goddess Durga	
Ketu	Shri Ganehsa	

Although the table above emphasizes the Hindu deities, by understanding the nature and essence of each graha, it is easy to modify your worship to fit your particular spiritual orientation. For instance, Chandra embodies a maternal loving and nurturing energy. Thus, the worship of any motherly divinity such as Mother Mary or Goddess Tara is appropriate for Chandra.

Chapter 18: Yogas for Spiritual Growth

Introduction

In the previous chapter, our focus was on the purushartha of dharma, or the purposeful pursuit of our individual path and higher duty. Yet, we are each born for the purpose of fulfilling all four aims in life. In order to live out our dharma, our mundane needs and those of our family must be tended to (artha). Similarly, enjoying the pleasures of the world and engaging in intimate relationships (kama) adds richness to life and is an important ingredient of the human experience. To evolve and mature as spiritual beings (moksha) is another goal of our existence. But the layout of the Vedic birth chart makes it readily apparent that living a spiritual life is no easy task.

This is supported by the fact that two of the three moksha sthanas are classified as trik-dusthanas. Unlike the upachaya (and artha) trik-dusthana 6B that offers the hope of overcoming the obstacles it poses, the moksha 8B and 12B hold no such promise. Instead, their proposition is one of inner growth, often at the expense of outer success. Face your deepest fears and vulnerabilities and brave the rollercoaster of sudden upheavals and transformations (8B) and you might open the gateway to the soul. Or, surrender to a life of loss and separation from others (12B) and spiritual liberation may be possible (12B). Just as a lotus that grows from its muddy origin reaches upwards towards the light, braving the dusthana aspects of the 8B and 12B inspire us to rise above our often murky mundane existence.[1]

As for the seemingly benign moksha sthana 4B, this bhava represents the nadir of the sky, or that area completely concealed at the time of birth. *Naraka sthana* (place of hell or torment) is one of its Sanskrit names, for this bhava shows the depths of the subconscious, which can be dark and foreboding.

Of course, only under certain birth chart configurations do the extremes of the moksha bhavas play out. More often, we experience a few transformative events that help propel our spiritual life forward (8B). At other times, we remove ourselves from the hustle and bustle of daily life, opting for a period of quiet exclusion (12B). We may even seek occasional professional help to assist us in revealing our dark shadows and hidden emotional motives (4B). Each of these experiences is a doorway into the soul and a gentle reminder that a spiritual life is important.

In this chapter, we move beyond the moksha sthanas and examine other birth chart configurations and yogas that promote spiritual development or provide unique skills that can aid us on our spiritual path.

---

[1] Recall, however, that there are also many positive aspects of the trik-dusthanas. Refer to Chapter 6: "Vikruti and the Trik-Dusthanas".

Pravrajya Yoga, Yogas for Renunciation

We begin with an examination of yogas for renunciation. In ancient times, it was customary for spiritual aspirants to remove themselves from society, relinquishing householder responsibilities and as much material attachment as possible. Thus, shastra-cited karma phala for yogas of asceticism include vows of celibacy, life as a naked mendicant, begging for alms or residing in the forest.

In our more modern day and age, we would expand the consequences of these yogas to include an extended period of time spent in an ashram, monastery or convent, or a sincere dedication to the spiritual path while engaged as a productive and contributing member of society. There are many versions of what a spiritual life could be.

Kalyana Varma dedicates an entire chapter in *Saravali* to *pravrajya* (wandering about) *yogas*, citing over 30 such yogas for renunciation. Varma was a king by birth but gained expertise in astrology through various masters.

Pravrajya yoga forms when four or more grahas (except, or in addition to, Rahu and Ketu) occupy a single bhava. Why might a person with this particular birth chart configuration be inclined towards worldly renunciation?

Under this scenario, the person looks to a particular area of life for fulfillment of mundane necessities and satisfaction of multiple interests and desires. He puts all his eggs in the proverbial basket.

When four or more grahas occupy a single bhava, it increases the odds that one or more of them are weak, be it by planetary war or rashi sandhi, or greatly destabilized. Moreover, many pravrajya yogas require the participation of Surya, which increases the odds of planetary combustion. Others stipulate that Surya *and* Chandra must participate in the yoga. In this case, Chandra is weak, i.e., the moon is dark.

We have learned that any weak graha undermines the affairs of its bhava and those of its bhava placement. Now consider the consequences when multiple grahas forming pravrajya yoga are weakly conditioned or greatly destabilized. In this case, the area of life most important to the individual, as indicated by the occupation of four or more grahas, is inherently unstable.

Sooner or later, problematic grahas participating in pravrajya yoga are triggered by stressful dashas and/or transits, and the person suddenly finds himself without a Plan B. For instance, perhaps an individual pours his heart and soul into his career. He may even make it to the top of the corporate ladder, for when multiple grahas occupy a single bhava, there are likely to be yogas for success (raj and dhana yogas) as well as downfalls (daridra and arishta yogas). Then, when the dasha of a problematic graha or one involved in daridra yoga is triggered, suddenly the corporate red carpet is pulled out from under him. Having down-played other aspects of life, such as hobbies, friends, marriage or a family, the person finds himself without a safety net. It is during these times of great disappointments that

Chapter 18: Yogas for Spiritual Growth

many people tend to take a more spiritual approach to life.

In addition to the requirement that four or more grahas (except, or in addition to, Rahu and Ketu) must occupy a single bhava, at least one graha must be strongly conditioned, while not also weakly conditioned (i.e., the graha should not be of mixed condition). Should the graha with strength also be combust the sun, the person will have "an earnest desire to be initiated into the religious order but will not attain fruition of his aim".[2] If the graha of strength possesses a factor of weakness other than combustion, "the native will give up the (religious) order after being initiated into it."[3] Notice that these exceptions do not negate dedication to a spiritual path, but only deny formal or fully committed initiation into a religious sect by a guru.

Lastly, of the four or more grahas occupying a single bhava, should Surya be the sole graha with strength, "there will only be faith in the religious order, while competence (to fulfil the order) will lack."[4]

As stipulated below, the graha with strength determines the type of spiritual order the aspirant is ordained into.[5]

> The Sun rules the ascetics of the following orders: Those who worship Agni (the fire god) in forests or on river banks, those who worship the Sun God, elephant-faced Ganesha and his benevolent mother Parvati, those who recite the hymns of Gayatri (mantra to the sun), those who make a vow to bathe in the sacred Ganges every day and those who maintain celibacy.

> The religious order belonging to the Moon attracts the following various persons: Those disciples who smear their bodies with sacred ashes, those who worship the feet of Lord Shiva, those who are abandoned by the society, those who are devoted to Bhavavati, those who give up company of others, those who take Soma Siddhanta and those who carry bowls in their hands for begging alms.

> The Buddhist monks, the tonsured (shaved head), those who wear white apparels, these who beg wearing good robes, those who wear blood-red clothes and those that have conquered their five senses; all these mendicants are ruled by Mars.

> Mercury denotes an alms-seeker, a conjurer, a snake poison curer, and one who wears the crest of a peacock.

> The ascetics ruled by Jupiter are: those who hold a single mace, those who hold three maces, those who wear red colored apparels, those who are in the third

---

[2] *Saravali of Kalyana Varma*, R. Santhanam (translator and editor), Vol. 1, 20.21. Ranjan Publications, 2005.
[3] Ibid, Vol. 1, 20.20.
[4] Ibid.
[5] Ibid, Vol. 1, 20.30-36

stage of their religious life, those who pull on their lives with fruits and water alone, those who still are attached to family ties, those who maintain celibacy and those who take to visiting shrines, etc.

Venus rules the mendicants of Saivite and Vaishnavite sects.

Religious hypocrites, bare mendicants and ascetics who sit under shadowy trees in forests are ruled by Shani.

Should there be more than one strongly conditioned graha, then the person is ordained into multiple religious sects. In this case, the first initiation corresponds with the graha whose dasha runs first. When the dasha of the next graha runs, the person relinquishes the holy order and accepts initiation into the order signified by the second graha, and so on.

Spiritual Yogas Involving Chandra

Chandra is central in many yogas indicating spiritual austerity. In Chapter 13: "Emotional Health and Wellbeing", the example is given of an influence from Shani on natal Chandra. Varma offers additional renunciation yogas that involve papa graha influences on the moon or its rashi ruler.[6]

> The native will attain religious order if the Moon, posited in a decanate (D-3) of Saturn, is aspected by Mars and Saturn. The same effect is produced if the Moon occupies the Navamsha of Aries or Scorpio in aspect to Saturn.
>
> If the waxing Moon, that also possess strength (i.e., a strongly conditioned Chandra), aspects the Lagnesha, who is bereft of strength (weakly conditioned) and not in association with another planet, the native will be devoid of wealth and own men (i.e., slaves), be miserable, sorrowful, will take to asceticism and will obtain his food with great inconvenience.
>
> If the planetary ruler for the rashi of the Moon receives only an aspect from Saturn, one will enter a religious order.
>
> If the planetary ruler for the rashi of a Moon that is bright with rays (a bright moon) lends its aspect to Saturn, while Saturn is in a kendra, the native will lose his fortunes only to enter into a religious order.
>
> If the planetary ruler for the rashi of the Moon aspects all the other planets, while the other planets are together in a single rashi, the native will become an ascetic.
>
> If one among the Sun, the Moon or Jupiter is devoid of strength and occupies the Lagna or the 10th or the 12th bhava and is aspected by a strong (strongly conditioned) Saturn, the native will become a distressed ascetic.

---

[6] Ibid, Vol. 1, 20.25-29.

The Dharma of Nicha Bhanga Grahas

A soul enters embodied life at the exact moment that the planetary patterns in the sky are synchronized with the events, desires and aversions that it is here to experience. This means that the position and condition of *each* natal graha is meticulously chosen by the soul to aid in the physical, mental-emotional and spiritual evolution of the individual. As a Jyotishi, it is our responsibility to understand the potential each graha holds for individual evolution and maturation and share this with the client.

To this end, in this section, we examine the potential of debilitated grahas. Debilitation is a factor of weakness that limits the worldly gains attainable from the graha. Under certain conditions, a debilitated graha is declared *nicha bhanga*, 'a reversal in low status'.[7] Take note that the operative word is *modified*, rather than *cancelled*. Nicha bhanga grahas convey significant life teachings, which will be discussed later in this section.

For a debilitated graha to receive nicha bhanga status, certain birth chart configurations must exist. These configurations involve natal grahas that have the ability to add strength to the graha, thereby modifying the otherwise challenging outcomes associated with its debilitation. The grahas are defined below and identified using the example of debilitated Mangala.

1. The graha that rules the debilitation rashi of the graha, i.e., Chandra rules Cancer, Mangala's debilitation rashi.
2. The graha that rules the exaltation rashi of the graha, i.e., Shani rules Capricorn, Mangala's exaltation rashi.
3. The graha that is exalted in the rashi that the debilitated graha occupies, i.e., Guru is exalted in Cancer, Mangala's debilitation rashi.

In our example, the three grahas that have the potential to modify Mangala's debilitation status are Chandra, Shani and Guru.

Having identified the grahas capable of such modification, answer the following questions, assigning one point to each occurrence. Does one or more of these grahas associate with or aspect the debilitated graha? Does one or more of these grahas occupy a kendra from the Udaya Lagna *or* Chandra Lagna? If the tallied result is three points or more, the debilitated graha is declared nicha bhanga.[8]

Let us practice applying nicha bhanga rules, beginning with Frank's Gemini-ruled Lagna birth chart. Notice in Frank's chart that Guru occupies Capricorn, its rashi of debilitation.

---

[7] Nicha bhanga does not apply to the nodes of the moon.
[8] Note that nicha bhanga does not override the health impact associated the debilitated graha.

Chapter 18: Yogas for Spiritual Growth

Which grahas have the potential to modify Guru's debilitation? Shani (ruler of Guru's rashi placement), Chandra (ruler of Guru's exaltation rashi) and Mangala (the graha exalted in Capricorn).

Frank: Gemini Lagna

Next, answer the following questions, assigning 1 point to each occurrence.

Does Shani, Chandra or Mangala associate with or aspect Guru? Yes, Shani is in association with Guru (1 point).

Does Shani, Chandra or Mangala occupy a kendra from the Udaya Lagna or Chandra Lagna? Yes, Mangala occupies a kendra (7B) from the Udaya Lagna (1 point) and Chandra occupies a kendra from the Chandra Lagna (1 point).

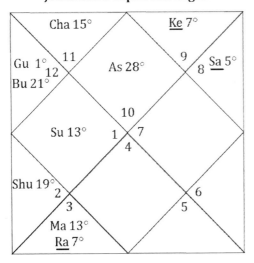

Johnathan: Capricorn Lagna

Our tally is 3 points. Thus, Guru is nicha bhanga.

Now let us do this same exercise using Johnathan's Capricorn-ruled Lagna birth chart. In this case, Budha is debilitated, for it occupies Pisces.

Which grahas have the potential to modify Budha's debilitation? The grahas are Guru (ruler of Budha's rashi placement) and Shukra (the graha exalted in Capricorn). Since Budha is exalted in its own rashi of Virgo it does not qualify.[9]

Now, answer the following questions, assigning 1 point to each occurrence.

Does Guru or Shukra associate with or aspect Budha? Yes, Guru is in association with Budha (1 point).

Does Guru or Shukra occupy a kendra from the Udaya Lagna or Chandra Lagna?

---

[9] The other exception occurs with debilitated Chandra. In this case, no graha (excepting Rahu and Ketu) is exalted in Scorpio.

141

Yes, Shukra occupies a kendra (4B) from the Chandra Lagna (1 point).

In this case, our tally is 2 points. Thus, Budha is not nicha bhanga.

Lessons learned from nicha bhanga grahas

As mentioned earlier, each natal graha has a precise role in manifesting the circumstances needed for the person's advancement. One must wonder, therefore, about the purpose of a nicha bhanga graha.

We can get insight into this question by first examining an individual's natural response to weakly conditioned grahas. A weakly conditioned graha indicates some area of "deficiency". Most often, consciously or subconsciously, the person is aware of the deficiency, but may chose to ignore or downplay its significance. Perhaps, defensive walls are built around such deficiencies and/or stories are construed to justify such actions. "Who needs money anyway?" "Why invest in a committed relationship when I'm perfectly happy being by myself?" "I don't care that my efforts aren't appreciated by others."

Yet, a person's response to a nicha bhanga graha often differs vastly. This could be because a graha's debilitation status does not automatically carry through to the vargas or sub-charts. Thus, its weak condition is less "fixed" than other factors of weakness.

Regardless of the reason, I have witnessed time and again, that rather than quarantining the graha or denying its existence, the person embraces the nicha bhanga graha, determined to develop and perfect its significations. Over time and with dedicated effort, improvement occurs.[10] In some cases, the nicha bhanga graha becomes the platform to launch a career. For example, the person with nicha bhanga Mangala may become a great athlete or surgeon, one with nicha bhanga Guru, a prominent attorney, nicha bhanga Shukra, a stellar artisan, and so on.

Often, it is in the initial dasha years of the nicha bhanga graha that the person first rallies around the areas represented by the graha, intent upon maximizing its potential. By the mid- to latter part of its dasha, the person makes personal progress it the areas of life indicated by the nicha bhanga graha and those of its karaka significations.

---

[10] As with all birth chart configurations, other factors such as graha destabilization, bhava placement and overall strength of the Lagna-Lagnesha must be considered.

Chapter 19: Chakras, Energetic Portals for Graha Consciousness

Introduction

Spiritual paths come in many forms and involve different practices. Yet, most paths have the common goal of enlightenment. In Tantra Yoga, the chakras are emphasized as part of this path.

In this chapter, we journey deeper into understanding the energetic construct of the individual by integrating our knowledge of Jyotisha with the chakra system. The chakras are psycho-spiritual centers aligned along the sushumna; the central energy channel that travels the length of the spinal column. In the area of each chakra a myriad of energetic pathways called *nadis* intersect. In total there are over 72,000 nadis.

Around the central sushumna circulate two major nadis that crisscross before and after each chakra. The *ida* is the nadi for the feminine, lunar energy and the *pingala*, the nadi for the masculine, solar energy. These lunar and solar channels begin at the *muladhara chakra* and merge at the *ajna chakra*.

Figure 11: Alternating Ida and Pingala Nadis

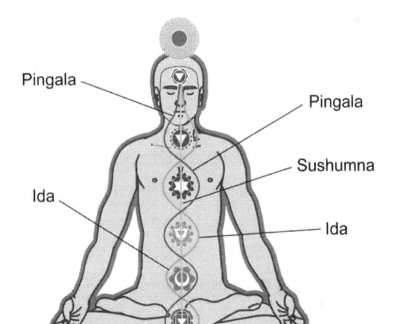

Chapter 19: Chakras, Energetic Portals for Graha Consciousness

Each chakra, a funnel-shaped vortex of energy, contains its own peculiar orientation, as highlighted in the table below.

Table 7: The Seven Major Chakras

Sanskrit (English) Name	Nature of Consciousness
Muladhara (root chakra)	physical needs, self-preservation
Svadhishtana (sacral chakra)	creative expression, hope, inspiration, values
Manipura (solar plexus chakra)	projection of personality, will-power, drive
Anahata (heart chakra)	compassion, harmony, union with others
Vishuddha (throat chakra)	speaking our truth
Ajna (3rd eye chakra)	union of consciousness (Purusha) with power (Shakti)
Sahasrara (crown chakra)	union with absolute Spirit (Brahman)

Kalapurusha and the Chakras

The notion of Kalapurusha, a cosmic being whose image overlays the twelve rashis in the sky, is introduced in Chapter 8: "The Kalapurusha of the Birth Chart". Here, Kalapurusha's body, limbs and organs are mapped to the natal birth chart to assist in evaluating the individual's physical health.

There is another mapping of the Kalapurusha to the birth chart, one revealed by Paramahamsa Yogananda. Yogananda perceived that each rashi in the sky corresponds to a chakra center in the Kalapurusha: ". . . the six spinal centers (*chakras*) correspond to the twelve astral signs of the zodiac (and) the symbolic Cosmic Man . . ."[1] Yogananda explains that since man is a reflection of the Kalapurusha, the twelve rashis also correspond to the six chakras in each of us and are arranged in polar pairs. "The astral system of a human being, with six (twelve by polarity) inner constellations revolving around the sun of the omniscient spiritual eye, is interrelated with the physical sun and the twelve zodiacal signs. All men are thus affected by an inner and an outer universe."[2]

The six pairs of rashis include the masculine and feminine rashi ruled by each graha, along with Surya-ruled Leo (a masculine rashi) and Chandra-ruled Cancer (a feminine rashi). For example, Budha is the ruler of Gemini (a masculine rashi) and Virgo (a feminine rashi). Masculine rashis are akin to the solar pingala nadi and are energetically outflowing, extroverted, expressive and initiatory. In contrast, feminine rashis are similar to the lunar ida nadi, as they are receptive, internally focused and intuitive.

---

[1] *Autobiography of a Yogi*, Paramahamsa Yogananda, Chapter 26, pg. 171. Self-Realization Fellowship, 2007.
[2] Ibid.

Chapter 19: Chakras, Energetic Portals for Graha Consciousness

To illustrate, the masculine-oriented rashi of Gemini represents our desire for communication with others and supports an inquisitive, exploratory mental nature. In contrast, the feminine-oriented rashi of Virgo denotes our internal thoughts and the conversion of incoming information into ideas and concepts. A graha occupying Gemini requires constant stimulation and does well in environments of outer change and movement. But this same graha placed in Virgo is cautious and internally centered.[3]

In the figure below, the six pairs of masculine and feminine rashis are mapped to the first six chakras. They begin at the base of the muladhara chakra with Capricorn (a feminine rashi) and Aquarius (a masculine rashi) and end at the ajna chakra with Leo (a masculine rashi) and Cancer (a feminine rashi). Just as the ida and pingala crisscross around each chakra, the masculine and feminine rashis alternate at each chakra.

Figure 12: Rashis, Grahas and Chakras

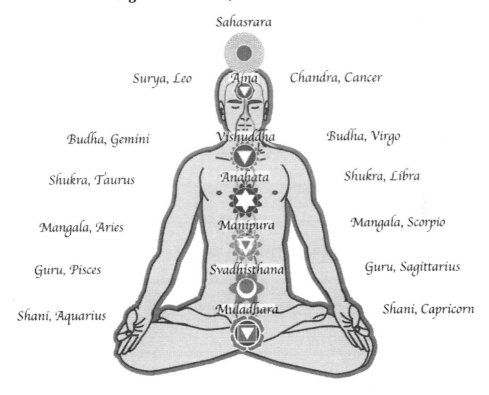

This rashi scheme also shows the alignment of each graha with a particular chakra, e.g., Shani and the muladhara chakra, Guru and the svadhisthana chakra, and so on. Beginning with the vishuddha chakra and ending with the muladhara chakra, the

---

[3] Refer to *Your Healing Stars: Volume I, Fundamentals of Vedic Astrology* for a descriptive of each rashi.

sequence of graha correspondences is the same as that of the grahas from the sun: Budha, Shukra, Mangala, Guru and Shani. This symmetry reveals the inner reflection of the cosmic universe, as illumined by Yogananda: as above, so below; as without, so within.

Chakras and Graha-Rashi Correspondences

The consciousness of a graha is transported by cosmic prana and broadcast through the chakra system. Due to its unique physiological function and psychological orientation, each chakra is the optimal repository for the consciousness of one of the seven grahas, excluding Rahu and Ketu. For instance, the ajna chakra is the natural recipient of solar and lunar consciousness, the anahata, for Shukra consciousness, and so on.

In this section, the chakras and their graha-rashi correspondences are described. Illustrations are given of the range of behavior possible for each graha and its corresponding chakra. A graha's precise expression is based on a myriad of birth chart factors, including strength, graha influences and yogas. In Chapter 20: "Enlightenment through the Stars", we examine how the rashi placement of a graha impacts the person's energetic make-up. Then in Chapter 21: "Chakra Evaluation Process", a methodology is presented to help assess a client's chakra construct.

Muladhara (rooted in support)

Positioned at the base of the charka system, the muladhara is governed by the earth element. Consciousness embodied in earth is dense, hard and crystallized. The earth of the muladhara gives form and structure to life. It causes us to identify with the physical body and perceive ourselves as being separate from all others. The downward flow of apana vayu in this region fixes our relationship with the material realm. This same flow of prana supports the purification function of purisha vaha srotas (channel of feces).

The muladhara is the portal for Shani's planetary consciousness. Just as the muladhara makes us feel we are separate to others, Shani distances us from whatever personal relationships are represented by its natal bhava position. Moreover, it is the karaka for apana vayu (downward flowing prana) and purisha vaha srotas.[4]

By keeping us grounded and practical, Shani helps us to provide for our physical needs such as food, clothing, shelter and a daily income, and those of our family. It does this by mandating that we keep both feet planted firming on earth and honor our limitations—necessary attributes for surviving in the mundane, material world. Without these higher expressions of Shani, we can be overcome by fear around self-preservation. Under this scenario, anxiety and anguish or despair and self-destruction become operative in our life. These are the lower expressions of Shani and the muladhara. From this position, our thoughts and actions might be colored by manipulation, scheming, suspicion or control.

---

[4] See Appendix F: "Channels of Nourishment and Elimination".

Capricorn (feminine): Like the muladhara chakra, Capricorn is governed by the earth element. This gives Capricorn a dependable, stable, grounded and self-sufficient nature. These are positive characteristics that correspond with the muladhara chakra. In addition, Shani-ruled Capricorn provides the strength, discipline and persistence to overcome fears related to self-preservation, a muladhara issue.

Aquarius (masculine): Aquarius introduces the air element to the muladhara, and stimulates its dense earth element. Air inspires movement and gives us a higher perspective on our earthy plights. With its extroverted, masculine orientation, Aquarius encourages us to lend a helping hand to others in need. Ruled by Shani, the graha of structure and democracy, Aquarius represents survival of the masses by promoting the bonding together of people around common needs and goals.

Svadhisthana (dwelling place of self)

The svadhisthana lies just above the practical, survival-oriented muladhara chakra. With its broader perspective and loftier viewpoint on life, this chakra allows us to see past the limitations of physical survival. The svadhisthana chakra confers a sense of unlimited possibilities and a better tomorrow. These features make the svadhisthana a ready recipient of Guru's planetary consciousness. Guru and the svadhisthana chakra give trust in the future. This trust might motivate some to bring children into the world, and Guru is a karaka for children.

Whereas Shani connects us with the earth of the muladhara for the purpose of survival, Guru merges us with the water of the svadhisthana in order to give birth to our creative self-expression. Water is soft, flowing and pliable, qualities that on a mental/emotional level relate to compassion, forgiveness and tolerance. These are the traits of the svadhisthana chakra and the psychological attributes of meda dhatu (fat tissue) that has Guru as its karaka.

Guru's planetary consciousness provides a broader definition of who we are by helping us integrate the values, morals, ideologies and spiritual beliefs that guide our lives. Without hope, faith and a meaningful set of values and morals, we are prone to fall into despair over what the future might hold or blindly adhere to outdated or overly orthodox beliefs. Alternatively, we may become intolerant of others' beliefs and spiritual orientation or apathetic towards spirituality. These are examples of Guru's lower aspects and those of the svadhisthana that can surface under certain graha conditions and influences.

Pisces (feminine): The watery svadhisthana chakra resonates well with dreamy, imaginative and water-ruled Pisces, a well-spring of creative expression. Feminine in orientation, Pisces is the more introspective, emotionally compassionate and receptive side of the svadhishtana chakra.

Sagittarius (masculine): Sagittarius introduces the expansive, exuberant and energizing aspects of fire to the water-dominated svadhisthana chakra. With Guru as its planetary ruler, Sagittarius incites us to live a purposeful life guided by higher principles. The muladhara's preoccupation with survival and self-preservation are replaced with spiritual ideals and philosophical doctrines that help us define ourselves within a broader context. The masculine, outgoing nature of Sagittarius encourages us to share those values and beliefs with others.

Manipura (city of lights)

The manipura is governed by the fire element and is located in the region of the solar plexus. It is connected with the digestive fire and *samana vayu*, a consolidating force often compared to a power station. Samana vayu fuels our hunger to experience life to its fullest. The hope that is central to the svadhisthana chakra becomes invigorated by the confidence that each of us has the power to make the world a better place. In the manipura chakra, dreams and ideals give way to action and goals.

As the chakra of personal power and assertiveness, the manipura is a natural receptacle for the fiery, independent and ambitious frequency emitted by Mangala. Consciousness-penetrating, the intensity of fire is radiant, courageous and dynamic. These are the psychological attributes of the manipura chakra as well as rakta dhatu (red blood cell tissue) that has Mangala for its graha karaka.

Mangala gives us the drive to express our will and a sense of being free to choose our destiny. It helps us meet challenges head-on as we claim a place for ourselves in the world. These are positive attributes of Mangala's consciousness and the manipura chakra.

When we doubt our self-worth or surrender our personal power to others, resentfulness, cowardliness or rage takes over and we miss out on what life has to offer. Alternatively, we cross the line between assertion and aggression or are driven by a self-centered desire for power, prestige, fame and domination. These feelings and actions are the result of the lower nature of Mangala and the manipura chakra. Others include excessive criticism, recklessness and vindictiveness.

Aries (masculine): Just like the manipura, Aries is governed by the fire element. Fire represents our need for freedom and desire for independence, attributes also related to this chakra. Corresponding to the solar pingala of the manipura, masculine-oriented Aries is excitable, enthusiastic, spontaneous and self-reliant. This rashi supports our ability to project our personality freely and fearlessly into the world. The flames of Aries also inspire originality in thought and in action.

Scorpio (feminine): Intuitive and perceptive, the feminine, water-ruled rashi of Scorpio offsets the scorching and often blinding flames of Aries. There is a balancing act between Scorpio and Aries, the ida and pingala aspects of the manipura chakra. Water and fire are inherently antithetical—water puts out fire and fire dries up water. Yet, as exemplified with the pitta dosha, their relationship is quite useful. Take for example the stomach, located in the area of the manipura chakra. Here, water and fire work together to transform food into chyle. Scorpio and Aries symbolize this notion of transformation applied to all levels of our being.

Anahata (unstruck)

Moving upwards from the manipura, the anahata is positioned at the center of the seven major energy centers. In one grand movement, we transition from the self-involved manipura to the socially-oriented heart chakra, governed by the air element. Here, one's attention shifts from belief in oneself and desire for independence to caring for others and cherishing the interdependent nature of human life. This center of love, harmony and union is the portal for the planetary consciousness of Shukra.

The anahata chakra is the root of mano vaha srotas where the physical heart, emotional heart, mind and soul unite.[5] It is the seat of *vyana vayu* whose movement is circular and expansive. Vyana vayu circulates the sensations, feelings and thoughts that originate from this chakra center and expands our sense of soul-consciousness seated in the region of the spiritual heart.

The air-ruled anahata chakra allows us to rise above the limitations of the earth-ruled muladhara, the attachment of the water-ruled svadhisthana, and the self-involved nature of the fire-ruled manipura. When we operate from the heart center, we are sensitive and connected to others and graceful in our actions. It is in this subtle region of the anahata where the emotional heart and mind come together that we find the ability to refine our aesthetic sense and express beauty.

When we are possessive in relationships, insensitive to others' needs or use personal charisma to influence people, it reflects the lower aspects of Shukra's consciousness and of the anahata chakra. This same planetary consciousness can be the force behind melodrama, overindulgence in or addiction to sense pleasures, vanity, narcissism and unwillingness to reciprocate the love and affection we receive from others.

Libra (masculine): Libra is the masculine, air-ruled rashi aligned with the anahata chakra, also governed by the air element. Denoted by its upward and outward movement, the air of Libra takes us to a higher plane. Supported by the detached nature of this element, Libra represents our ability to love people unconditionally. Shukra-ruled Libra also imbues a refined sense of taste that is instrumental for artistic expression.

Taurus (feminine): Were it not for the counterbalancing force of earth-ruled Taurus, the anahata-oriented person would remain forever airborne. Taurus gives endurance, practicality and reliability, necessary traits for stable, lasting relationships. Its feminine, ida-like energy aligns well with the receptive and devotional nature of this chakra. Ruled by the earth element, Taurus also gives us an appreciation for the beauty all around us.

Vishuddha (pure and clear)

The vishuddha chakra is located in the throat region and is aligned with the

---

[5] Refer to "Introduction to Section V".

planetary energy of Budha. Mirroring this graha's proximity to the sun, the vishuddha chakra lies closest to the ajna chakra, governed by Surya.

Budha is the graha karaka for majja dhatu (nerve tissue) that is responsible for two-way communication between the body and brain. The psychological attributes of majja dhatu and vishuddha chakra are curiosity, intelligence, open-mindedness and clarity. Hence, this charka and Budha govern effective and truthful communication as well as creative verbal expression. Other functions include proper understanding, orientation to a healthy lifestyle and equanimity.

The vishuddha chakra is governed by the ether element. Ether is the first element to appear in creation and the one nearest in essence to infinite and unbounded Spirit. In the space created by ether, all other elements unfold to produce the manifest world. This makes the vishuddha chakra and Budha a portal between Spirit and Matter. Here, we dance in both worlds, connected to spirit *and* to earthly existence. From this perspective, we are able to witness the delightful play of the Divine in every aspect of life.

Grounded in the diaphragm but centered in the throat, *udana vayu* governs the upward movement of the life force. It allows for self-expression of our thoughts and ideas and mental perceptions through speech. The ascent of prana in this region of the vishuddha chakra carries consciousness upwards towards the light of the luminaries, the sun and moon, and the ajna chakra, the gateway to universality in body, mind and soul.

When Budha's consciousness streams undistorted through the vishuddha chakra, it gives the power of detached perception and the ability to witness ourselves objectively. Its consciousness is well aligned with the flexible and adaptable vishuddha chakra. These qualities help us adjust to the ever-changing circumstances of life, optimizing each moment. Remaining open and receptive to life experiences, we are better able to grasp the purpose behind them.

When these qualities are absent in our life, we become obstinate and stuck in our habits. This closes us off to opportunities and experiences. In contrast, we may be so adaptable and changeable that we find ourselves in a perpetual state of indecisiveness. The constant stimulation and movement drains our physical energy, taxes our nervous system and makes us unable to balance our spiritual life with our mundane existence. These are all lower tendencies of Budha's consciousness and the vishuddha chakra.

Gemini (masculine): Masculine, Budha-ruled Gemini represents our mental versatility, inquisitiveness and desire to learn and to bestow knowledge. Governed by the air element, Budha-ruled Gemini is aligned with the social side of the vishuddha chakra. It gives us an ability to remain detached and adaptable. It favors movement, stimulation and change.

Virgo (feminine): As the feminine side of the vishuddha chakra and governed by the earth element, Virgo is introspective, patient and practical. It inclines a person to use information to improve himself/herself. Virgo expresses its creativity in utilitarian skills and talents.

Just as earth-ruled Taurus favors a handful of meaningful relationships over the endless acquaintances that socially oriented, air-ruled Libra enjoys, a similar comparison exists between earth-ruled Virgo and air-ruled Gemini. Virgo is discerning in its information-gathering, preferring to go deeply into a few subjects. In contrast, curious air-ruled Gemini is an intellectual butterfly, flittering here and there, dabbling in a diverse range of topics. Furthermore, the earth of Virgo connects, while the air of Gemini disperses. Hence, Virgo gives the ability to interconnect a myriad of data through analyses and comparisons.

Ajna (command)

Crisscrossing all the way up from the muladhara charka, the lunar ida and solar pingala merge into the sushumna at the ajna chakra. Located in the space between the eyebrows, the ajna chakra is frequently referred to as the "third eye". This chakra gives the capacity to move beyond the world of the maha bhutas (the five elements) and enter the realm of universal consciousness. It is the domain of divine revelation.

Depicted as a two-petalled lotus, the ajna chakra symbolizes creation. The center of the lotus is the pre-creative state of the universe; a timeless period when Purusha (pure consciousness) and Prakruti (the power to create) are one. For the purpose of manifestation, Prakruti separates from Purusha and begins her dance of creation.[6] On the subtlest level, the right petal is Purusha and the portal for Surya's consciousness, while the left petal is Prakruti and the portal for Chandra's consciousness. In the center, their energies intermingle.

Directly behind the ajna chakra and located in the cranial cavity is prana vayu. Prana vayu gives heightened sensitivity to inner awareness and creates a union of outer cosmic prana and inner prana. When prana vayu is stilled, we experience a state of pure awareness.

The planetary consciousness of Surya brings consistency, purposefulness and illumination of truth. But when blocked, its energy, and that of the Ajna chakra, can manifest as spiritual pride, a sense of superiority, pretentiousness or a need for recognition and admiration. Rather than serving as a guiding light for others, one turns the spotlight on himself.

Chandra's consciousness is equally noble in its higher state. It imbues sensitivity, nurturance and creative imagination. But even kind and gentle Chandra has a lower expression under certain chart configurations. Attachment, sentimentality, emotional instability, moodiness and greed are illustrations of Chandra's (and those of the Ajna chakra) less attractive attributes. Alternatively, broodiness,

---

[6] Refer to Chapter 12: "The Interplay of the Tridoshas and Trigunas" for a discussion of Sankhya philosophy and its 25 tattvas.

selfishness, self-absorption, emotional stagnation, hoarding and self-pity can manifest.

Leo (masculine): The fire of Leo is universal, giving light, vision, clarity, and beneficence to all. As with the other fire rashis of Aries (muladhara) and Sagittarius (svadhisthana), Leo is creative and dynamic. It seeks unbounded freedom. Yet, its fire is refined and discerning. Compare the consistent, radiating warmth of Leo's fire to the all-consuming and scorching fire of Aries and the endless fireworks of Sagittarius, bursting with idealism and grandiose notions of right and wrong.

Cancer (feminine): The water of Cancer is like a meandering stream or gently flowing river that encourages life to grow along its banks. Its feminine and watery nature makes Cancer a rashi of intuition and compassion. Cancer perceives the world from its highly developed emotional orientation and with sensitivity to others. It unites people with its loving, affectionate energy. As a reflection of Surya's light, Chandra and its rashi hold the memory of our sacred origin.

Sahasrara (thousandfold petal)

The two-petalled lotus of the ajna chakra blossoms into the thousand-petalled lotus of the sahasrara chakra, located outside the sushumna channel at the top of the head. The energy of all nadis flows together at this chakra, generating the brilliance of a million suns.

When we master and integrate the higher consciousness of each of the seven grahas and their corresponding chakras, we transcend earthly experiences and enter into spiritual enlightenment through the sahasrara chakra. This chakra is the gateway to Supreme Spirit, which has always been and will always be. It represents our own immortality and unbounded vastness.

Chapter 20: Enlightenment through the Stars

Introduction

The consciousness of a graha is transported by cosmic prana and broadcast through the chakra system. As illustrated in the previous chapter, each graha and its rashis naturally align with a particular chakra. This alignment is based on the symmetry between the consciousness of the graha and the physiological and psychological functions of the charka.

Figure 13: Rashis, Grahas and Chakras

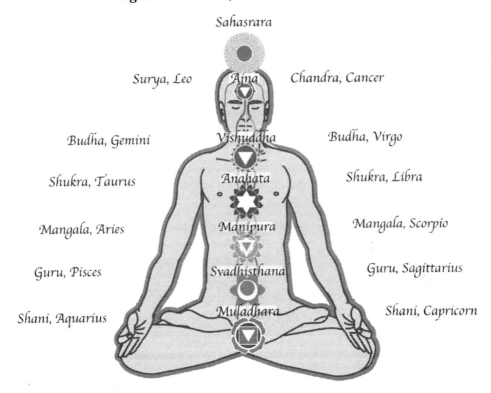

In this chapter, we explore different factors of graha strength based on rashi placement. The condition of a graha has an impact on the functioning of the chakra it governs *as well as* its recipient chakra. (We can use this same approach to evaluate the effect that other factors of strength, such as retrogression, combustion, planetary war, etc., have on the energetic make-up of the individual.)

A simplified process for evaluating the chakras is then presented in Chapter 21: "Chakra Evaluation Process". This methodology incorporates the unique influence of Rahu and Ketu on the chakra system.

Rashi Placement of Grahas

When a graha occupies its own rashi, its energetically-related chakra receives and processes its energy directly. For example, when Mangala occupies Aries or Scorpio, its consciousness of strength, courage, assertiveness, risk-taking, insight and resilience is transmitted through the manipura chakra, which has these same attributes. This is akin to a bhavesha that occupies its own rashi (i.e., is sva rashi). Such a graha readily manifests its affairs as a bhavesha and its significations as a graha karaka.

But what is the effect on the energetic construct of a person when a natal graha is not sva rashi? In this case, its consciousness is received by the chakra that corresponds to its rashi placement. Depending on the rashi-based condition of the graha, the chakra either effectively and efficiently utilizes the graha's conscious to meet its needs and responsibilities or struggles to do so.

To illustrate, assume that natal Mangala occupies Capricorn, the Shani-ruled, feminine rashi aligned with the muladhara chakra. As described in the previous chapter, the muladhara chakra is oriented towards self-preservation and supports our capacity to provide for our own physical needs and those of our dependents. With its structured, practical perspective and raw endurance, this earth-ruled chakra gives adeptness in material manifestation, just like earth-ruled Capricorn.

When Mangala's energy is transmitted through the muladhara chakra, its consciousness of bravery and buoyancy is applied to surmount basic survival-based fears. Mangala's intellectual insight and exploratory nature is also leveraged to discover innovative means of manifesting resources in the physical world. Because Mangala is exalted in Capricorn the muladhara chakra optimizes Mangala's consciousness seamlessly.

Moreover, since Mangala is strongly conditioned, the manipura chakra is also well-supported. This is true to our principle that a strongly conditioned graha supports its bhava affairs and karaka significations.

Similarly, but to a lesser extent, when a graha is ordinary in condition because of its rashi placement, the person manages to leverage the consciousness of the graha in a manner somewhat consistent with its chakra-aligned rashi placement. For instance, assume that Mangala occupies Sagittarius. In this case, its consciousness is transported to the visionary and faith-inspired svadhisthana chakra. Here, Mangala's self-motivation, courage and passion are directed towards developing ideals and beliefs that guide us in our daily life. The new territory pioneered by Mangala is the world of spiritual ideals and philosophical speculation. Since freedom-loving Mangala is self-focused, the person tends to apply values and philosophical constructs to define himself and bring a sense of freedom.

Thus, even when a graha is ordinary in condition by rashi placement, its recipient chakra leverages its consciousness in a fairly productive manner, according to its function. Further, its condition supports the expression and functioning of its own chakra.

Now consider what happens when a graha occupies its debilitation rashi. For example, assume Guru occupies Capricorn. How might the muladhara chakra redirect the expansive consciousness of Guru? The muladhara is concerned about daily survival techniques, and promotes a structured, cautious approach to life. Guru and the svadhisthana chakra are about future possibilities, grandiose visions and rising about the limitations of our physical existence. As one can imagine, Guru's consciousness of optimism, expansiveness and a belief that all things are possible is grossly misaligned with the mundane, practical concerns of the muladhara chakra. This is why Guru is considered debilitated in Capricorn.

The condition of natal Shani, the graha aligned with this chakra, is pivotal to the muladhara chakra's ability to successfully leverage Guru's consciousness.[1] Consider a bhava occupied by a debilitated graha whose bhavesha is likewise weak, in contrast to one whose bhavesha is ordinary or strong.

If Shani is ordinary or strong, than the person acquires knowledge and develops values and morals (Guru's consciousness) that are conducive to material manifestation. He may take a strong interest in business and be a successful administrator in a large company. On the other hand, if Shani is weak, the person is more likely to compromise his or her values and morals due to fear of survival and the need to provide for basic needs in life. Under this scenario, self-destructive tendencies, secretive or manipulative behavior or grief and anguish are some of the likely consequences.

Just as importantly, the debilitation of Guru in Capricorn adversely impacts the functioning of the svadhisthana chakra, now colored by the survival concerns, insecurities and limitations of the muladhara charka. The svadhisthana chakra, responsible for providing a sense of hope, joy and trust in others, struggles to maintain its natural, lofty perspective on life and instead, assumes a cautious, contained and self-doubting manner. The person may lack faith and belief in future possibilities, or doubt his ability to access higher knowledge. He may cling to outmoded values, be overly orthodox in his beliefs and/or view ritualistic practices as ends in themselves. The person may also have little faith and trust in gurus and be apprehensive about having children.

Summary

In summary, when sva rashi, the graha expresses itself purely through the chakra it governs. When not sva rashi, a graha's consciousness is modified by its rashi placement and funneled through the chakra aligned with its rashi placement. Moreover, the chakra that is naturally aligned with the graha assumes the psychological perspective of the recipient chakra.

This means that the health of each chakra depends on the condition of the graha(s) whose energy is channeled through its portal as well as the condition of its governing graha.

---

[1] This same principle holds true for all chakras.

Chapter 20: Enlightenment through the Stars

Although our focus in this chapter is on rashi-based factors of strength, equivalent principles apply to other graha conditions such as combustion, retrogression, dark moon, and so on. Note that because dig bala is bhava-specific, directional strength is not applicable to our rashi-based chakra evaluation.

Readers are encouraged to try a similar exercise for each remaining factor of strength and weakness. Imaginatively step into the shoes of each natal graha and envision how its consciousness mutates according to its condition. What is the impact on the recipient chakra as well as on the chakra that the graha governs? Use this same process to consider the impact of various graha influences on a chakra. This perspective improves your interpretative techniques in all areas of chart reading, including evaluating the energetic make-up of an individual.

Alternatively, a simple chakra evaluation process is outlined in the next chapter. This process identifies those chakras that require remedial support, but it does not capture the underlying reason for why a chakra functions in a particular manner. For this, a deeper understanding of the impact that various graha conditions and influences have on a chakra is required, as illustrated in the examples provided in this chapter.

Chapter 21: Chakra Evaluation Process

Methodology

By using the following process, we can quickly identify the chakras that require support.

1. Begin your evaluation with those chakras that are naturally aligned with the rashis of the Lagna and Lagnesha. These chakras are important, because one's personality is largely shaped by their perspective and orientation.

   For instance, in a Taurus-ruled Lagna chart with the Lagnesha (Shukra) placed in Scorpio, the focus is on the anahata and manipura charka, respectively. In this case, we would want to stress the importance of these two chakras when consulting the client and suggest practices and remedial measures that ensure their proper functioning.

2. Next, identify any graha that is weakly conditioned.[1] For each such graha, determine the chakra it governs and the recipient chakra based on its rashi placement.

   For example, assume Budha is combust and occupies Mangala-ruled Aries. Budha governs the vishuddha chakra, and the manipura is the recipient of its consciousness. Both chakras are adversely impacted by Budha's weak condition. Also consider the condition of Mangala, which impacts the ability of the manipura to effectively utilize the consciousness of any graha placed in Aries or Scorpio.

Prioritize your findings and review the 2-3 chakras of most concern with your client, explaining its psychological orientation and functions that are likely impaired.[2] Suggest remedial measures that support these grahas and chakras, such as those suggested in Section VI: "Healing through the Grahas".

You may also want to recommend non-Jyotisha chakra-healing techniques, including Ayurveda chromotherapy, chakra-based yoga asanas, pranayama or professional therapy.

Case Illustration: Joshua

Let us practice the above methodology using a hypothetical Gemini-ruled Lagna birth chart belonging to a client named Joshua. Right away we know that the vishuddha chakra is an important conduit for developing Joshua's personality and the perception he has of himself. As a masculine rashi aligned with the solar nadi of the vishuddha chakra, Gemini emphasizes the worth of truthful communication and "walking our talk." It is important that Joshua speaks his authentic truth and in

---

[1] If no grahas are weakly conditioned, consider those that are greatly destabilized (i.e., that have two or more factors of destabilization).
[2] Refer to Chapter 19: "Chakras, Energetic Portals for Graha Consciousness".

Chapter 21: Chakra Evaluation Process

a clear and concise way.

Interestingly, Surya's placement in Virgo activates the lunar nadi of this same chakra. This adds to the significance of the vishuddha chakra for Joshua and indicates that it is an important channel for soul development and self-realization. (Surya represents our soul nature and governs the solar nadi of the ajna chakra, a chakra of universal consciousness and divine revelation.)

Thus, Joshua will want to make sure that the vishuddha chakra remains open and balanced. This can be done through planetary remedial measures such as recitation of Budha's mantra, nakshatra rasayana practices, wearing an emerald or jade, and so on.[3] Activities that resonate with Budha's higher frequency, such as proper communication, truthful speech and writing are also recommended.

Joshua may also consider *bhramari pranayama* (Bee breath) which stimulates the vishuddha chakra or yoga asanas that keep this chakra open, such as the fish (*matsyasana*), supported shoulder stand (*salamba sarvangasana*) and upward plank (*purvottansana*) asanas.

Joshua: Gemini Lagna

Shu 4° (5, 4)	As 19° (2, 1) Sa 28°
Su 2° Ra 20° (6)	3 / 12 Ke 20°
Ma 15° (7) Bu 24° (8)	Cha 28° (9) 11 / 10
Gu 8°	

Now that we have evaluated the rashi of the Lagna and its chakra, we need to consider the rashi placement of the Lagnesha (Budha) and its corresponding chakra. The Lagnesha occupies Libra, the solar nadi of the anahata chakra. Libra relates to the social, expressive aspect of the heart center that seeks beauty, harmony and balance in relationships. The Lagnesha's placement here shows that Joshua's heart center is activated by Budha's consciousness, but in a manner consistent with Libra and the anahata chakra. This may include heart-inspired expressions of poetry, music or song, and heart-centered communications with others, perhaps as a personal coach or mentor.

Notice that the planetary consciousness of Mangala, graha ruler of the manipura chakra, is likewise channeled through the anahata chakra. Mangala's consciousness is one of courage, insight and personal power. These attributes are more naturally compatible with the manipura chakra (Aries and Scorpio) and might seem at odds with the heart chakra. It is important for Joshua to find ways to express this martian consciousness in a tender and harmonious way (anahata chakra).

---

[3] Refer to Section VI: "Healing through the Grahas".

Next, consider any weakly conditioned grahas. Debilitated in Aries, Shani is the only weakly conditioned graha in Joshua's chart. Just as we recommended remedial measures for Budha and the vishuddha chakra, we should support Shani and the manipura chakra as well as the muladhara chakra, both which are harmed by Shani's consciousness. Jyotisha remedial measures can help align the consciousness of a natal graha prior to its entering the chakra system. In contrast, chakra practices enhance a chakra's ability to process the incoming consciousness of a weak or greatly destabilized graha.

For insight into the adverse impact of Shani's debilitation on the muladhara and manipura chakra, we could apply the technique demonstrated in the previous chapter. First consider why Shani is debilitated in Aries and how that placement modifies its consciousness, thereby impacting the functions of the manipura chakra. Aligned with the fiery, solar nadi of the manipura chakra, Aries is related to personal empowerment, spontaneity, enthusiasm, risk-taking, courage and originality. These qualities are at odds with cautious, conservative, calculating, disciplined, reserved and serious Shani and the muladhara chakra. When Shani is placed in Aries, its consciousness is modified to accommodate the excitable, adventuresome and impulsive nature of this rashi and the manipura chakra. This is much like mixing oil and water, and precisely the reason that Shani is considered debilitated in Aries.

Joshua may doubt his personal power or surrender his power to others. He may vacillate between cruising down the road of life with the "pedal to the metal" one moment and the emergency break fully engaged the next moment. This can lead to passive-aggressive behavior. Notice, however, that Mangala is ordinary in condition and aspects back on its own rashi, Aries. This reduces (but does not cancel) Shani's adverse impact on the manipura chakra. We would want Joshua to examine his sense of personal power and his openness to adventure and willingness to take chances in life. The manipura and Mangala also supports our quest for independence, another important area for Joshua to reflect upon.

Now consider the impact that Shani's debilitation has on its own muladhara chakra. The earth-ruled muladhara requires prudence, consistency, focus and determination to ensure that our material needs are met. When Shani is debilitated, the muladhara chakra struggles to deliver on these important psychological attributes. Joshua may waffle when it comes to accepting long-term commitments and responsibilities and/or find it difficult to remain grounded and practical in his approach to life.

As every Jyotishi can attest, it is Shani that teaches us our most profound lessons, and the particular psychology and orientation of Shani's recipient chakra becomes the portal for such lessons. This highlights the importance of muladhara issues for Joshua. Similarly, Mangala's recipient chakra is the portal for developing our courage; Guru's recipient chakra, fostering our vision and hope; Surya's recipient chakra, enlarging our soul consciousness, and so on.

Rahu and Ketu

Although Rahu and Ketu are shadow grahas, they are influential forces. In *Your Healing Stars: Volume I, Fundamentals of Vedic Astrology*, it was shown that the bhava placements of Rahu and Ketu represent opposite areas of life. The process of integrating and balancing these two areas becomes an important lesson for the person. For example, if Rahu and Ketu occupy the 4B and 10B, one's home life and the emotional security derived from this area of life is to be balanced with one's professional life and the material security it provides.

Because we use a rashi-based system to evaluate chakras, we can apply a similar notion to the rashi placement of the lunar nodes. The rashi placements of Rahu and Ketu represent divergent psycho-emotional perspectives as symbolized by the chakras that require balance and integration.

To illustrate, let us return to Joshua's birth chart. Notice that Ketu occupies Pisces and Rahu occupies Virgo. Thus, the svadhishtana and vishuddha chakras receive the consciousness of Ketu and Rahu, respectively. This shows that Joshua must balance the watery lunar nature of the svadhisthana chakra, i.e., the imaginative, free-flowing and surrendering nature of Pisces, with the earthy lunar nature of the vishuddha chakra, i.e., the discerning and thought-structured perspective of Virgo.

Summary

Jyotisha is an effective means for providing spiritual insight and guidance to the client, provided that you communicate your birth chart findings in a manner he or she can understand. I have many clients in the yoga community who are well-versed in the meaning and use of the chakras. For these clients, there is a natural receptivity and an ease of comprehension of a chakra-based evaluation using the birth chart.

For those clients not familiar with the chakras and their representations, take time upfront to educate them on this spiritually-oriented system and its relationship with the cosmic forces of the universe.

Introduction to Section VI

In ancient cultures, people lived in alignment with the natural rhythms and cycles of nature, as governed by the celestial bodies. Many such civilizations designed calendars based upon particular planetary cycles. In India, two systems evolved—a solar and lunar calendar. To this day, India's nakshatra-based lunar calendar is used to determine when to plant seeds and harvest grains, auspicious times for weddings, advantageous days for surgery and the best times for preparing and administering medicine.

In these civilizations, the planet's movements are viewed from Earth's perspective, and read as omens. A brilliant star in the night sky leads three wise men to baby Jesus, and the birth of the Dalai Lama is predicted based upon auspicious planetary alignments. Occultation of other planets signals an imminent natural disaster, such as an earthquake, hurricane or fire.

Since the ancient Vedic times, planetary-based rituals and celebrations have been an integral part of Indian life. Ceremonies for the new and full moon are performed to ensure the on-going exchange of giving and receiving between the gods and mankind. The Agnihotra (oblations to the fire), a practice that survives to this day, is performed twice daily by married couples to honor Surya and Agni (the fire god). In these and many other ways, people maintain a sacred connection with the planets.

It seems that in modern day society, we have all but forgotten this connection that was once deeply ingrained in every aspect of living. Disconnected from the sacredness of our existence, we bear witness to rampant abuse of Mother Earth, needless loss of human life due to war and domestic violence, and a growing discontent within each of us, as we miss a sense of purpose and meaning.

As holograms of the heavenly forces, each cell in our body contains the memory of our sacred connection with the universe. All that is needed to awaken this connection is remembrance. When we align our daily life with the planetary forces, that memory gradually rises to the surface and becomes part of our waking day. By remembering this sacred connection, I believe we can resolve many of the plights now facing mankind and Mother Earth.

You have already begun this process by appreciating that the grahas manifest their energy in our physical, mental-emotional and spiritual sheaths. This knowledge is the beginning of a personal alignment with the cosmic forces. By aligning our daily life with the grahas, we awaken within ourselves their unique wisdom, which helps us navigate through difficult times.

In this section, several planetary practices are illustrated. Incorporating them into your daily life consciously and consistently supports the blossoming of an intimate relationship with the grahas. This relationship is the doorway into remembering our sacred connection with the cosmos.

SECTION VI: Healing through the Grahas

Chapter 22: Celestial Prayers to the Grahas

The Power of Chanting

There are many forms of meditation that help one enter into communion with the planetary forces. Chanting Sanskrit syllables (*bijas*) and prayers (*mantras*) is one such practice. The vibrational sounds of the grahas activate various energy centers in the body, promoting healing and transformation.

A bija, or 'seed syllable', is often compared to the seed of a tree. When we plant and water a seed, we activate its innate creative potential, causing a beautiful tree to grow and blossom. In similar fashion, a planetary bija sound contains powerful creative energy and, when chanted, it releases the graha's inherent potential in our life.

By way of illustration, Budha's bija sound is *ai* (pronounced aye). *Ai* contains the potency of knowledge and instruction as well as the capacity for right speech. The vishuddha chakra is also activated by *ai*, as Budha is the graha that corresponds with this energy center.[1]

Notice that when you pronounce *ai*, the energy flows outwards, away from the body. By adding the sound "m" to the end of any seed syllable, in this case, making it *aim*, the energy is redirected inwards, causing the sound to reverberate within each and every cell. This is why bijas commonly end with the sound "m".

There are also longer chants containing one or more bijas. Many of these begin with *om*, the primeval sound of the universe, and end with *namah*, translated as, 'with adoration' or 'in veneration'. To illustrate, the celestial prayer for Budha is: *om aim Budhaya namah*. Notice that this mantra begins with *om* and the bija *aim* and ends with *Budhaya namah*, 'to Budha, with adoration'.

One can recite planetary bijas and mantras in order to invite the wisdom of a graha into his life or to strengthen its natal birth chart condition. For example, if you want to usher in the curiosity and teaching energy that Budha offers, recite his bija and planetary mantra.

Planetary Bija-Mantras

The following are the bija sounds for each of the seven grahas, followed by their planetary mantras.

Surya	*hrim* (pronounced hreem), the power to energize, hold, attract and vitalize *Om hrim sum Suryaya namah*
Chandra	*shrim* (pronounced shreem), the power of love, peace, tenderness and delight *Om shrim som Somaya namah* (Soma is another name for Chandra)
Mangala	*krim* (pronounced kreem), the power of transformation, motivation and

---

[1] See Chapter 19: "Chakras, Energetic Portals for Graha Consciousness".

Chapter 22: Celestial Prayers to the Grahas

	action *Om krim kum Kujaya namah* (Kujaya means 'born of the earth)
Budha	*aim* (pronounced I'm), the power of articulation, learning, guiding and teaching *Om aim bum Budhaya namah*
Guru	*strim* (pronounced streem), the power of expansion, abundance and wisdom *Om strim brahm Brihaspataye namah* (Brihaspati is another name for Guru)
Shukra	*klim* (pronounced kleem), the power of love, beauty, creativity and fulfillment *Om klim shum Shukraya namah*
Shani	*hlim* (pronounced hleem), the power of delaying, stopping or terminating *Om hlim sham Shanaye namah*

Beginning a Mantra Practice

It is recommended that a chanting practice last at least 40 days. This is the minimum length of time required to establish the energy of a graha firmly in the gross and subtle bodies.

Start your practice on the day of the week that is ruled by the graha you wish to honor or propitiate. Then chant the mantra 108 times, morning and evening, for 40 consecutive days. Should you forget to recite the mantra on any particular day, just pick up your practice the next morning.

You may wish to use a mala to help guide your mantra practice. The word *mala* means 'garland'. A mala is a strand of 108 beads by which prayers, mantras and chants are counted. The number 108 has spiritual significance, and is associated with the heart chakra and the lunar nakshatras.[2]

The typical Indian mala is made of Rudraksha beads, the sacred seed of Lord Shiva. The larger stone bead at the center of the mala is called the guru (teacher) bead. It represents the inner teacher.

To use the beads, hold the strand in your right hand. Position the first bead next to the guru bead between your thumb and middle finger. Say your mantra over the first bead, then move your fingers to the next bead, and repeat your mantra. Continue this practice for all 108 beads. If you wish to continue chanting when you get to the guru bead, turn the strand around and continue back the other way, since the guru bead should not be crossed over when doing multiple rounds of beads.

---

[2] Each nakshatras is divided into *padas* or quarters. The total number of nakshatras (27) multiplied by the number of padas (4) gives us 108 sacred spaces in the sky.

You may chant your mantra out loud or silently in your mind. A powerful practice is to say one round out loud and a second round silently. During the second round, you will notice that the vibration of the mantra still resonates, almost as if you are saying it audibly. Repeating Sanskrit sounds out loud helps clear blockages throughout the body, while saying them silently instills the sound within every cell.

Planetary malas

Planetary malas are made of precious or semi-precious gemstone beads that resonate at the frequency of that graha. (See Chapter 23: "Choosing the Right Gemstones".) Hence, a planetary mala is a powerful way for enhancing your mantra practice.[3] The following table lists the planetary mala gemstone beads for each graha.

Table 8: Planetary Mala Gemstones

Graha	Primary Gemstones	Secondary Gemstones
Surya	Ruby	Red Spinel, Rhodolite Garnet
Chandra	Pearl	Moonstone
Mangala	Red Coral	Carnelian, Red Agate
Budha	Emerald	Jade, Peridot, Green Tourmaline
Guru	Yellow Sapphire or Topaz	Yellow Citrine
Shukra	Diamond	White Sapphire, White Topaz
Shani	Dark Blue Sapphire	Lapis Lazuli, Amethyst, Turquoise
Rahu	Hessonite	
Ketu	Cat's Eye	Tiger's-eye

A nice way to honor all nine grahas is by wearing a Navagraha mala crafted of precious or semi-precious planetary gemstone beads. The beads in this mala follow the graha rulership of the seven week-days, followed by Ketu and Rahu: rhodolite garnet (Surya), moonstone (Chandra), jade (Budha), yellow citrine (Guru), clear quartz (Shukra), lapis lazuli (Shani), cat's eye (Ketu) and hessonite garnet (Rahu).

Attuning a Mala to your Energy

When you first purchase a mala, it will need to be attuned to your energy. Regardless of the mantra you plan to recite, the first round of chants should be the sound *hrim*, the bija of Surya and the spiritual heart. Hold the mala at the level of your heart. Visualize your heart opening to your mala and to your upcoming practice as you recite 108 *hrim* bijas.

Next, pick a particular graha you wish to honor or to strengthen. For example, if you are facing a difficult situation and are unable to find a way past it, you might choose to propitiate Shani, the likely planetary trigger of this situation. Chanting Shani's mantra will bring

---

[3] For an assortment of planetary prayer malas visit the author's website: celestialgazing.com.

qualities of fortitude, focus and disciplined action to your life. Alternatively, if the situation is caused by a lack of courage, then consider chanting the mantra for Mangala, a graha of great valor. Or, if you are beginning a spiritual discourse, you should honor Guru, the guru amongst the grahas.

Repeat the mantra 108 times in the morning and evening, commencing on the day ruled by the graha. Continue this practice for at least 40 days.

Navagraha Mantra

Before beginning your morning spiritual practice, it is auspicious to call in all the grahas, including Rahu and Ketu. When invoked together in mantra, the grahas surround you with their protective energy and guide you throughout the day.

I also recite the Navagraha mantra before commencing study or work involving the grahas, be it writing, instructing or advising on Jyotisha. Opening with the Navagraha mantra during an astrological consultation is particularly auspicious. In this way, we invite the grahas to serve as channels for information that might be useful or important for the client to hear. Often, such information is revealed to the client several days afterwards, through mediation, contemplation or dreams.

The Navagraha mantra is given below in transliteration and in English translation.[4]

Navagraha Mantra

brahma murari tripurantakari
To the creator Brahma, the sustainer Murari (a name for Vishnu), and the destroyer Tripurantakari (a name for Shiva)

bhanuh shashi bhumisuto budhashcha
To the shining one (Surya), the hare (Chandra), son of the earth (Mangala), the intelligent one (Budha)

gurushcha shukrah shani rahu ketavah
To the wise one (Guru), the bright one (Shukra), the slow-going one (Shani), the smoky one (Rahu), and to the comet (Ketu)

kurvantu sarve mama suprabhatam
May all of you please be auspicious for me today

om shanti, shanti, shanti
om peace, peace, peace

---

[4] For proper pronunciations of the Navagraha Mantra, visit celestialgazing.com.

Chapter 23: Choosing the Right Gemstones

Outwitting the Stars

It is natural to be skeptical about astrological *upayas* (planetary remedial measures), including the wearing of gemstones. In a dialog between Shri Yuktesvar and his student Paramhansa Yogananda, even the wise Yogananda questions the validity of Jyotisha and the use of planetary remedial measures. He queries Master Yuktesvar about how one can mitigate the ill-health effects of certain planetary transits just by wearing a simple armlet made of particular metals. A firm proponent of astrology, Yuktesvar enlightens Yogananda on the validity of using metals, gemstones and plants as astrological upayas.

The following excerpts are taken from this dialogue between Yuktesvar ("Master") and Yogananda ("Student").[1]

Master: Mukunda *(Yogananda)*, why don't you get an astrological armlet?

Student: Why should I, Master? I don't believe in astrology.

Master: It is never a question of *belief*; the only scientific attitude one can take on any subject is whether it is *true*. The law of gravitation worked as efficiently before Newton as after him. The cosmos would be fairly chaotic if its laws could not operate without the sanction of human belief...

Astrology is the study of man's response to planetary stimuli. The stars have no conscious benevolence or animosity; they merely send forth positive and negative radiations. Of themselves, these do not help or harm humanity, but offer a lawful channel for the outward operation of cause-effect equilibriums which each man has set into motion in the past.

A child is born on that day and at that hour when the celestial rays are in mathematical harmony with his individual karma. His horoscope is a challenging portrait, revealing his unalterable past and its probable future results.

The message boldly blazoned across the heavens at the moment of birth is not meant to emphasize fate or the result of past good and evil but to arouse man's will to escape from his universal thralldom. What he has done, he can undo. None other than himself was the instigator of the causes of whatever effects are now prevalent in his life. He can overcome any limitation, because he created it by his own actions in the first place, and because he has spiritual resources which are not subject to planetary pressure.

... God is harmony; the devotee who attunes himself will never perform any action amiss. His activities will be correctly and naturally timed to accord with astrological law. After deep prayer and meditation he is in touch with his divine consciousness; there is no greater power than that inward protection.

---

[1] *Autobiography of a Yogi*, Paramahamsa Yogananda, Chapter 16, pg. 171. Self-Realization Fellowship, 2007.

Student: But, dear Master, why do you want me to wear an astrological bangle? (I ventured this question after a long silence, during which I had tried to assimilate Sri Yuktesvar's noble exposition.)

Master: It is only when a traveler has reached his goal that he is justified in discarding his maps. During the journey, he takes advantage of any convenient short cut. The ancient Ashvins discovered many ways to curtail the period of man's exile in delusion. There are certain mechanical features in the law of karma which can be skillfully adjusted by the fingers of wisdom.

All human ills arise from some transgression of universal law. The scriptures point out that man must satisfy the laws of nature, while not discrediting the divine omnipotence. He should say: 'Lord, I trust in Thee, and know Thou canst help me, but I too will do my best to undo any wrong I have done.' By a number of means by prayer, by will power, by yoga meditation, by consultation with saints, by use of astrological bangles the adverse effects of past wrongs can be minimized or nullified.

Just as a house can be fitted with a copper rod to absorb the shock of lightning, so the bodily temple can be benefited by various protective measures. Ages ago our yogis discovered that pure metals emit an astral light which is powerfully counteractive to negative pulls of the grahas. Subtle electrical and magnetic radiations are constantly circulating in the universe; when a man's body is being aided, he does not know it; when it is being disintegrated, he is still in ignorance. Can he do anything about it?

This problem received attention from our Ashvins; they found helpful not only a combination of metals, but also of plants and most effective of all, faultless jewels of not less than two carats. The preventive uses of astrology have seldom been seriously studied outside of India. One little-known fact is that the proper jewels, metals, or plant preparations are valueless unless the required weight is secured, and unless these remedial agents are worn next to the skin.

Rasashastra

Ayurveda recognized long ago the medicinal properties of various metals and precious and semiprecious stones and their correlation to the grahas in a special branch known as Rasashastra (alchemy). To illustrate the principle of Rasashastra, gold (containing the properties of the sun) acts as a nervine tonic, strengthens the heart muscle and improves intelligence. Silver (similar to the moon) promotes strength and stamina, reduces excess pitta conditions and remedies certain liver disorders. Copper (and its planetary equivalent, Mangala) alleviates excess kapha and is useful in the treatment of obesity and lymphatic obstruction.

This same science prescribes the internal use of the nine planetary gemstones (Navaratna), which are reduced to powdered form (*bhasma*): ruby (Surya), pearl (Chandra), red coral (Mangala), emerald (Budha), yellow topaz (Guru), diamond (Shukra), blue sapphire (Shani), hessonite (Rahu) and cat's eye (Ketu). True to their planetary correspondences and in accordance with Rasashastra, ruby bhasma increases the life span, strengthens bones and improves the digestive fire, emerald bhasma enhances the nervous system and helps correct health issues such as epilepsy and stammering mental hysteria, diamond bhasma is an aphrodisiac and rejuvenator, and so on. (At the current time, medicinal gemstone bhasmas

Chapter 23: Choosing the Right Gemstones

are forbidden for use in the U.S.)

Jyotisha likewise acknowledges the powerful effects of gemstones. According to Jyotisha, gemstones are recipients of planetary consciousness and their structural patterns are similar to those of the grahas. When one wears a gemstone, the gross and subtle bodies absorb its energy field immediately and continuously. Gemstones are potent planetary upayas, and one must be prudent about which gemstones to wear.

In this chapter, guidelines are provided to assist the Ayurvedic practitioner in recommending the use of gemstones. Additional information, such as which metals to use for gemstone settings, the quality and size of gemstones and the proper hand and finger on which to wear different gemstone rings, is covered in Chapter 24: "Other Important Gemstone Considerations".

Table 9: Graha Gemstones

Graha	Primary Gemstones	Secondary Gemstones
Surya	Ruby	Red Spinel, Rhodolite Garnet
Chandra	Pearl	Moonstone
Mangala	Pink Coral	Carnelian, Red Agate
Budha	Emerald	Jade, Peridot, Green Tourmaline
Guru	Yellow Sapphire, Yellow Topaz	Yellow Citrine
Shukra	Diamond	White Sapphire, White Topaz, White Zirconium
Shani	Dark Blue Sapphire	Lapis Lazuli, Amethyst
Rahu	Hessonite	
Ketu	Cat's Eye	

Gemstone Evaluation Process

It is essential to observe the following guidelines when recommending gemstones. If you follow these standards, the right gemstone for your client usually becomes readily apparent. However, due to the *many* possible birth chart nuances, these guidelines are not intended to be all-inclusive. If you are new to the science of Jyotisha, it is advised that you not recommend gemstones to your clientele until you are more qualified. In this case, consider reviewing your recommendations with an experienced Jyotishi.

1) Evaluation of the Lagna-Lagnesha and Chandra

Determining the proper gemstone requires first and foremost a consideration of the Lagnesha. As a general rule, the Lagnesha is the best candidate for gemstone usage when it is ordinary or poorly-conditioned or when the Lagna or Lagnesha are destabilized by multiple papa grahas.

In contrast, when the Lagna-Lagnesha are well-conditioned there is little need to wear their gemstone. Adding strength to *any* well-conditioned natal graha can result in exaggerated or erratic expressions of its energy in the individual's life. For example, suppose that for a Leo-ruled Lagna, the Lagnesha (Surya) occupies the Aries-ruled 9B. In this case, Surya is strong (exalted). If the client strengthens Surya by wearing a ruby, conditions of excess pitta could surface, such as skin rashes, dominating behavior or excessive pride.

Or, consider a Cancer-ruled Lagna with the Lagnesha (Chandra) placed in the Lagna and Surya occupying the 7B. In this case, Chandra possesses two factors of strength: sva rashi and bright moon. If the client wears pearls on a regular basis, we can predict heightened emotional sensitivity that can lead to manas imbalance.

Because Chandra is an important graha in Jyotisha, we next consider its condition using the same general guidelines stipulated above. When Chandra is ordinary or poorly-conditioned or destabilized by multiple papa grahas, it is a good candidate for gemstone treatment.

2) *Grahas ruling positive bhavas or the money bhavas*

Having evaluated the Lagna-Lagnesha and Chandra, we are now ready to consider gemstone usage for grahas that rule the other trikonas (5B, 9B) and kendras (4B, 7B, 10B) or the money bhavas (2B, 11B). When the dharma bhavas are supported, the person displays intellectual discrimination (5B) and aligns himself with higher values and morals (9B). When the kendras are powerful, the person is likely to have a nourishing home life (4B), happy marriage (7B) and satisfying job (10B). Lastly, someone with strong money bhavas will reap the benefits of a stable income (2B) and financial gains (11B).

Once again, apply our standard rule to each graha and its bhava: when the bhava-bhavesha are ordinary or poorly-conditioned or destabilized by multiple papa grahas, consider using a gemstone as an upaya. (See "Important qualifiers for papa grahas" in this same section.)

When recommending gemstones for grahas that rule dharma, kendra and/or money bhavas, be sure that the graha does not also rule a trik-dusthana (6B, 8B, 12B). For example, assume that your Gemini-ruled Lagna client is experiencing financial difficulties. Chandra (2B) and Mangala (11B) rule the money bhavas in a Gemini-ruled Lagna chart. Should Mangala occupy the last degree of Pisces (i.e., is rashi sandhi), we would not consider recommending its gemstone, for this graha also rules the trik-dusthana 6B. By strengthening Mangala, support is given to the 11B, but also the 6B of short-term debt, litigation, enemies, obstacles and acute illnesses.

When a graha ruling one positive and one negative bhava requires added support, we can consider the gemstone for its dispositor. By strengthening its dispositor, the affairs of the bhavas ruled by the graha and karaka significations of the graha are fortified. This principle is evidenced in parvata yogas, as demonstrated in Chapter 5: "Constitutional Strength and Vitality". For our Gemini-ruled Lagna client, we can recommend a gemstone for Guru, Mangala's rashi ruler *and* the bhavesha for two positive bhavas, the 7B and 10B.

The exception to the above rule is when the Lagnesha also rules a trik-dusthana bhava, as in an Aries-ruled Lagna. A graha's role as the Lagnesha overrides its role as a dusthana bhavesha.

3) *Confluence from Chandra Lagna*

It is *imperative* that gemstone recommendations are congruent with the Chandra Lagna. Of course, when Chandra occupies the Udaya Lagna, there is automatic confluence for gemstone recommendations.

4) Important qualifiers for papa grahas

The following special considerations apply to the five papa grahas.

Surya: When recommending a gemstone for Surya, be sure that no natal grahas are combust the sun, as strengthening Surya would further harm these graha. For instance, suppose that for an Aries-ruled Lagna, Surya (ruler of the auspicious 5B bhava) is of ordinary condition and in close association with Budha (i.e., Budha is combust the sun). When Budha is combust, the person's mind is often excessively active and reactive. Strengthening Surya exaggerates this situation. It also harms Budha's other graha karaka significations and the affairs of the bhavas ruled by Budha.

A similar result occurs when Surya associates with Chandra. Here, Surya's close proximity creates a dark moon. Strengthening Surya harms natal Chandra, its graha karaka significations and the affairs of the bhava it rules.

This principle holds true any time a graha is in association with another graha. Be mindful that by strengthening one graha, you could harm one or more others.

Mangala: Notice that Mangala's primary gemstone is red coral. However, by wearing red coral, we also strengthen Mangala's papa nature, including its confrontational and combative ways. Furthermore, should Mangala be placed in the Lagna, 2B, 4B, 7B, 8B or 12B, it forms kuja dosha, which can spell trouble for one's marital life.[2] As an alternative, recommend pink coral to your client. An important exception is when Mangala is the Lagnesha *and* poorly-conditioned. In this case, the wearing of a red coral can strengthen the physical constitution and improve a person's overall vitality.

Shani: Shani's papa nature has the ability to create obstacles, difficulties, loss and ill-health. Hence, I typically do not recommend the wearing of a dark blue sapphire. As with Mangala, an important exception is when Shani is the Lagnesha *and* poorly-conditioned. Wearing a dark blue sapphire can fortify the constitution and support one's resistance to sickness and disease.

Rahu and Ketu: This brings us to the nodes of the moon. Rahu and Ketu are not only papa grahas, but their behavior is erratic and unpredictable, particularly when they are exalted or debilitated. For this reason, I rarely recommend strengthening Rahu or Ketu by wearing gemstones. Notably, this is contrary to several Jyotisha shastras. However, because of the potency of gemstones, I am particularly cautious about using them.

When Rahu or Ketu are problematic, consider instead strengthening the graha karaka for the affairs of the bhava they occupy. For example, for a Virgo-ruled Lagna, Rahu and Ketu are debilitated in the Taurus-ruled 9B, a bhava of higher education, gurus and spiritual instruction. Since Guru is the karaka for these same affairs and rules two positive bhavas (4B and 7B), the client could consider wearing a yellow topaz.

---

[2] Kuja dosha forms when Mangala occupies the Lagna, 2B, 4B, 7B, 8B or 12B.

Chapter 23: Choosing the Right Gemstones

Prioritizing Gemstone Recommendations

Most often, several grahas qualify for gemstone usage. In this case, give priority to the Lagnesha and Chandra. We don't get very far strengthening other natal grahas if the condition of the Lagnesha and Chandra are not first addressed.

To prioritize the remaining grahas, consider the relative strength of each, the current dasha period, stressful planetary transits and client objectives. For example, suppose that your client is in his Guru dasha. If natal Guru rules positive bhavas and is weak, wearing a yellow topaz will support its karaka significations and the affairs of its bhavas. Or, suppose that Shani is transiting natal Chandra. We could recommend that the person wear a strand of pearls in order to mitigate the emotional stress that such a transit brings. When prioritizing which graha to strengthen, you should also consider the client's objectives. Perhaps your client is hoping to marry and have children. In this case, evaluate the graha rulers of the 7B and 5B, respectively, and/or their graha karakas.

Finally, as an Ayurvedic practitioner, always consider the client's current condition and personal experiences. If the client has a Cancer-ruled Lagna and the Lagnesha (Chandra) is poorly-conditioned, wearing pearls is typically an appropriate recommendation. However, should your client be experiencing kapha *vruddhi* (excess kapha dosha) health issues, we would *not* recommend the wearing of strand of pearls, because pearls have kapha-increasing qualities.

Client Case Illustrations

Let us return to several clients and their birth charts to demonstrate the application of the guidelines presented in this chapter.

Alexandra

We determined in Chapter 3 that Alexandra's prakruti is vata and her primary health concern is emotional anxiety.

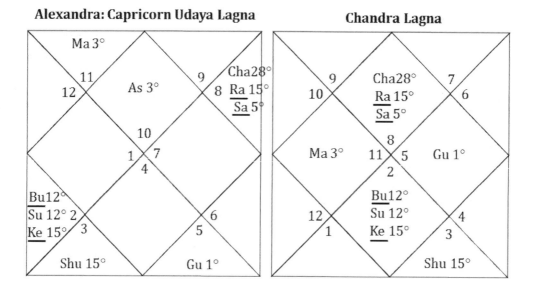

First consider the condition of the Lagna-Lagnesha and Chandra. The Lagnesha (Shani) is strongly conditioned (retrograde) and aspects its own Lagna. However, it is greatly destabilized by an exalted Rahu and debilitated and eclipsed Chandra. If we strengthen Shani, Chandra is further harmed, and so are any grahas aspected by Shani. Since Alexandra's main concern is emotional anxiety, consider recommending a strand of pearls. Pearls will calm Alexandra's emotional state and also support her marriage (Chandra is the 7B bhavesha). Furthermore, with their calming kapha qualities, pearls will soothe Alexandra's vata.

Frank

During Frank's first health consultation, he mentioned that he often flies off the handle when irritated (Budha combust the sun and in association with combust Mangala). Frank was also concerned about his recently diagnosed pre-diabetic state.

An emerald, the gemstone of the Lagnesha (Budha), would be beneficial for Frank and will strengthen Frank's overall constitutional health and vitality. It will also help stabilize Frank's reactive and explosive nature (Budha is the graha karaka for the mind). Notice that from the Udaya Lagna and the Chandra Lagna, Budha rules two positive bhavas.

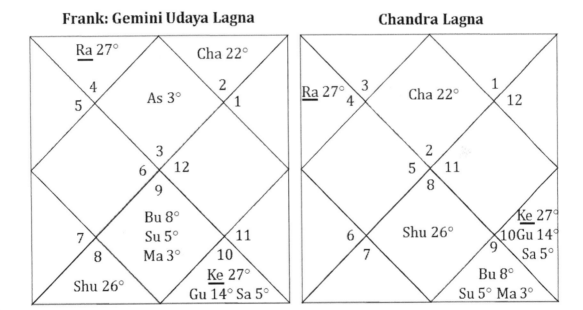

Concerning Frank's pre-diabetic state, Shukra is the primary karaka for the endocrine system as a whole.[3] However, Guru is responsible for monitoring the blood glucose levels in the body, which is the endocrine function of the pancreas.[4] Thus, Shukra and Guru are implicated in cases of diabetes. In Frank's chart, Shukra occupies the trik-dusthana 6B but is ordinary in condition. In contrast, Guru is poorly-conditioned (debilitated, associates with Shani and Ketu and occupies the trik-dusthana 8B).

---

[3] See Chapter 10: "Dhatus-Srotamsi and the Grahas".
[4] See Appendix F: "Channels of Nourishment and Elimination".

Chapter 23: Choosing the Right Gemstones

To address the Jyotisha aspect of Frank's pre-diabetic concern, a yellow topaz is appropriate. From the Udaya Lagna, Guru rules two positive bhavas (7B and 10B). However, from the Chandra Lagna, Guru rules the 11B (financial gains) and trik-dusthana 8B (upheavals and transformative events). Still, between the Udaya Lagna and Chandra Lagna, Guru is the bhavesha for three out of four positive bhavas. Most importantly, Guru is also the dispositor of the Lagnesha (because Budha occupies Sagittarius). For these reasons, a yellow topaz may be suggested. Importantly, a yellow topaz will help improve Frank's relationships (7B bhavesha) and support his career endeavors (10B bhavesha). Since yellow topaz is not compatible with emerald, Frank should purchase two separate jewelry settings.

Katrina

The reader is familiar with Katrina's chart, first presented in Chapter 3: "Dosha Prakruti".[5] Katrina's most significant health concern is her gradual loss of vision. As well, Katrina has had multiple bouts of kidney stones and often has trouble sleeping. Katrina attributes her insomnia to emotional stress and anxiety.

Shukra is the Lagnesha in Katrina's Taurus-ruled Lagna and also the karaka for vision and the kidneys. We noted earlier the problematic condition of Shukra.[6] Katrina should wear a diamond, the gemstone for Shukra. A diamond will fortify Katrina's overall constitution and promote good vision and well-functioning kidneys. From the Chandra Lagna, Shukra is the rashi ruler of Chandra. Thus, by strengthening Shukra, we also strengthen Chandra (which is destabilized by Rahu) and Katrina's emotional stress and anxiety.

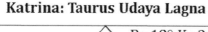

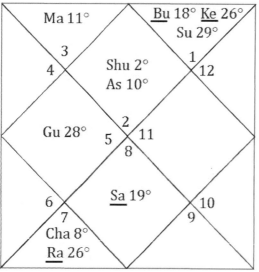
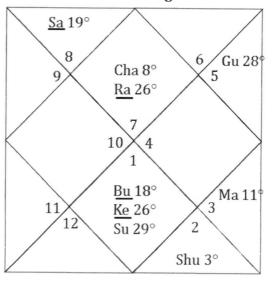

---

[5] See also Chapter 9: "Identifying Khavaigunyas" and Chapter 11: "Evaluating Dhatus using Graha Karakas".
[6] Lagnesha (Shukra) is of mixed condition (sva rashi and combust the sun) and destabilized by papa graha flanking and an aspect from Shani, who is strongly conditioned (retrograde and dig bala).

Terrance

We determined that Terrance has a vata-pitta prakruti.[7] Terrance has experienced several acute illnesses throughout his life, with some becoming chronic. Most life-threatening today is Terrance's Crohn's disease, which he first discovered at the age of 30. He has since had three operations to remove sections of his small intestines.

The 6B and its bhavesha (Guru) is the bhava of the small intestines and Budha is the graha karaka. Issues with the small intestines are indicated in Terrance's birth chart by the greatly destabilized 6B bhavesha (Guru) (influenced by strong Shani and Mangala) and papa graha flanking and poor placement of Budha (graha karaka for the small intestines).

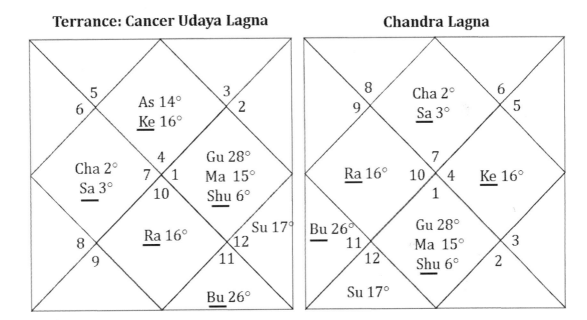

The Lagnesha (Chandra) has two factors of strength: dig bala and a bright moon. However, both the Lagnesha and the Lagna are greatly destabilized (influenced by strong Shani and Mangala). To support Terrance's overall vitality, we might recommend a gemstone for Surya (graha karaka for overall health) and Chandra (the Lagnesha). From both the Udaya Lagna and Chandra Lagna, Surya rules money bhavas (2B and 11B, respectively). I would suggest that Terrance wear a large red ruby ring with small pearls set on either side.

Specific to Terrance's Crohn's disease, since Guru and Budha rule trik-dusthanas from the Udaya Lagna and Chandra Lagna, we would not recommend that Terrance wear their gemstones. However, other graha upaya measures mentioned in Section VI can help remedy the ill-health affect that Guru and Budha has on Terrance's health. Terrance's Crohn's disease should also be more specifically addressed by various Ayurvedic measures.

---

[7] See Chapter 3: "Dosha Prakruti".

Chapter 24: Other Important Gemstone Considerations

Sacred Origin of Gems

According to the *Garuda Purana*, there once lived a formidable asura (demon) named Vala (cavern). So powerful is Vala that he defeats Indra (king of the gods) and takes all the gods as hostages. Staking his claim on their heavenly abode, Vala anoints himself ruler of the universe.

The wise gods devise a plan to regain heaven and their rightful rulership of the universe. As they prepare for ceremonial worship, they dare Vala to play the role of the sacrificial animal victim. Thinking the ceremony silly and assured of his invincibility, Vala consents to their request.

Soon, Vala is tied to the sacrificial stake. The gods enter into worship with the recitation of a mystical death-invoking mantra, which causes the vital pranas of this "invincible" demon to begin to escape his body.

Realizing his death is near, Vala pleads to the gods to grant him spiritual liberation. They award Vala his dying wish and, in return, he offers up his spirit for the good of the universe and the welfare of the gods. As Vala's liberated soul leaves his body, his limbs and body parts turn into the seeds of various precious gems.

The gods rush to gather up these valuable seeds. With their pockets full, they scurry off to reclaim heaven and, once again, they reign supreme. In their flurry of excitement, some of the seeds drop to earth. Wherever the seeds fall, precious gems spring up.

The seeds born from Vala's blood that fall upon riverbanks give rise to rubies (gemstone of Surya). The seeds born from Vala's teeth fall in the ocean and then into oysters, and give rise to pearls (gemstone of Chandra). The seeds born from Vala's bile are transformed into pools of emeralds (gemstone of Budha). Beds of dark blue sapphires (gemstone of Shani) spring up from the seeds born of Vala's dark eyes.

The seeds of Vala's parched skin fall upon the summit of the Himalayas, forming the treasured gemstone, golden topaz (gemstone of Guru). From the seeds of Vala's intestines that drop upon Kerala and nearby locales, brilliant red corals (gemstone of Mangala) are formed. Finally, the seeds born from Vala's semen are transformed into the most precious of all gemstones, diamonds (gemstone of Shukra).

As allegorically told by this ancient tale, gemstones originate from the liberated body-spirit of Vala. Of immense value and stunning beauty, they are offerings to the divine forces, who greatly prize them. A few are left behind for the benefit of mankind, who discover the healing power of these precious gems.

Important Gemstone Considerations

Quality

It is preferable for gemstones not to have inclusions, but this criterion is difficult to meet for certain stones, such as emeralds. In this case, select one with fewer inclusions.

Avoid gemstones that are dyed or treated with chemicals. Colorless topaz is sometimes irradiated (pounded with subatomic particles or radiation) and heated to transform it into a blue topaz. These treatments dramatically change the structure and clarity of the gemstone.

Size

For precious gemstones (diamonds, rubies, sapphires, emeralds), 2 carats is sufficient. Semi-precious gemstones should be 6-8 carats. In the case of pearls and gemstone beads, 5-7mm beads are appropriate.

Settings

A gemstone should be encased in a setting that is open in the back so that the gemstone touches the skin. Alternatively, wear a strand or mala of gemstone beads as a necklace.

Be sure that the jewelry setting is made of the proper metal—one that is compatible with the gemstone (see table below).

Table 10: Metal and Hand-Finger

Graha	Metal	Hand-Finger
Surya	Yellow Gold	right hand, ring finger
Chandra	White Gold, Sterling Silver	right or left hand, ring finger
Mangala	Yellow Gold, Copper	right hand, ring finger
Budha	Yellow Gold, White Gold	right or left hand, little finger
Guru	Yellow Gold	right hand, index finger
Shukra	Yellow Gold, White Gold	right or left hand, ring finger
Shani	Sterling Silver	right hand, middle finger
Rahu	Sterling Silver	left hand, middle finger
Ketu	Yellow Gold	left hand, middle finger

Gemstone rings

Most often in India, gemstones are worn on the right hand (the right hand is aligned with solar energy), as the left hand is used for cleansing. However, rings for Shukra and Chandra may be worn on the left hand, as the lunar energy is associated with the left hand. A ring for Budha may also be worn on the left hand, although the right hand is preferred.

Each finger corresponds to one of four grahas: the index finger, Guru; middle finger, Shani; ring finger, Surya, and little finger, Budha. Gemstone rings should be worn on the finger that corresponds with the gemstone.

Gemstones for the remaining grahas are worn on the following fingers: Chandra, Mangala and Shukra, the ring finger; Rahu and Ketu, middle finger (left hand). (See above table.)

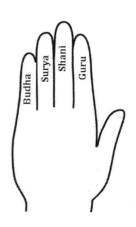

In those cases where two different gemstones are placed in a single setting, wear the ring on the finger that corresponds to the larger gemstone.

Gemstone Combinations

I usually encourage the client to consider separate jewelry pieces for each gemstone, such as a ring for one and a necklace or mala for another. If this is not possible or the client prefers a single setting, take care to ensure that the 2 gemstones are compatible. The following table lists several compatible gemstone combinations. (Note that this is not an all-inclusive list.) Only the "primary" gemstone is mentioned for each graha in the table below. This can be substituted with any secondary gemstones.

Table 11: Compatible Gemstone Combinations

Gemstone (Graha)	Complementary Gemstones (Grahas)
Ruby (Surya)	Pearl (Chandra) or Yellow Topaz (Guru)
Pearl (Chandra)	Ruby (Surya) or Yellow Topaz (Guru)
Emerald (Budha)	Ruby (Surya) or Diamond (Shukra)
Yellow Topaz (Guru)	Ruby (Surya) or Pearl (Chandra)
Diamond (Shukra)	Emerald (Budha)

When two different gemstones are placed in the same jewelry setting, both of them should be of approximately the same quality. Determine which graha requires more attention. The gemstone of that graha should be roughly twice as large as that of the other gemstone. For example, when designing a ring primarily for Chandra and secondarily for Guru, you can set a large pearl in the center of the ring and two smaller yellow topazes on either side.

Favorable Times for Putting on Gemstones

It is highly recommended that a muherta be constructed to determine the day and time that a new gemstone is first worn. A muhurta is an auspicious time to engage in a particular activity. We can ascertain the right time for putting on gemstones through a myriad of methods, including planetary transits, lunar phases, nakshatras, sun-moon relationship and the natal birth chart placement of the graha for which the gemstone is to be worn.

Determining a favorable muhurta is a science onto itself, requiring expertise that is beyond the scope of this book. As an Ayurvedic practitioner, the best course of action is to establish a working relationship with an experienced Jyotishi whom you can ask to construct a muhurta.

Other Suggestions

Keep in mind that the cost of certain gemstones may be prohibitive for some clients. In these cases, recommend less expensive, secondary gemstones. Alternatively, suggest other upaya measures to support the graha. These include recitation of planetary mantras, worship of planetary deities, nakshatra rasayanas and others, as described elsewhere in Section VI.

Needless to say, when the birth chart indicates that gemstones are not necessary or no single gemstone meets the qualifications outlined in Chapter 23: "Choosing the Right Gemstones", you should not recommend the use of a gemstone.

Chapter 25: Planetary Aromatherapy

Introduction

In their book *Ayurveda & Aromatherapy*, Drs. Light and Bryan Miller tell the story of how rose oil was discovered by a king during ancient Indian times.[1] In preparation for his daughter's grand wedding ceremony, the king requests for the castle moat to be filled with hundreds of thousands of rose petals. In the days following the wedding, a thin film coats the water. People notice that the oily film contains the essence of the rose petals. This simple observation is the beginning of the first production of essential rose oil in India. To this day, rose oil remains an important Ayurvedic essential oil. Its cooling properties make it useful for treating excess pitta conditions.

Essential oils are valued in Ayurveda for their subtle, yet concentrated energetics. Attars (essential oils made of flower petals and having sandalwood oil as a base), nasyas (essential oils mixed with medicated oils that are applied to the nostrils) and abhyanga oils (massage oils infused with essential oils) are just a few examples of how Ayurveda incorporates the healing benefits of aromatherapy.

Everything on earth is a vessel for planetary light, and the same is true for plant life. Well-known botanist and physician Nicholas Culpeper (1616-1654) identified the planetary energy of hundreds of plants and herbs.[2]

Two centuries later, Dr. Edward Bach suggested correlations between several florals used as Bach Flower Essences and the 12 astrological rashis. In this chapter, we look at correlations between all 38 Bach Flower Remedies and the seven grahas. Recognizing the efficacy of Bach Flower Essences, many Ayurvedic practitioners incorporate these subtle medicines into their practice. My Ayurvedic herbology instructor, also a certified aromatherapist, first drew my attention to the marvelous healing properties of these essences.

In addition to the planetary correspondences of the Bach Flower Remedies, the following sections include the same for more commonly used Ayurveda essential oils. In most cases, the planetary associations are based on the oil's therapeutic actions as an antioxidant, adaptogen, nervine tonic, and so on. For example, as the name implies, adaptogens helps us to adapt to internal and external stressors. This is also the function of Chandra. Hence, when natal Chandra is poorly-conditioned or afflicted by taxing planetary transits, essential oils that serve as adaptogens may be recommended to the client.

Be sure to check with your health professional for proper dosage, combination and duration of use for the specific medicinal remedies referenced to in this chapter.

Dr. Edward Bach

Trained in conventional medicine, Dr. Bach began his career as a surgeon. One day, while

---

[1] *Ayurveda & Aromatherapy*, Dr. Light Miller, ND & Dr. Bryan Miller, DC, p. 70. Lotus Press, 2012.
[2] *Culpeper's Complete Herbal: a book of natural remedies for ancient ills*, Nicholas Culpeper, Ware: Wordsworth Editions, 1995.

tending to injured French soldiers, he suddenly collapsed from a severe hemorrhage and was told he had only three months to live. The three months came and went, and Bach continued to improve. He attributed this remarkable recovery to his positive outlook on life and his strong sense of purpose. His brief dance with death forever changed his life, leading him to understand first-hand the critical role that one's mental-emotional state plays in physical illness and disease.

With this realization, Bach began exploring unconventional healing modalities that would address the psychological state of his patients. Experimenting with various plants, he discovered that the flower, the most developed part of the plant, has a high vibrational frequency that resonates with the subtle spiritual, mental and emotional bodies. Even in minute doses, floral essences quickly improve a patient's outlook on life. Bach noticed that this shift in the patient's psychological state promotes recovery of his physical symptoms.

Encouraged by his results, Bach dedicated the rest of his life to exploring and testing various floral essences and their efficacy in specific psychological states. One by one, Bach uncovered the healing properties of 38 floral remedies. He cataloged the effects of each flower essence, assigning a particular mental-emotional "quality" to each one, and a corresponding "fault" that it corrects. Each flower strengthens the psychological quality it is associated with, so that the person can overcome the fault that is the stumbling block. For example, Bach found that Clematis is effective in instilling the desire to live in the present moment, and he recommended it to people who live in the memories of the past.

Bach was not an astrologer, but he was certain that many of his flower essences correlate to the rashis. This hypothesis is consistent with the premise presented in Section VI: the cellular structure and vibrational frequency of a specific color, mantra, plant, gemstone or deity resonates at a frequency that corresponds to one of the nine grahas. Indeed, this foundational principle is readily accepted by most Jyotishis, who routinely advise clients on planetary remedial measures.

The author has extended Bach's notion of rashi correspondence to graha correspondences for all the 38 Bach Flower Remedies. This is done by matching each essence to a particular graha based on its psychological "quality" and corresponding "fault", as identified by Bach. The fault addressed by a particular Bach Flower Remedies results from an excessive *or* insufficient amount of graha energy in the person's life. An excessive level is most often caused by a graha having two or more factors of strength in the natal birth chart. The opposite is true for an insufficient level of graha energy. This occurs when the graha is weak or greatly destabilized in the birth chart. Certain transits over natal grahas can also result in an excess or deficient amount of planetary energy.

Let us take, for example, the solar energy. When natal Surya is excessively strong (i.e., has two or more factors of strength), it often appears as pride or egotism, "faults" addressed by Water Violet. An insufficient level of solar energy caused by a weak natal Surya, manifests as a poor self-image and low confidence, the "faults" addressed by Crag Apple and Larch, respectively.

Vata Grahas
Budha
Budha represents our intellectual capacity and our ability to organize our daily lives. When

this vata graha's energy is out of alignment, we experience scattered thinking, mental restlessness, nervousness and an inability to translate experiences into knowledge. Back Flower Essences ("BFEs") that address these specific psychological conditions are the following.

BFE	Fault	Quality
Cerato	over-reliance on advice from others	trusting one's judgement
Chestnut Bud	failure to learn from experience	experiences translated into knowledge
Scleranthus	indecisiveness	resolve or steadfastness
Sweet Chestnut	mental anguish	peace and calmness of mind
White Chestnut	unwanted thoughts, inner chatter	mental quietness

Along with Shani, Budha governs majja dhatu. A primary function of this dhatu is to facilitate communication between the brain and the rest of the nervous system. Curiosity, intelligence, calmness, open-mindedness and clarity are the results of a healthy majja dhatu and a well-conditioned natal Budha.

Budha's essential oils are those that are sweet and warming nervine tonics that strengthen, restore and nourish the majja vaha srotas and the mind. These include: Bergamot, Cedarwood, Clary Sage, Frankincense, Jatamamsi, Lemon Balm, Melissa, Orange Blossom (Neroli), Roman Chamomile, Periwinkle and True Lavender.

Shani

Without this weighty graha, we would rarely be able to deliver on our commitments and obligations. But when Shani's energy is insufficient, we can become overwhelmed, exhausted or discouraged by adversities and challenges. In contrast, an excessive level of Shani energy results in a dominating, overly controlling and inflexible attitude. The following BFEs address these concerns.

BFE	Fault	Quality
Aspen	vague or unspecified fear and anxiety	courage, trust
Cherry Plum	irrational behavior, fear of loss of control	calm thoughts and actions
Elm	exhausted or overwhelmed by responsibilities	confidence in handling responsibilities
Gentian	despondency, discouraged by setbacks	strength to overcome difficulties
Mimulus	shy, withdrawn, fearful	inner strength and courage
Oak	overworked and exhausted	fortitude and strength
Rock Rose	hidden fears	coping with threats and fears
Rock Water	rigid, inflexible	flexible and open
Vine	domineering, overbearing	friendship without domination

When the saturian energy is unbalanced, it can create a host of phobias and exaggerated or unfounded fears. Neuroses, including depression, obsessive behavior and hypochondria, stem for an imbalance of saturian energy. Whereas nervine tonics help tone and fortify Budha's energy, nervine relaxants and anti-depressants are often more suitable for an imbalance of Shani's energy.

Nervine relaxants help cushion the impact of shock, fear or nervous debility. Essential oils that function as nervine relaxants include: Angelica, Bay Laurel, Cedarwood, Juniper Berry, Lavender, Magnolia and Rose.

Anti-depressants inhibit feelings of depression and provide mental and emotional upliftment. Anti-depressants are used to address major depression disorders. Essential oils that function as anti-depressants include: Bergamot, Geranium, Lavender, Lime, Magnolia, Sweet Orange, Patchouli, Rose.

Pitta Grahas

Surya

When there is insufficient solar energy in our life, it creates a lack of confidence and self-esteem or makes us indifferent to our higher purpose and duty. In contrast, excessive solar energy exhibits as unwarranted pride and egotism. The following Bach Flower Essences address imbalances in our solar energy.

BFE	Fault	Quality
Crab Apple	poor self-image, self-criticism	positive self-image, self-acceptance
Larch	lack of confidence, fear of failure	confidence, belief in oneself
Pine	feeling of being underserving	self-value and respect
Water Violet	pride, egotism	recognizing and honoring others
Wild Oat	uncertainty or indifference to one's path	purpose and clarity of life path

Of the seven grahas, Surya is most important to our overall health, vitality and longevity, for the strength and warmth of solar energy protects us against ill-health and disease. Antioxidants contain an abundance of solar power and aid in maintaining a state of optimal health. Acclaimed as "fountains of youth", they defend against the damage free radicals cause to the body. Recommended essential oils that function as antioxidants are: Bay Laurel, Blue Yarrow, Cedarwood, Citronella, Clary Sage, Clove, Coriander, Douglas Fir, Fennel, German Chamomile, Melissa, Nutmeg, Palmarosa, Petitgrain, Winter Green.

Mangala

Mangala's pitta energy is a tricky one to marshal. Yet, its energy is crucial in our lives. Without a healthy dose of martian energy, we lack passion, enthusiasm and drive. Tip the scale just a bit either way and the lower qualities of Mangala rear their ugly heads. An excessive level of martian energy creates intolerance and criticism of others, impatience, irritability and aggression. Insufficient martian energy manifests as physical fatigue, apathy and cowardice. Several BFEs address these concerns.

BFE	Fault	Quality
Beech	intolerance, critical of others	tolerance and compassion
Hornbeam	weariness, fatigue	vitality, vigor
Impatiens	impatient, easily irritated	patience, calmness
Olive	exhaustion, chronic fatigue	restoration of energy
Rock Rose	terror due to feeling threatened	coping with threats, inner courage
Wild rose	apathy, lack of spunk	zest for life

Mangala provides us with abundant energy and drive. If your energy level needs a jump-start, invigorate yourself with essential oils that function as stimulants. Stimulants strengthen the metabolism and provide vigor to the physical, mental and emotional bodies. Recommended essential oils include: Basil, Bergamot, Cardamom, Carrot Seed, Cedarwood, Lemon, Niaouli, Nutmeg, Pink Grapefruit, Vetiver.

Kapha Grahas
Chandra

An imbalance in lunar energy may take several forms, such as an inability to live in the moment, being too easily influenced by one's environment, over-protecting others or emotional anxiety and worry. These kapha-type responses are addressed by the following BFEs.

BFE	Fault	Quality
Clematis	dreaminess, living in the past	live in present reality, enjoy the now
Honeysuckle	nostalgic, homesick	live in present reality, enjoy the now
Red Chestnut	overprotection of others due to fear	caring for others without fear
Star of Bethlehem	after effects of shock or trauma	emotional calmness and security
Walnut	easily influenced by others and the environment	steadfast despite others and the environment
Willow	blaming others, self-pity	forgive and forget

Just as the gravitational pull of the moon causes high- and low-tides, the lunar energy creates a state of constant flux. This ebb and flow can, at times, overtax our emotional body. Thus, essential oils that act as stress relievers are most helpful in handling everyday anxieties and restoring us to a state of emotional calmness. This is the action of adaptogens. Recommended essential oils that function as adaptogens: Bergamot, Cedarwood, Frankincense, Geranium, German Chamomile, Jasmine, Lavender, Marjoram, Roman Chamomile, Tulsi.

In Jyotisha, Chandra represents the immune system, the body's natural defense against viruses, bacteria and other disease-producing organisms. Extended periods of mental or emotional stress weaken the immune system, making the body more susceptible to outside invaders. Immunostimulants strengthen the body's response to disease. Essential oils that support this function include: Bergamot, Cardamom, Cinnamon, Clove Bud, Eucalyptus, Niaouli, Patchouli, Peppermint, Tea Tree, White Thyme.

Guru

Guru provides the beneficial and uplifting qualities of faith and optimism. When these qualities are absent, we can fall into despair and despondency. Over an extended period, such lack of hope and positivity impairs the physical body, causing disease and ill-health.

Imbalanced jupiterian energy may disguise itself behind a façade of enthusiasm. But look beneath the surface to see if such enthusiasm is grounded in reality. If not, the person aims for the stars . . . and misses. His lofty jupiterian visions are outside the limits of his abilities and resources.

BFE	Fault	Quality
Agrimony	hiding behind a cheerful face	displaying our true self
Gorse	hopelessness, despair	hope, despite roadblocks in life
Mustard	deep gloom with no known origin	joy and upliftment
Vervain	overenthusiastic, fanatical beliefs	broader perspective, grounded optimism

Guru invigorates and enlivens us by providing a belief in something larger than ourselves. This divine graha is credited with our deep inner knowing that guides us to the right action. At times, we may lose touch with this part of ourselves. Essential oils that function as rejuvenatives are helpful in these cases. As the name implies, rejuvenatives uplift the spirit and engender higher wisdom and inner knowing. Recommended rejuvenating essential oils include: Betony, Blue Lily of the Nile, Citrus Labdanum, Frankincense, Myrrh, Patchouli, Rose Attar, Sandalwood, White Lotus.

Shukra

Shukra is a graha of respect for others *and* oneself. If we too readily give in to the needs of others at the expense of our own needs, it signals a misalignment of venusian energy. Shukra is also a graha of unconditional love. Conditional love, envy, excessive self-focus, craving for the attention of others and lack of compassion are illustrative of an imbalance in venusian energy. The following BFEs help correct these mental-emotional conditions.

BFE	Fault	Quality
Centaury	easily imposed upon	courage to express our own needs and desires
Chicory	selfish possessiveness of others	selfless love
Heather	self-concern, always talking about oneself	concern and empathy for others
Holly	jealousy and envy	kindness, compassion, generosity

The root of many venusian imbalances is self-doubt and uncertainty about our own inner and outer beauty. When we are unable to see our own attractiveness and inner splendor, we can feel unworthy of love. This impacts our need to be touched and our desire for intimacy with a spouse or partner. A group of essential oils considered "beautifiers" can increase one's sense of inner and outer beauty. Recommended essential oils that are beautifiers include: Carrot seed, Jasmine, Neroli, Pomegranate, Rose.

To stimulate the libido, consider essential oils that are aphrodisiacs. Recommended essential oils for women include: Geranium, Orange Blossom (Neroli), Rose Absolute. Recommended essential oils for men: Cypress, Jasmine, Rosemary Officinalis, Ylang-Ylang.

How to use essential oils

Because essential oils are in concentrated form, you will want to dilute them before using. To dilute an essential oil use one part ethyl alcohol and three parts water. Alcohol helps to preserve the tincture. If you prefer not to use alcohol, you may use cider vinegar. For each fluid ounce (30 ml) of dilution mixture, add 2-3 drops of an essential oil.

Apply 4-6 drops of the diluted tincture under the tongue four times a day. Hold the drops under the tongue for a few seconds before swallowing. Be sure to shake the bottle prior to usage. Under severe conditions, the same dosage may be taken every hour. This level of treatment should be restricted to several days.

Since essential oils are very potent, the fewer administered the better! Try to restrict your usage to no more than two or three essential oils at one time.

If you are using an essential oil on a short-term basis, just put 2-3 drops directly into an 8-oz glass of water and sip three to four times throughout the day. Keep the glass of water refrigerated when not using.

An alternative application is to add an essential oil to your bath water. Add 8-10 drops of an undiluted essential oil to the bath and soak for 15-20 minutes. This method is particularly effective for remedies intended to relax the body and mind, including Geranium, Jasmine, Lavender, Marjoram and Roman Chamomile. However, if the problem persists, oral application may be required.

Venusian beautifiers (Carrot seed, Jasmine, Neroli, Pomegranate and Rose) can be added to your daytime or nighttime face and body cream. In a small bottle, combine 8-10 drops of several undiluted beautifiers and shake well. Apply by adding one drop of the mixed essential oil tincture to a small amount of face or body cream.

Chapter 26: The Sacred Nature of Plant Life

The Divine Nature of Trees

The subject of the classical Ayurvedic texts is the health and happiness of human beings and the medical treatment of illness and disease. This concern for health and wellness is extended to trees, because trees are considered to have the same divine origins and life force as humans. To this day, planting and caring for a tree is viewed as a meritorious act symbolizing a long and fruitful life.

Adoration of plant life is as ancient as the *Rigveda*, the oldest scripture in India. Here, a 23-verse hymn called *Praise to the Plants* (RV 10.97) is cognized by Rishi Atharvan. Atharvan extols the virtues of various plants and categorizes them according to their medicinal properties. In this hymn, he declares Soma, the divine ecstasy-producing plant, as king of the plant world.

> I know the hundred and seven applications of the brown-tinted plants, which have been growing since ancient times, much before men were born and thriving during the three seasons (spring, rains and autumn). (1)

> You are like mothers of mankind; a hundred are your applications, a thousand fold is your growth; may you who fulfill a hundred functions make this man free from disease. (2)

> Rejoice, plants, bearing abundant flowers and fruit, triumphing together (over disease) like victorious horses, sprouting forth, bearing men safe beyond disease. (3)

> "Plants!" thus I hail you; you are the divine mothers of mankind. Oh physician, I shall give you a horse, a cow and a garment, even myself (in case you cure the sick). (4)

> Your abode is in the holy Asvattha tree, your dwelling is established in the Palasa leaves; you shall assuredly become the winner of cattle, you could effectively cure and thus save this man for me. (5)

> Where, plants, you are congregated like princes in battle, thereby the sage is designated a physician, the destroyer of evil infections and extirpator of virus disease. (6)

> I praise here the virtues of belonging to four categories: asvavati (horse-possessor), the curatives; somavati (soma-possessor), the sedatives; urjayanti (the strengthener), the energizing, and udojas (the overpowering one), the rejuvenators. All these plants, I praise for the purpose of overcoming this disease. (7)

> O man, the healing virtues of the plants stream forth (from these herbs) like cattle from the stall; they have the competency of restoring the richness of health to you. (8)

> (O plants), verily your mother is Iskriti (unmaker of disease) by name, the Reliever, and therefore, you are called Niskrti, the Restorer; whomsoever a man is ill, you cure him. (9)

> The universal all-pervading plants assail diseases as a thief attacks a cow-shed; they drive out all types of infirmities from the body. (10)

As soon as I take these plants in my hand, the vanished strength is restored, and the soul or the root of the malady perishes before the sick succumbs to disease. (11)

From him, O plants, in whom you creep from limb to limb, from joint to joint, you drive away disease like some strong arbiter of strife. (12)

Fly forth, sickness, with the jay, with the blue jay, with the velocity of the wind; vanish together with the wind. (13)

O plants, let each of you go to the other, lend assistance to the other; thus being all mutually joined together, attend to this my invocation. (14)

Whether bearing fruit or barren, whether flowering or flowerless, may they, the progeny of the supreme protector, liberate us from our pain and grief. (15)

May they liberate me from the pain and sickness produced by negligence and ignorance, from the sin caused by a disregard to natural ways of life. May they liberate us from the fetters of death, and from all guilt caused by disobeying Nature's bounties. (16)

The plants, descending from heaven, said, "No evil shall befall a man, whom, while he lives, we nourish." (17)

Of all the plants, you Soma are the divine elixir (i.e., the nectar of immortality), the master cure. Numerous people seek you, O Soma, the best one. Be prompt to the wishful and sweet to the heart. (18)

May the plants, which have Soma for their king, which are scattered all over the earth, which are the offspring of our supreme protector, give vigour to this infirm body. (19)

Let not the digger hurt you, not the sick person for whom I dig you up; may all my bipeds and quadrupeds be free from disease. (20)

All the plants that hear this invocation and those which are removed far off, come together and give vigour and health to this (sick body). (21)

All the plants, in the presence of Soma, the king, declare, "O king, we save him whom on the advice of the Brahmana physician, administer us, we cure him, we save him from death." (22)

O divine herb, Soma, you are the best of the plants; to you other plants pay obeisance and salute. Let him be subject to us whosoever attacks us. (23)

The much later Puranic scriptures acknowledge the divinity of plant life allegorically in their tales of the birth of plants from different godheads. The lotus sprouts from the navel of Lord Vishnu (the sustainer god), the palasha tree, from the right side of Lord Yama (god of death), the bilva tree, from Shri Lakshmi (goddess of fortune and luck), and kurchi flowers, from the palms of Parvati, Shiva's wife. Elsewhere, trees and plants give birth to gods. Agni (god of fire) is birthed from the sacred Shami tree and Brahma (the creator god), from a lotus growing out of Vishnu's navel.

As well, great sages are enlightened under trees. Buddha gains self-realization under the Asvattha, Rishi Kasyapa, under the Nyargrodha, and Muni Kanaka, under the Udumbara.

The Puranas also tell of the gods having their "favorite" plant. The tulsi plant is sacred to Shri Krishna, durva grass, to Shri Ganesha, the amalaki tree, to Lord Vishnu and the rudraksha tree, to Lord Shiva.

The grahas, as well, are identified with and/or compared to particular plants. Surya is as bright as the red japa flower, Budha is like the priyangu bud (a creeper plant whose flowers open up being touched by a woman), Shukra has the fragrance of the lotus root and Ketu has the appearance of the palasha flower.

Many of the 27 divine godheads that rule the lunar nakshatras are intimately familiar with the medicinal properties of various trees. For instances, the Aswhini Kumars (ruler of Aswhini) are celestial healers adept in using the mystical soma plant, which contains the nectar of immortality. Rudra (ruler of Ardra) carries a small pouch filled with rare botanical medicines. His specialty is healing poisonous bites, such as that from a snake and scorpion. Nirrti (ruler of Mula), a fierce goddess of destruction, cures hereditary diseases with the roots of various herbs bundled together.

As with all other lifeforms, trees are receptacles of planetary light and responsive to the movements of the grahas. The blossoms of heliotrope flowers track the sun as it moves from east to west each day. Poppies open as the rays of the sun touch their blossoms, and close when sunlight fades on the western horizon. Other flowers bloom or release a soft scent under the light of the moon

Vrikshayurveda

The science of caring for trees and treating their diseases is called Vrikshayurveda. Like Ayurveda, Vrikshayurveda is a sacred science. Surapala, a scholar in the court of King Bhimapala and a prominent Ayurvedic physician, authored the first book on this subject, called *Vrikshayurveda*. Written around the time of the major classical Ayurvedic texts, *Vrikshayurveda* is dedicated to the cultivation and supervision of trees.

Surapala also writes about subjects such as divining groundwater, proper selection of planting grounds, productivity of land, and so on. A poet at heart, he eloquently describes the type of land that is best suited for planting: "Bluish like sapphire, soft like a parrot's feather, white like conch, jasmine, lotuses, or the moon, and yellow like heated gold or blooming champaka is the land recommended for planting."[1]

Leveraging his knowledge of Ayurveda, Surapala also describes different types of plant diseases as doshic imbalances. Vata vruddhi (excess vata) shows signs such as thinness and crookedness of the trunk, knots on the trunk or leaves and hard fruits with little juice or sweetness. Pitta vruddhi (excess pitta) is evidenced by yellowness or paleness of leaves,

---

[1] *Surapala's Vrikshayurveda: the Science of Plant Life,* Surapala, Nalini Sadhale (translator), pg. 45. Asian Agri-History Foundation, 1996.

flowers and fruits and premature dropping of fruits. Kapha vruddhi (excess kapha) is present when it takes a long time for the tree to bear fruits, when its fruits are tasteless or its leaves are pale and excessively small.[2]

Nakshatra Van

According to the science of *Vrikshayurveda*, each nakshatra is related to a particular plant whose energy and healing properties resonate with it. This plant will also be harmonious with the person who is born under its related nakshatra. Scripture recommends that a person plant, care for and even worship the nakshatra tree that corresponds to his or her moon nakshatra. It is also good for a person to meditate under such a tree. Ayurveda refers to such practices as *rasayana chikitsa*, a rejuvenative or restorative therapy that uses foods, herbs and various practices to renew, regenerate and restore the body, mind and spirit.

Since many of the nakshatra trees grow only in India, an alternative remedial measure is to donate money towards the conservation of one's nakshatra tree or to scientific research into its medicinal value. Alternatively, a financial contribution can be made to organizations that, in general, support plant conservation or plant research for the cure of diseases. Many organizations exist for these purposes.

In any case, the reader is encouraged to familiarize himself with his nakshatra tree: its habitat, medicinal properties and mythology. A monograph of each nakshatra tree is provided in the next chapter, Chapter 27: "Nakshatra Rasayana Chikitsa", along with a listing of nakshatra trees.

One Indian tradition is for a community to plant all 27 nakshatra trees sequentially in a circle, forming a nakshatra yantra. The yantra begins in the north with *Nux vomica*, the sacred tree for Ashwini (the first nakshatra) and proceeds counterclockwise with Amala, the sacred tree for Bharani (the second nakshatra), and so on, until all 27 trees are planted. This circular yantra of the nakshatra trees is called Nakshatra Van.[3]

In modern times, Nakshatra Van serves to protect and conserve the several nakshatra trees that are classified as endangered. As importantly, people are encouraged to cultivate a Nakshatra Van garden in a community space to support biodiversity, beautify the earth and promote healing energy.

---

[2] Ibid., pg. 52-53.
[3] A similar tradition correlates the 9 grahas (e.g., Navgraha Van) and the 12 rashis (e.g., Rashi Van) with specific trees. See Appendix H: "Navgraha Van and Rashi Van".

Chapter 26: The Sacred Nature of Plant Life

Figure 14: Nakshatra Van

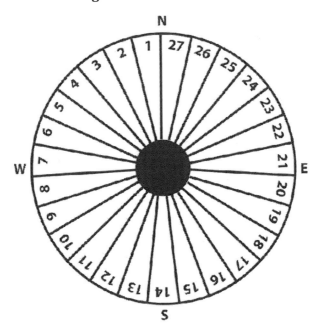

We have an ancient spiritual connection with Mother Earth, and we need to preserve her resources to sustain the world's prosperity. The earth's importance is emphasized in countless Indian scriptures. For example, a hymn in the Atharvaveda (the oldest Indian medical scripture) called *Hymn to Goddess Earth* lauds Mother Earth, comparing her to a milch cow that generously nourishes mankind with her milk. The poet, a vigilant sage, prays that he will not pierce Mother Earth's skin or heart as he digs up her healing medicines. It is not only an obligation, but also a privilege to honor and care for Mother Earth by conserving her resources and supporting her bio-diversity.

Chapter 27: Nakshatra Rasayana Chikitsa

Introduction

In this chapter, the tree sacred to each nakshatra is presented.[1] In many cases, the correlation between the nakshatra's ruling devata and designated tree is readily apparent.[2] For example, the sacred tree of Magha, a nakshatra ruled by the Ancestors, is the Akshayavat (eternal air-born) tree. Traditionally, one spreads the ashes of deceased loved ones under its wide-spreading roots. One of the most deadly of the 27 nakshatra trees, the Vishadru (poisonous) tree is assigned to Ashwini and its ruling devatas, the Ashwini Kumars. Only these celestial healers are adept enough to administer this potentially fatal herbal medicine. (See table on following page for a listing of the 27 nakshatras, their ruling devatas and sacred trees.)

Ayurvedic properties and usages of each nakshatra tree, its effect on the doshas (vata, pitta, kapha) as well as its gunas (qualities), rasa (taste), *virya* and *vipaka* are listed. Virya is the quality of energy released by the herb of the plant upon digestion. Viryas are classed as either cooling or heating. Vipaka relates to the post-digestive effect of an herb, which especially affects the colon. Vipakas can be sweet, sour or pungent. All vipakas act on the excreta (urine and feces).

Where applicable, the *prabhava* (supernatural power) of the tree is also described. Prabhava is a mystical action that is unexplainable by scientific laws. For example, in Jyotisha, wearing gemstones or reciting planetary mantras has the *prabhava* of healing. Likewise, planting and caring for your sacred nakshatra tree brings prosperity, a long life and many blessings. These benefits are beyond modern scientific explanation.

Your nakshatra tree is the tree associated with your natal moon nakshatra. Surapala advises that one treat his nakshatra tree as he would his own son, or even better since, as he says, trees are always reliable, whereas sons are not. Your nakshatra tree, or any of its parts, should not be harvested to make medicines, nor should its fruits be eaten.

A special section under each nakshatra, "Did you know", elaborates on the mythology associated with the nakshatra tree.[3]

---

[1] Please note that the description of several nakshatra trees is sourced from *Biodiversity Complex*, Commemoration of CoP-11 to CBD, October 01-19, 2012, Hyderabad, India. National Biodiversity, Ministry of Environment, Forests & Climate Change, Government of India, Andhra Pradesh State Biodiversity Board.
[2] Refer to *Your Healing Stars: Volume 1, Fundamentals of Vedic Astrology* for a description of each nakshatra devata.
[3] Several legends are sourced from: *Medical Botany: Plants Affecting Human Health*, Walter H. Lewis, Memory P. F. Elvin-Lewis. Wiley, 1977. *People Trees*, Haberman, David L. Oxford University Press, 2013. *Sacred Plants of India*, Krishna, Nanditha and Armirthalingam, M. Penguin Group, 2014.

Chapter 27: Nakshatra Rasayana Chikitsa

Table 12: Nakshatra Trees and Plants

#	Nakshatra	Devata	Sanskrit	English	Botanical Name
1	Ashwini	Aswhini Kumars, celestial healing twins	Vishadru	Nux Vomica	Strychnos nux-vomica
2	Bharani	Yama, lord of death	Dhatri	Indian Gooseberry	Phyllanthus emblica
3	Krittika	Agni, lord of fire	Hemadugdha	Cluster Fig	Ficus racemosa
4	Rohini	Prajapati, the creator god	Jambu	Indian Blackberry	Syzygium cumini
5	Mrigashira	Soma, the moon	Khadira	Cutch	Acacia catechu
6	Ardra	Rudra, an ancient form of Shiva	Krishna	Kashmir	Gmelina arborea
7	Punarvasu	Aditi, mother earth	Vamsha	Bamboo	Bambusa bambos
8	Pushya	Brihaspati, preceptor of the gods	Asvattha	Sacred Fig	Ficus religiosa
9	Ashlesha	Nagas, celestial serpent snakes	Nagakesara	Messua	Mesua ferrea
10	Magha	Pitris, ancestors	Akshayavat	Banyan	Ficus benghalensis
11	Purva Phalguni	Aryaman, god of traditions	Palasa	Flame of the forest	Butea monosperma
12	Uttara Phalguni	Bhaga, god of bliss	Plaksha	Indian laurel	Ficus microcarpa
13	Hasta	Savitar, sun god	Ambashta	Hog plum	Spondias pinnata
14	Chitra	Tvashtar, celestial architect	Bilva	Bael	Aegle marmelos
15	Svati	Vayu, wind god	Arjuna	Arjuna	Terminalia arjuna
16	Vishakha	Indra-Agni, dual gods Indra and Agni	Vikamkata	Governor's plum	Flacourtia montana
17	Anuradha	Mitra, god of friendship	Sakesara	Bullet Wood	Minusops elengi
18	Jyeshta	Indra, king of heaven	Sabara	Lodh	Symplocos cochinchinensis
19	Mula	Nirriti, goddess of destruction	Sarja	White dammar	Vateria indica
20	Purva Ashadha	Apas, water goddesses	Vanchula	Powder-puff Mangrove	Barringtonia racemosa
21	Uttara Ashadha	Visvedevas, all the gods collectively	Panasa	Jackfruit	Artocarpus heterophyllus
22	Shravana	Vishnu, the sustainer of the universe	Arka	Giant Swallow	Calotropis gigantia
23	Dhanishta	Vasus, earthly gods	Shami	Indian Mesquite	Prospopis specigera
24	Shatabhishak	Varuna, lord of the waters	Kadamba	Kadam	Anthocephalus indicus
25	Purva Bhadrapada	Aja Ekapada, one-legged serpent	Amra	Mango	Mangifer indica
26	Uttara Bhadrapada	Ahirbudhnya, cloud serpent	Nimba	Margosa	Azadirachta indica
27	Revati	Pushan, lord of cattle	Madhuka	Indian Butter tree	Madhuca nerifolia

Ashwini: Vishadru (poisonous tree)
Botanical Name: *Styrox nux vomica*, Loganiaceae
Other names: Kuchala (H), *Nux vomica* (E)

Ayurvedic properties of Vishadru, holy tree of Ashwini

Parts used	inner, hard button-like seeds
Dosha	V- P+ K-
Guna	light
Rasa	pungent, bitter
Virya	heating
Vipaka	pungent

Nux vomica belongs to the Loganiaceae family of plants. It is a moderate-sized tree whose trunk is often crooked. It has small flowers and orange-red colored fruits about the size of an apple. Inside the fruit are several coin-like seeds surrounded by a jelly-like pulp. These inner seeds act as stimulants in very small doses but can be poisonous in larger doses. Thus, *Nux vomica* is dangerous when used in excess and should be taken internally only under the advice of an Ayurvedic professional or doctor.

Administered in medicinal doses, *Nux vomica* is a remedy for atony of the gastro-intestinal tract, cholera, constipation and chronic dysentery.

Due to the minute dosages required when administering this "poison nut", *Nux vomica* is a popular homeopathic remedy used in acute conditions such as headaches, emotional stress, back pain and menstrual problems.

It seems fitting that this potentially deadly herb is assigned to Ashwini nakshatra, whose divine rulers are the Ashwini Kumars. Renowned celestial physicians to the gods and mankind, the Ashwini Kumars possess the medical expertise required for proper administration of *Nux vomica*.

Did you know?

In many parts of the world, *Nux vomica* seeds are hidden within fish bait. When fish eat it, they become stupefied or intoxicated, making them an easy catch.

It is said that Cleopatra, in search of a suicidal poison, considered *Nux vomica*. She felt it superior over other methods, because its effects were instantaneous. However, once Cleopatra realized that, taken in large doses, *Nux vomica* produces convulsions that result in distorted facial features at death, she elected the bite of a cobra instead.

Bharani: Dhatri (foster, mother)
Botanical Name: *Phyllanthus emblica*, Euphorbiaceae
Other names: Amla (H), Indian Gooseberry (E)

Ayurvedic properties of Dhatri, holy tree of Bharani

Parts used	leaves, fruits, bark, root bark
Dosha	VPK
Guna	cooling, heavy
Rasa	sour, sweet, astringent, pungent, bitter
Virya	cooling
Vipaka	sweet

The Amla tree is called the Indian Gooseberry and is well-known and cherished throughout India. Its Sanskrit name means 'one who fosters or mothers'. Thus, Amla is considered the universal caregiver and nurturer of health and vitality.

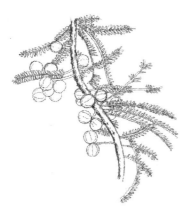

The Amla tree yields gooseberry-like fruits which are used medicinally when ripe (consumed directly), pickled (as a digestive aid) or dried. They are often infused into massage oil that is used to promote hair growth. The Vitamin C content of this fruit is one of the highest in the vegetable kingdom—over 15-20 times that of an orange.

Amla is famed as a rejuvenative, adaptogen, aphrodisiac and heart, mind and hair tonic. It slows aging, increases virility and boosts the immune system.

It is a major ingredient in Cyavanaprasa, a tonic containing many herbs mixed in a ghee and honey base that is a superb rejuvenative for all three doshas. Amla is also one of the three herbal ingredients in Triphala, a well-known formula used to promote gentle cleansing and good digestion.

Amla is used in a wide spectrum of illnesses, including eye disorders, sexual impotence, fever, loss of hair, skin diseases, piles, diabetes, anaemia, diarrhoea, jaundice, bronchitis and asthma. The prabhava of Amla includes mental clarity, promotion of sattvic qualities and an increase in ojas.

Did you know?

Lord Vishnu dwells within the Amla tree. This explains why the tree is worshipped on Amalaki Ekadashi, a day sacred to Vishnu. Amalaki Ekadashi occurs on the 11th day (Ekadashi) of the waxing moon in the lunar month of Phalgun (February/March). Vishnu's consort, Shri Lakshmi, the goddess of prosperity, abundance and grace, is said to reside within its fruits. The Amla tree is sometimes called Amala (shinning, spotless, pure), which is one of the 108 divine names of Lakshmi. People worship this tree to reap its promise of spiritual blessings and divine grace.

Because of the nurturing qualities of Amla, later mythology associates this holy tree with Mother Earth. A special festival occurs in its honor on Amla Navami, the ninth day of the bright half of the lunar month of Kartik (October/November). Worshippers wrap the Amala tree nine times with red and yellow string in hopes of having their wishes fulfilled. This same day marks the first day of Holi, the celebration of spring.

The origin of the Amla tree is narrated in the legendary "Churning of the Ocean" myth, in which the devas (gods) and asuras (demons) churn the bottom of the ocean in search of amrita (the divine nectar of immortality or soma). Once the nectar is retrieved, the gods anxiously partake of it, spilling a few drops of soma that fall upon the earth. From these drops, an Amla tree sprouts. Birthed from the nectar of immortality, this tree cures many illnesses and promotes longevity.

Krittika: Hemadugdha (golden-juiced)
Botanical Name: *Ficus racemosa* or *Ficus glomerata*, Moraceae
Other names: Gular or Udumbara (H), Cluster Fig (E)

Ayurvedic properties of Hemadugdha, holy tree of Krittika

Parts used	fruit, leaves, latex, bark
Dosha effect	VP-K-
Guna	heavy, dry, cool
Rasa	astringent
Virya	cooling
Vipaka	pungent

The Cluster Fig is found all over India and frequently referred to as Udumbara (copper-colored). Unlike other members of the fig family, this tree is devoid of aerial roots.

A distinctive aspect of the Cluster Fig is its dense clusters of red, furry figs that grow directly out of its trunk. The sweet taste of the figs attracts many birds. Small worms frequently burrow in the fruit. Like its fruits, the bark of the Cluster Fig has a reddish hue. Its reddish hue explains why the Cluster fig is the holy tree for Krittika, a nakshatra ruled by Agni (god of fire).

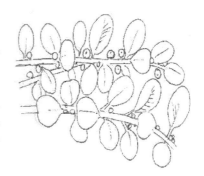

Different parts of the Cluster Fig are used medicinally to treat dysentery, diarrhoea, bleeding rectum, hemorrhagic disorders, menorrhagia, leucorrhoea and diabetes.

The latex mixed with sugar treats sperm debility. No doubt, this is why a Cluster Fig tree is planted to honor Shukra, the graha representing sexual fluids.[1]

Did you know?
Various trees are referred to as Bodhi (awakening) trees, because great saints and sages have been enlightened while mediating beneath them. Buddha was enlightened under the Asvattha (*Ficus religiosa*) (see Pushya nakshatra), Muni Kasyapa, under the Nyagrodha (*Ficus benghalensis*) (see Magha nakshatra), Vipasvi, under the Asoka (*Saraca indica*) and Muni Kanaka under the Cluster Fig (*Ficus glomerata*).

Flowers are rarely seen on the Cluster Fig tree. According to Buddhist scriptures, the Cluster Fig last blossomed prior to the birth of Buddha and will only blossom again 3,000 years from this time, when the next Buddha is born. Indian mythology explains that the Cluster Fig is flowerless because on Diwali (the festival of the

---

[1] Refer to Appendix H: "Navagraha Van and Rashi Van".

lights) the gods ascend to earth and pick the flowers for themselves.

The *Vrikshayurveda* (science of trees) recommends that a person plant a Cluster Fig on the south side of the house to protect the household against inauspicious outside influences and to purify the environment. The *Atharvaveda* advises that one wear an amulet made from the bark of this tree for protection.

During the sacred Brahmanic Somayajnas (Soma ceremonies), the soma plant (the divine nectar of immortality) is placed on a throne carved from Cluster Fig wood before being anointed King Soma. The wood of this tree is reddish-brown, the same color as the nectar of the soma plant and the sacrificial fire.

Rohini: *Jambu (rose apple)*
Botanical Name: *Syzygium cumini*, Myrtaceae
Other names: Jamun (H), Java Plum, Indian Blackberry (E)

Ayurvedic properties of Jambu, holy tree of Rohini

Parts used	fruit, leaves, stem bark, root bark
Dosha effect	V+P-K
Guna	light, dry
Rasa	sweet, astringent, sweet
Virya	cooling
Vipaka	pungent

The Jambu, a member of the Myrtaceae family of plants, is an evergreen tree that is of great interest because of its medicinal applications. It is also referred to as Jamun, Java Plum, Rose Apple and Indian Blackberry. The Jambu has a silvery grey bark with dark flaky patches and greenish-white, sweet-scented flowers that grow in dense clusters.

The fleshy oblong fruit of the Jambu is high in Vitamin A and Vitamin C. Medicinally, the fruit is considered astringent, stomachic, carminative, antiscorbutic and diuretic. It is cooked to a thick jam and eaten to alleviate acute diarrhea. The juice of the ripe fruit is administered in cases of enlargement of the spleen, chronic diarrhea and urine retention.

An alcohol extract of the seeds and leaves of the Jambu tree is administered to patients with diabetes mellitus. A decoction of the bark is taken internally for dyspepsia, dysentery and diarrhea. It also serves as an enema. Ashes of the bark mixed with water are spread over local inflammations. Jamun is considered a brain and liver tonic.

Did you know?

In India, trees are often associated with divine godheads. Goddess Lakshmi resides within the fruit of the Amala tree and Goddess Shitala dwells within the Neem tree. Lord Agni hides in the Shami tree and the Bilva tree originates from Lord Yama. As for the Jambu, this tree holds special significance to two gods: Brahma (Prajapati), devata ruler of Rohini, and Lord Shiva.

In the Puranas, Mount Meru is considered the sacred abode of Brahma. On its summit is Brahmapuri, the 'city of Brahma'. Brahmapuri is encircled by a grove of giant Jambu trees, the holy tree of Rohini.

There is also an ancient tale that connects the Jambu tree with Lord Shiva. According to this legend, an ascetic sat beneath a Jambu tree mediating upon the Lord. Suddenly a fruit falls from the tree, landing directly in front of him. The ascetic travels to Mount Kailash, Shiva's abode, and offers the fruit as *prasad* (sacrificial offering) to the Lord. Graciously accepting the prasad, Shiva eats the fruit and then spits out its seed.

Realizing the seed has been touched by Shiva, the ascetic quickly picks it up and swallows it. Soon, a Jambu tree takes sprout inside ascetic. The tree gets so big that its branches splits open the ascetic's head as it continues to grow. From that day forward, the ascetic faithfully follows Shiva, constantly offering his leafy branches as a shady place for the Lord to rest.

Mrigashira: Khadira (strong, stable)
Botanical Name: *Acacia catechu or Acacia chundra*, Mimosaceae
Other names: Khairkatha (H), Cutch (E)

Ayurvedic properties of Khadira, holy tree of Mrigashira

Parts used	heartwood extract, gum, stem bark, leaves, fruits
Dosha	V+P-K-
Guna	light, dry
Rasa	bitter, astringent
Virya	cooling
Vipaka	pungent

The Cutch tree is part of the Mimosaceae family. It is a deciduous, thorny tree that grows to about 50 feet in height. It is found on mountain slopes up to 5,000 feet above sea level. The flowers of the Cutch tree are pale yellow in color and have cylindrical spikes. The flattened and glabrous fruit of this tree have oblong purplish colored pods.

The Cutch tree is also known as Black Cutch or Black Catechu, for the gummy extract of its heartwood yields a dark, concentrated aqueous extract (cutch). The heartwood extract is used to treat coughs, sore throat, dysentery, diarrhoea, wounds and skin sores. It is the main ingredient in Khadirarishta, a well-known Ayurvedic skin tonic.

Other medicinal applications of the Cutch tree include the treatment of liver disorders, swelling of the spleen, worm infestations, chronic fever, colitis, fungal growths, mouth ulcers and skin disorders. Combined with other herbs, it acts as a natural birth control.

Did you know?
Interestingly, the sacrificial bowl from which the gods and priests partake of the soma nectar is carved from the hard wood of the Cutch tree. As a divine godhead, Soma is the ruler of Mrigashira. According to the ancient Brahmanic texts, a person who wants to attain heaven should use sacrificial instruments made from the wood of this tree.

In the Navagraha Van (the planting of a tree for each of the nine grahas), the Cutch tree is planted in reverence to Mangala, the planetary ruler of Mrigashira.[1]

---

[1] Refer to Appendix H: "Navagraha Van and Rashi Van".

Ardra: Krishna (dark blue)
Botanical Name: *Gmelina arborea*, Verbenaceae
Other names: Gumari or Gamar (H), Kashmir or White Teak tree (E)

Ayurvedic properties of Krishna, holy tree of Ardra

Parts use	Root bark, stem bark, leaves, flower, fruits
Dosha effect	V-P+K-
Guna	heavy
Rasa	astringent, bitter, sweet
Virya	heating
Vipaka	pungent

The Kashmir tree is a fast-growing deciduous tree and a member of the teak family. It produces oval-shaped yellow fruit that is sweet and astringent to taste. The leaves of the tree are dark blue, explaining its Sanskrit name Krishna (dark blue), and its trunk is off-white. Both colors are associated with Rudra, the divine ruler of Ardra, who is later known as Shiva. Shiva is frequently referred to as Nilakantha or 'the blue-necked one', for Shiva's neck turns blue after consuming the poison produced during the churning of the ocean for the nectar of immortality.[1] The off-white trunk of the Kashmir tree is much like the off-white, ash-smeared body of Lord Shiva.

The Kashmir is used as a brain tonic and for treating vertigo. The ripe fruit and its juice serve as a cardiac and nutritive tonic. It is also considered an aphrodisiac. The root is anti-inflammatory and administered to reduce pain and swelling.

In the classical Ayurvedic texts, Gumari is cited as a pacifier for vata dosha. It is one of ten herbal ingredients in dasamula (ten roots), a well-known Ayurvedic formula used to treat vata. Its warming nature also pacifies kapha.

---

[1] Refer to Your Healing Stars: Volume I, Fundamentals of Vedic Astrology for the legend of the Churning of the Ocean.

Punarvasu: Vamsha (family, dynasty)
Botanical Name: *Bambusa bambos*, Bambusaceae
Other names: Thabaseer (H), Bamboo (E)

Ayurvedic properties of Vamsha, holy tree of Punarvasu

Parts used	root, seeds, siliceous matter, leaves
Dosha effect	V-P-K+
Guna	light, dry, sharp
Rasa	sweet, astringent
Virya	cooling
Vipaka	sweet

Bambusa bambos is a species of clumping bamboo native to India. It belongs to the Bambusaceae or Poaceae grass family. Rising from an underground rootstock, Bamboo grows straight up without branches. *Bambusa bambos* is a one of the important commercial bamboo species and finds its use in construction, scaffolding and wood chip industry.

The Bamboo tree is highly reputed for its medicinal properties. It is most noted for the silica-rich secretion contained in the knots of its shoots. This difficult-to-harvest secretion is used in Vanshlochan (bamboo eye), an Ayurvedic remedy for

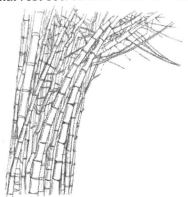

generalized weakness and loss of strength. It is often recommended as a tonic to assist in repairing and strengthening lung tissue.

More generally, Bamboo is used as an astringent, laxative and diuretic. A decoction of its shoots dislodges worms and extracts of its leaves treat leprosy, amenorrhea, dysmenorrhea and eye troubles. The leaf juice strengthens the cartilage, preventing and treating osteoarthritis and osteoporosis. The siliceous matter helps repair connective tissue.

Did you know?
The bamboo tree is considered as sacred as the Pipal tree, the tree that symbolizes the universe and Brahman.

Lord Krishna plays a flute made out of a young green bamboo shoot, charming the gopis (milkmaids) of Vrindavan with its sweet and tender melodies. Lord Shiva (ruling devata of Ardra), in his ancient Pashupata (lord of wild animals) form, carries a bow made from bamboo shoots.

Bamboo grows in clusters, symbolic of prolific progeny. This explains its Sanskrit name Vamsha, 'family dynasty'. In parts of India, women hang cradles on the Bamboo tree hoping for a large family.

In a similar manner, a king wishing to expand his kingdom would plant a grove of Bamboo trees. One particular king, King Vasu of the Puru Dynasty, initiated the ceremonial practice of planting a bamboo pole each year to honor Indra (devata ruler of Jyeshta), king of the gods. The pole is decked with golden cloths, garlands and various other ornaments. The king then prays to Indra to help him expand his kingdom.

Pushya: Asvattha (under which horses stand)
Botanical Name: *Ficus religiosa*, Moraceae
Other names: Pipal (H), Sacred Fig (E)

Ayurvedic properties of Asvattha, holy tree of Pushya

Parts used	stem bark, root bark, leaves, flowers, fruits
Dosha effect	VP-K-
Guna	heavy, dry
Rasa	astringent
Virya	cooling
Vipaka	pungent

The holy tree of Pushya is best known by its Sanskrit name Asvattha and Hindi name Pipal. Asvattha means 'under which horses stand', for horses rest under the shade of this tree. Another popular name is Bahupada, or 'one with many feet'. As with most *Ficus* trees, its aerial-hanging adventitious roots (or feet) extend to earth to support the tree.

Birds eat the small, reddish-purple figs of this tree when they ripen. Its seeds pass through them unharmed, and so take root at the most obscure places, such as on a rooftop, or the walls of a house or temple.

The leaves and the bark are used for controlling dysentery and diarrhea. Coated with clarified butter and applied as a poultice, the leaves are also used to relieve boils and swollen salivary glands as in cases of the mumps. The latex is used for relieving warts. The powdered fruit is useful in asthma. The bark of the tree has cooling, astringent, laxative and hemostatic properties.

Freshly burnt ashes of the bark are mixed with water and allowed to steep for some time. This mixture is useful in relieving obstinate cases of hiccups and control vomiting. Oil made from the root bark can be applied externally to relieve skin diseases like leprosy, eczema and also useful in relieving rheumatism.

Ayurveda also considers it effective in the treatment of diabetes. A combination of the fruit, root and bark combined with milk, sugar and honey is an aphrodisiac. It is also used to treat infertility.

Did you know?
Because of its mythological, spiritual and medicinal value, Indians consider the Asvattha as one of the most sacred trees on earth. In the Gita, Lord Krishna says, "Amongst all the trees, I am the Asvattha." This may explain why the tree is closely associated with Lord Vishnu, who incarnates as Krishna as mankind transitions

into the Kali yuga.

In the Navagraha Van (the planting of a tree for each of the nine grahas), the Asvattha tree is planted in reverence of Guru.[1] Guru is exalted in Pushya nakshatra and frequently depicted as Lord Brihaspati, devata ruler of Pushya.

The Asvattha is associated with divine revelation and spiritual achievement, since Buddha Siddhartha attained enlightenment under its branches. Hence, the Asvattha tree is sometimes called the Bodha (awakening) tree.

It is also regarded as the symbol for a man. In Indian villages, the Asvattha (symbolizing a man) and Neem tree (symbolizing a woman) are planted side by side and depicted as a married couple. Their branches intertwined, these two trees represent conjugal love and happiness.

In India, women worship the Asvattha on the new moon (amavasya, 'dark moon') that falls on Monday. This day is called Somavati Amavasya Vrat. Water and milk are poured on its roots, and offerings of sandal paste, vermillion, wet rice and flowers are made. Circumambulating the Asvattha tree one hundred and eight times, women place sweetmeat or fruit at its base after each round. After the last circumambulation, they kneel at the base of the tree and affectionately stroke its trunk. The worship of the Asvattha tree promotes domestic happiness and the birth of sons, and helps one avoid widowhood.

---

[1] Refer to Appendix H: "Navagraha Van and Rashi Van".

Ashlesha: Nagakesara (serpent stamens)
Botanical Name: *Mesua ferrea*, Clusiaceae, syn. Guttifereae
Other names: Nagakesar (H), Ironwood or Messua tree (E)

Ayurvedic properties of Nagakesara, holy tree of Ashlesha

Parts used	flower, stamen, seed, seed oil, stem, root bark
Dosha effect	V+P-K-
Guna	light, dry, sharp
Rasa	astringent, bitter
Virya	heating
Vipaka	pungent

Belonging to the Clusiaceae family, the Mesua tree is an evergreen with bluish, round stems and plenty of leaves. It bears large white fragrant flowers. Because this tree has particularly strong wood, it is often called Iron Wood.

The holy tree of Ashlesha is aptly named Nagakesara (serpent stamens), for divine serpents are the rulers of Ashlesha. Also known as the Messua tree, its flowers, leaves and bark serve as antidotes for snake and scorpion bites. It is elsewhere known as Cobra's saffron.

Parts of the Messua tree are used as a brain tonic in cases of mental debility and hysteria. It is also used as a digestive aid and vermicide. The seed oil is applied as an anti-inflammatory agent for arthritis, and to treat skin itches and eruptions. The fresh flowers are used to treat bleeding piles and menorrhagia. Ashes of the leaves are used to treat sore eyes.

Nagakesara is an ingredient in several Ayurvedic formulations, including Nagakesharadi churna (used for bacillary dysentery) and Nagakesara yoga (used for piles).

Did you know?
Kamadeva (god of desire) is the Hindu god of love who arouses passion in those struck by his five-tipped arrow composed of sweet-scented flowers. One inflicted with Kamadeva's arrow falls helplessly in love. Because of its alluring aroma and beautiful white flowers with golden centers, the flower of the Messua tree is one of these five flowers.

Even the great ascetic Lord Shiva is susceptible to the potency of the five-tipped floral arrow. One day Parvati visits the lord in hopes of marriage. But Shiva is deeply engaged in mediation. Observing Parvati's dismay, the gods request Kamadeva to shoot a love arrow at Shiva. When the arrow hits the lord, Shiva is jolted from mediation. Beholding lovely Parvati standing in front of him, he falls in love with her and the two are soon married. To this day, the fragrant stamens of the Messua tree is used to the stuff pillows on bridal beds.

Magha: Akshayavat (eternal air-born)
Botanical Name: *Ficus benghalensis*, Moraceae
Other names: Vatah (H), Banyan (E)

Ayurvedic properties of Akshayavat, holy tree of Magha

Parts used	stem and root bark, milky latex, leaves, fruit
Dosha effect	V+P-K-
Guna	heavy, dry
Rasa	astringent, sweet
Virya	cooling
Vipaka	pungent

From the branches of this massive tree hang clumps of brown aerial roots, thus its Hindi name is Vataja (air-born). It is also known as Nyagrodha (downward growing), for its downward growing roots eventually unite and take root in the earth. Here, the roots grow into separate pillars that support the crown of the tree and can even grow out as separate trees. Its most popular name is the Banyan tree, the symbol of long life and prosperity.

Its diverse medicinal properties make the Banyan tree ideal for treating a wide range of symptoms. The crushed seeds and the milky latex from the twigs are applied externally to relieve pains, sores, ulcers and bruises. The same mixture is also used for healing cracked and burning soles. The seeds are considered cooling and tonic. A paste of the leaves or the heated leaves is applied as poultice to promote healing of abscesses. The infusion of the bark is a powerful tonic and useful for treating diabetes, dysentery and diarrhoea. The red tips of the young aerial roots are eaten to cure obstinate vomiting.

Other medicinal uses include the treatment of inflammation of joints, toothache, pain, skin diseases, eye diseases, impotence, premature ejaculation, urinary tract infection and impurity of blood.

Panchavalkala churna is an Ayurvedic formula made from the bark of five major trees belonging to the *Ficus* family, including *Ficus benghalensis*. It is a remedy for various skin disorders and is particularly useful for wound healing.

Did you know?
The Banyan tree is a symbol of immortality. By dropping vertical aerial roots that grow into a ring of trees around the original one, it extends its existence in perpetuity. This is the reason that the Akshayavat (eternal air-borne) tree is connected to the forefathers. In hopes that their recently deceased ones also

become immortal, family members deposit the ashes of their beloveds under an Akshayavat tree.

According to the Narada Purana: "He who, with special efforts, performs the rite of Shraddha (offerings to the ancestors) at the place of an Akshayavat tree and salutes and worships Vatesha (the lord of the Banyan tree) with concentration and purity of mind shall take his ancestors to the everlasting and eternal city of Brahma."[1]

The Banyan tree is honored and worshipped on Vat Purnima, the full-moon day during the month of Jyeshta (May-June). On this day, people join together to hear the legend of Savitri (the daughter of the Sun god). The legend tells how Savitri brings her dead husband, Satyavan, back to life by worshipping the Banyan tree. Hence, on Vat Purnima, wives all over India revere this sacred tree for the protection of their husbands.

---

[1] *People Trees*, Haberman, David L., pg. 164. Oxford University Press, 2013.

Purva Phalguni: Palasa (red lac)
Botanical Name: *Butea monosperma*, Fabaceae
Other names: Palas (H), Flame of the Forest (E)

Ayurvedic properties of Palasa, divine tree of Purva Phalguni

Parts used	bark, flowers, leaf, gum, roots, fruits, seeds
Dosha effect	V-P-K+
Guna	light, dry
Rasa	pungent, bitter, astringent
Virya	heating
Vipaka	pungent

The Palasa tree grows up to 50 feet in height. It is known for its stunning red flowers which are compared to the rays of the sun. This gives it its English name: Flame of the Forest. Its trunk is usually crooked and twisted with irregular branches.

The rough, grey bark of the Palasa tree contains gum which is used to relieve the symptoms of dysentery. Its seeds are ground and powdered and used to kill intestinal and stomach worms and its leaves, ground and powdered to reduce blood sugar levels. The whole plant is considered an excellent overall tonic.

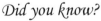

Externally, the various parts of the Palasa tree are applied to skin disorders, including eczema, itching and inflammation.

Other applications include the treatment of night blindness, bone fractures, piles, ulcers, menstrual disorders, cough, stomatitis, sperm debility, vaginal discharges, liver disorders, gonorrhea and dysmenorrhea.

Did you know?

The following legend conveys the connection between Soma, the nectar of immortality, and the Palasha tree.

Devata Soma had been captured by the asuras and hidden in a faraway universe. After much time traveling far and wide, an eagle locates Soma in a hidden realm and scoops him up with his sharp claws. As he takes flight, the eagle is struck by the arrow of an archer who has been closely guarding Soma. The eagle escapes injury, but loses a feather, which falls to earth. As it touches the ground, the feather turns into a Palasha tree. Because of its association with Soma, the Palasha tree is believed to contain within its shoots the nectar of immortality (soma).

The tenth mandala (book) of the *Rigveda* contains a "Wedding Hymn". It recounts the divine marriage of Surya (the daughter of the Sun) to Soma (Chandra). This occasion is of great extravagance and festivity, the likes of which have never been witnessed by the gods. Surya rides upon a wedding chariot decked with stunning red flowers from the Palasha tree, as Aryaman (devata ruler of Purva Phalguni) and Bhaga (devata ruler of Uttara Phalguni) chaperon her to the wedding ceremony, where she is wedded to Soma.

According to Navagraha Van, the Palasha tree is planted in reverence to Chandra, also known in the Vedas as Soma.[1]

---

[1] Refer to Appendix H: "Navagraha Van and Rashi Van".

Uttara Phalguni: Plaksha (roots growing downwards)
Botanical Name: *Ficus microcarpa*, syn. *Ficus aggregata*, Moraceae
Other names: Pakar (H), Indian laurel (E)

Ayurvedic properties of Plaksha, holy tree of Uttara Phalguni

Parts used	fruit, bark, milky latex, leaves, adventitious roots, buds
Dosha effect	V+P-K-
Guna	heavy, sharp, dry
Rasa	astringent, sweet
Virya	cooling
Vipaka	pungent

The Plaksha is a spreading evergreen tree with large branches and numerous aerial roots hanging from the trunk and branches. Many eventually reach the soil and form pillar-like roots. This tree is also known as the 'strangling fig' tree, as it often grows on a host tree, surrounding it with its own roots and pulling the other tree down with its weight.

The pounded leaves and bark are applied as poultice in rheumatic headache, wounds and bruises. Ashes obtained by burning the roots are applied to aching teeth. The juice of the bark mixed in milk is considered as useful in liver disease. Its figs are used as a pain killer and its leaves and buds treat conditions related to conjunctivitis.

The Plaksha tree is used as a medicine to treat ulcers, skin disorders, edema, wounds, bruises, diarrhea, dysentery, diabetes mellitus, kidney disorders, cholesterol and other lipid problems, inflammatory conditions and osteoporosis. The milk of the bark is used to address liver disease.

Did you know?
Just as Bhaga (ruling devata of Uttara Phalguni) is the godhead of conjugal bliss and bestower of children,[1] the Plaksha tree is a symbol of fertility, for a single large Plaksha can produce upwards of 100,000 fruit. Women circumambulate the tree 108 times in hopes of progeny and prosperity.

Legend tells of Indra's grand coronation during which the gods anoint him as king of heaven on the full moon day of Uttara Phalguni. Perhaps this explains why a person who plants four Plaksha trees is granted the boon of *rajasuya*, the status of a king.

---

[1] Refer to *Your Healing Stars: Volume I, Fundamentals of Vedic Astrology* for a description of each nakshatra devata.

Hasta: Ambashta (situated in the mother)
Botanical Name: *Spondias pinnata*, Anacardiacea
Other names: Amra (H), Hog plum, Wild mango (E)

Ayurvedic properties of Ambashta, holy tree of Hasta

Parts used	root bark, stem bark, leaves, fruits
Dosha effect	V-P+K-
Guna	heavy
Rasa	astringent, sour
Virya	heating
Vipaka	sweet

The Ambashta tree is a medium-sized deciduous tree with a pleasant smell. Its flowers are small and yellowish green. Its plum-shaped fruit hangs down in pendulous clusters. Rich in vitamin A, iron and other minerals, the fruit of the Ambashta is used in the preparation of chutney, curries and different types of spicy delicacies. Its sour fruit makes excellent pickles.

The pulp of the fruit is acid and astringent, and is considered useful in bilious dyspepsia. The bark is sometimes used as a refrigerant medicine. The juice of the leaves is used for ear-aches. Various parts of the Ambashta tree are used to treat dysentery, diarrhea, vomiting, articular and muscular rheumatism, gonorrhea, irregular menstruation, rheumatism, sore throat and burning sensations.

Did you know?

The Ambashta tree belongs to the mango family of trees. It is stated in the ancient scriptures that "He who plants five mango trees will never go to hell." When planted on the eastern side of a house, the mango tree is said to give wealth and fortune to the householder. It is also considered to be the tree of destiny or fate and is involved in many rites of passage, such as wedding ceremonies.

Because the fruit of the Ambashta tree is not as sweet as that of other varieties of Mango trees, it was considered somewhat inferior and given the English name 'Hog Plum". Still, the juice of this fruit makes an excellent cider.

Chitra: Visva (universal) or Bilva
Botanical Name: *Aegle marmelos*, Rutaceae
Other names: Bel (H), Bael (E)

Ayurvedic properties of Visva, holy tree of Chitra

Parts used	leaves, fruits, stem bark, root
Dosha effect	V-P+K-
Guna	light, dry
Rasa	bitter, astringent
Virya	heating
Vipaka	pungent

The Bilva or Bael is a small to medium-sized thorny tree with a short, erect trunk. The signature of the Bale tree is its trifoliate leaves that emit a spicy fragrance when crushed. With its strikingly beautiful greenish-yellow tender foliage in the spring and the conspicuous cannon-ball like pendulous yellowish-orange ripening fruits from the downward-arching branches in the blazing sun of summer, Bael is an unmistakable tree to locate in the dry deciduous forest. Traditionally referred to as 'fruit of plenty', its fruit is described in Indian literature as the breasts of the Goddess of Plenty.

The root of the Bael tree serves as a nerve tranquilizer and is used in the treatment of insomnia, epilepsy and hysteria. It is one of ten herbal ingredients in Dasamula (ten roots), a well-known Ayurvedic formula used to treat vata and tonify the nervous system.

The pulp of the fruit is often diluted with water and sweetened with tamarind to make a cooling drink during summer which is used as an appetizer. It is an excellent curative for dysentery, acidity and for purifying blood.

A decoction of leaves is a favorite remedy for ailments that often occur during seasonal changes, including fevers, influenza, and fatigue. Various other parts are used to treat rheumatism, edema, stomach problems, malabsorption, chronic diarrhea, insomnia, conjunctivitis, liver congestion and irritable bowel syndrome.

Did you know?
The Bael has been called "Shivadruma", or the 'tree of Shiva'. Its trifoliate leaf resembles Shiva's trisula (three-forked trident) or, alternatively, Shiva's three eyes. It is said that one who pays homage to the Shiva lingam while sitting under the Bilva tree will go to Shiva loka (the world of Shiva) upon death.

Of the Hindu Trinity, Shiva is the lord of dissolution. Perhaps this is why the wood of the Bael tree is often used for the funeral pyre or the cremation fire of the recently deceased. It would also explain why during the ancient Brahmanic sacrifices, the sacrificial animal is tied to a post (yupa) constructed out of Bael wood.

The Bael tree is worshipped on the 14th phase of the waning moon between the months of Magha (January-February) and Phalguna (February-March). This is Shivaratri, a day in honor of Shiva's first manifestation in his phallic form. The lingam is bathed in milk and wrapped with Bael leaves on this day.

The Bael is one of the *panchavati*, or five most sacred trees of India. The others, and their corresponding nakshatras, are: Asvattha (Pushya), Banyan (Magha), Amala (Bharani) and Nimba (Uttara Bhadrapada).[1] Each Panchavati tree is associated with one or more godheads. The Asvattha is the embodied form of Lord Vishnu and sacred to Lord Krishna; the Banyan is associated with the ancestors and Savitar, daughter of the Sun; the Amala is the abode of Shri Lakshmi and the Nimba, the abode of Shitala (the cooling goddess) and sacred to Goddess Durga. As noted above, Bael is sacred to Shiva.

---

[1] Several sources reference the Asoka tree in place of the Nimba tree.

Svati: Arjuna (white)
Botanical Name: *Terminalia arjuna*, Combretaceae
Other names: Arjuna, White Marudh (H), Arjuna (E)

Ayurvedic properties of Arjuna, holy tree of Svati

Parts used	root bark, stem bark, leaves
Dosha effect	V+ P- K-
Guna	light, dry
Rasa	astringent
Virya	cooling
Vipaka	pungent

The Arjuna is a large deciduous tree that reaches up to 70-85 feet in height. It is an evergreen with yellow flowers, conical leaves and smooth gray bark. Arjuna is found throughout India, especially in the Himalayas and Eastern India. Its botanical name is *Terminalia*, referring to its leaves that are crowded at the tips of its shoots. Arjuna means 'white' or 'bright' and its flowers are creamy white and its bark is shiny-bright.

According to Charaka, author of *Charaka Samhita*, Arjuna is also called *hridya* (heart), for it is acclaimed as the best herb for the heart. Many cardiovascular diseases are addressed by medicines made from this tree, such as hypertension, congestive heart failure and coronary artery disease. The bark extract is used to treat hypertension and, in powdered form, is considered a heart tonic. It strengthens the heart muscles and tones the capillaries, helping to prevent high blood pressure.

The prabhava (unexplained effect) of Arjuna is its ability to treat a "broken heart" and other similar emotional disturbances.

Did you know?
An ancient legend recounted in the *Bhagavatam* (the story of Krishna's pastimes) tells of a time when Kubera's (god of wealth) sons, Nalakuvara and Manigriva, grew idle and began to spend all their time romancing women and drinking wine.

Sage Narada (the god of music) happens by and notices their outrageous behavior. They fail to pay proper respect to Narada, and he curses them that they shall turn into twin Arjuna trees.

Before long, baby Krishna sits beneath the twin trees, mischievously playing games with the gopis (milkmaids). Suddenly, both trees come crashing down. As the Arjuna trees hit the ground, Nalakuvara and Manigriva are released from their trunks. As luck would have it, Narada had later modified his curse, stipulating that the day baby Krishna plays beneath the Arjuna trees, Kubera's two sons will be released.

Vishakha: Vikamkata
Botanical Name: *Flacourtia indica*, Flacourtiaceae
Other names: Katia (H), Governor's plum (E)

Ayurvedic properties of Vikamkata, holy tree of Vishakha

Parts used	fruit, bark
Dosha effect	VP-K-
Guna	light
Rasa	sour
Virya	cooling
Vipaka	sweet

The berries of the Governor's plum are red when ripe, and eaten raw or made into jelly. They are also fermented to prepare wine. The trunk of this demi-evergreen contains thorns and its bark is dark brown.

The leaf is carminative, astringent and used as a tonic, an expectorant and for asthma, pain relief, gynecological complaints and as an anthelmintic, and treatment for intestinal worms. An infusion of the bark is used as a gargle for hoarseness. The root and ash have been used as a remedy for kidney complaints.

The fruit contains medicinal constituents that aid in jaundice and enlarged spleen. Blood disorders such as abscess, skin disorders, bleeding disorders such as menorrhagia and nasal bleeding, as well as arthritis, intermittent fever, bacterial throat infection and cholera are treated by the Governor's plum.

Anuradha: Sakesara (containing many stamens)
Botanical Name: *Mimusops elengi*, Sapotaceae
Other names: Bakul (H), Bullet Wood, Spanish Cherry (E)

Ayurvedic properties of Sakesara, holy tree of Anuradha

Parts used	root bark, stem bark, fruits, flowers
Dosha effect	V+ P- K-
Guna	heavy
Rasa	pungent, astringent
Virya	heating
Vipaka	pungent

The Bakul is a mid-sized evergreen tree, branching low and forming a dense, rounded crown of numerous spreading branches. The fragrance exuded by the tiny, night-opening flowers of this towering tree is overpowering and lingers in the air. Due to its dome-shaped crown and creamy white, star-shaped flowers, the Bakul is often planted in Indian gardens. The many stamens in the flower explain its Sanskrit name Sakesara (of many stamens).

Other distinguishing features of the Bakul include its dark-grey scaly bark with deep fissures, exudation of milky juice when cut, and glossy green leaves with wavy margins and berries which are green at first and turn orange-yellow when ripe. Its fruit is edible and painters use the oil from its seed kernels.

The small, white, fragrant flowers of the Bakul grow in clusters and make a lovely garland. Krishna wears a garland of Bakul flowers; its fragrance attracts the gopis (milkmaids). Hence, the flowers of this tree are a symbol of love and beauty and considered an aphrodisiac.

The bark of the Bakul tree is astringent and, when made into a decoction, treats diarrhea, dysentery and intestinal worms. Powdered bark of the tree is used to strengthen gums and teeth. It is also believed to increase fertility in women.

The flowers serve as a nervine tonic and ease the mind. Heart disease is treated with an alcoholic extract of the flowers.

Did you know?
Legend tells that the Bakul is sensitive to the actions of women. Should a woman dine under the shade of this tree or sprinkle the tree with wine from their mouths,

its flowers blossom.[1]

Women circumambulate the Bakul and tie cradles to its branches in hopes of male progeny. Even today in parts of India, one finds cradles hanging from the branches of the Bakul tree.[2]

---

[1] *Sacred Plants of India*, Krishna, Nanditha and Armirthalingam, pg. 176. M. Penguin Group, 2014.
[2] Ibid., pp. 177-178.

Jyeshta: Sabara (lotus bark)

Botanical Name: *Symplocos cochinchinensis*, syn. *Symplocos racemosa*
Symplocaceae
Other names: Lodhra (H), Lodh (E)

Ayurvedic properties of Sabara, holy tree of Jyeshta

Parts used	flowers, leaves, stem bark, root bark
Dosha effect	V+P-K-
Guna	light, dry
Rasa	astringent, bitter
Virya	cooling
Vipaka	pungent

The Sabara tree is more popularly known as Lodhra. It is a small-to-medium sized evergreen found in northern and eastern India and Kerala. The leaves of the Lodhra tree are oblong, the bark is soft and its yellowish-white flowers are fragrant.

The Lodhra tree is reputed as a remedy for ophthalmia (severe inflammation of the eye or of the conjunctiva). Applied as a vaginal douche, it is particularly useful for inflammation of the uterus and reduces leucorrhea, menorrhagia and endometritis. It flowers are used to treat stomach ulcers.

The bark is used to treat diarrhoea and dysentery as well as liver issues. A decoction of the bark is administered for bleeding gums, menorrhagia and other uterine disorders. Externally, a paste made of the bark is used for skin diseases, swelling and bleeding wounds. It reduces pain and edema.

Did you know?

The seeds of the Lodhra tree are believed to have protective powers. After giving birth, women wear a necklace strung from the seeds of this tree to protect their newborns.

Mula: Sarja (casting out)
Botanical Name: *Vateria indica*, Dipterocarpaceae
Other names: Saphed dammar (H), White dammar (E)

Ayurvedic properties of Sarja, holy tree of Mula

Parts used	stem bark, root bark, gum
Dosha effect	V-P+K-
Guna	oily
Rasa	astringent, bitter
Virya	cooling
Vipaka	pungent

Saphed dammar is a large evergreen tree with rough, greyish-white bark and white flowers. The tree produces a fragrant resin from channels within its trunk and oil from its seed kernels. Both have a variety of domestic uses, such as soap, candle and incense manufacturing.

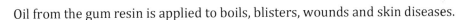

The resin from the tree is known as Sarja rasa. Recent studies indicate that Sarja rasa has anti-cancerous properties. It is also a tonic, carminative and expectorant and used in the treatment of respiratory disorders, throat troubles, tubercular gland, boils, piles, diarrhea and rheumatism. Other medicinal uses include the treatment of infected wounds, diarrhea, intestinal worms, earache, cough, asthma, intoxication, abscesses, deafness, rheumatism and dysentery.

Oil from the gum resin is applied to boils, blisters, wounds and skin diseases.

Purva Ashadha: Vanchula

Botanical Name: *Barringtonia racemosa*, Lecythidaceae
Other names: Samudraphal (H), Powder-puff Mangrove (E)

Ayurvedic properties of Vanchula, sacred tree of Purva Ashadha

Parts used	fruit, leaves, stem bark, root bark
Dosha effect	V+ P- K-
Guna	dry, light, sharp
Rasa	pungent, bitter
Virya	cooling
Vipaka	pungent

Powder-puff Mangrove is a small estuarine deciduous tree with an unbranched stem that leads to a rounded crown. The attractive pinkish white flowers in drooping long racemes and the pinkish-red foliage before leaf-fall are distinct in the coasts of mangroves. Half the flowers bloom simultaneously emitting a pungent, yet faintly sweet odor. Pollination of the night-opening fragrant flowers is generally by bats or insects (mainly moths), which are attracted to the copious nectar. After shedding the flowers, the inflorescences are often crowded with ants attracted by the nectar.

Found along the banks of rivers, this tree is aptly aligned with Purva Ashadha, whose ruling devatas are depicted as river goddesses (the Apas).

The Powder-puff Mangrove is widely known for its anti-inflammation and anticancer properties. The fruit is used as a remedy for cough, asthma and diarrhea as well as the treatment of pain, inflammation, rheumatic conditions and ear aches. The seeds are aromatic and useful in treating colic and ophthalmic problems. The leaves are traditionally used to treat ulcers and cancer.

The young shoots and leaves are eaten raw as a vegetable due to its medicinal values which is effective in high blood pressure treatment. The pounded leaves, roots and barks are used to reduce itchiness and chicken pox.

Other conditions treated by this tree include inflammation, rheumatism, boils, piles, gastric ulcers, skin diseases, syphilis, malaria and nasal catarrh.

Uttara Ashadha: Panasa (thorn)
Botanical Name: *Artocarpus heterophyllus*, Moraceae
Other names: Kathal (H), Jackfruit (E)

Ayurvedic properties of Panasa, holy tree of Uttara Ashadha

Parts used	root bark, stem bark, leaves, seeds, fruits
Dosha effect	V-P-K+
Guna	oily, heavy, slimy
Rasa	sweet
Virya	cooling
Vipaka	sweet

Jackfruit is a large tree belonging to the fig family. Jackfruit grows all over India, particularly in the southern region. It is valued for its edible fruit that is rich in sugar and can weigh up to a hundred pounds. The fruit has small thorns on its surface, which accounts for the tree's Sanskrit name, Panasa (thorns). Oblong in shape, the huge fruit hangs from the trunk and sometimes grows on exposed roots of the tree. A strong yellow dye obtained by boiling the saw dust from the tree is used to dye the robes of Buddhist monks.

The pulp of young fruit is cooked before consuming, but as the fruit ripens, it becomes sweeter and is often eaten raw. High in carbohydrates and protein, the seeds of the fruit are roasted and eaten.

The ashes of the leaves treat skin conditions such as ulcers, boils and wounds. The pulp and seeds of the fruit are used as a cooling tonic and the seeds are considered an aphrodisiac. The wood has sedative properties and its pith is used to induce abortion.

Latex extracted from the tree treats night blindness and, when mixed with vinegar, is used for glandular swelling. A paste made from the root is applied to ulcers and wounds. Other medicinal uses include: fevers, skin diseases, convulsions, constipation, ophthalmic disorders and snake bites.

Did you know?

Legend tells of the sacred connection between the Panasa tree and Lord Shiva. One day while out in the forest, Shiva happens upon a lower caste woman of great beauty named Koolivaka. In the heat of the moment, Shiva desires to make love to the young woman. He expresses his wishes and tells her he will soon return for her.

Koolivaka, a great devotee of Goddess Parvati (Shiva's wife), prays to the goddess for guidance, who reveals an ancient secret to her. Parvati tells Koolivaka that in a previous life, she was a servant to her and Shiva. Her name was Manasvini. Once, while tending to the needs of Parvati's baby, Lord Ganesha, Manasvini decides to breast feed the baby herself. This angers Parvati, who curses Manasvini that she will be born in her next life to an outcast family.

Before long, Parvati regrets her curse and modifies it. Although Manasvini will be born to an outcast family, she will have the opportunity to breast feed a son of Shiva's. Parvati tells the servant girl that she will take on her form for a brief period of time and entice Shiva into love making. A son will be born from their union and Koolivaka will mother the child. Before long, the child will defeat a mighty demon.

And so, Parvati assumes Koolivaka's form and swings on a creeper attached to a Jackfruit tree, anxiously awaiting her lord's arrival. When Shiva returns, the couple engages in love making. A child with divine power is born from this holy union. The child is named Vishnu Maya, as he is born out of Parvati's illusion. Shiva requests Koolivaka to tend to the needs of the baby. In the pursuant months, Koolivaka nurses baby Vishnu Maya.

Fulfilling his destiny, Vishnu Maya one day defeats the great asura Jalandhara in battle. To this day Vishnu Maya remains in his native land, living amongst the poor and offering them his protection.

Shravana: Arka (sun)
Botanical Name: *Calotropis gigantia*, Asclepiadaceae
Other names: Ak (H), Giant Swallow (E)

Ayurvedic properties Arka, holy tree of Shravana

Parts used	flowers, milky latex, root bark, leaves
Dosha effect	V+PK-
Guna	light, dry, sharp, spreading
Rasa	pungent, bitter
Virya	heating
Vipaka	pungent

The Arka belongs to the Asclepiadaceae family of trees, which includes latex bearing plants. The tree is found throughout India and grows best in dry soil. There are two species, identified by the color of their waxy flowers that grow in clusters. The flowers of the *Calotropis gigantea* are white and those of the *Calotropis procera* are bluish-red. The *Calotropis gigantea* is commonly referred to as Giant Milk Weed due to its milky latex.

Juice from the flower is applied as a nasya for headaches. If taken in excess, this milky juice causes extreme nausea and vomiting, stomach pain, cramping and irregular or slowed pulse, the latter producing dizziness, headache and general confusion. The leaves are used for diarrhoea and candida. In cases of skin disease, the latex from the Arka tree is mixed with mustard oil and applied topically. Black pepper is added to the root sap and used as an antidote for snake bites.

Other medicinal actions and uses include: purgative, cardiac stimulant, blood purifier, blood diseases, hemorrhagic disorders, expectorant, remedy for scabies and appetite stimulant.

Did you know?

The Sanskrit name for this tree (Arka) means 'sun'. Like the intense heat of the mid-day sun, the milky juice of the Arka tree can irritate or burn the skin. Arka also means 'flash of lightning'. There is an ancient Indian belief that one who carelessly approaches the Arka tree is blinded by lightning.

According to Navagraha Van (the planting of a tree for each of the nine grahas), the Arka (sun) tree is planted in reverence of Surya.[1] Ratha saptami is a Hindu festival falling on the seventh day after the sun begins its northerly movement (Uttarayana). On this day, a person is to bathe with Arka leaves on his body while

---

[1] Refer to Appendix H: "Navagraha Van and Rashi Van".

reciting the following: "The sun bestows happiness and success to people who bathe on this day with Arka leaves."

Arka bhasma (ash from the roots of the Arka tree) is applied when Surya is ill-placed in the natal birth chart, for it is said to instill confidence, self-esteem and a vibrant state of health.

Dhanishta: Shami (pacifying)
Botanical Name: *Prosopis specigera*, Lenguminoseae
Other names: Chomkar (H), Indian Mesquite (E)

Ayurvedic properties of Shami, holy tree of Dhanishta

Parts used	stem bark, root bark, leaves, fruit
Dosha	V+PK-
Guna	heavy, sweet
Rasa	light, sweet
Virya	cooling
Vipaka	pungent

The Shami tree is of medium height and is predominately found in extremely arid regions of India, but is indicative of the presence of a deep water table. Its branches are thorned along the internodes. The Shami tree is one of a genus of flowering plants in the pea family and has long, seed-bearing pods hanging from its branches. The flowers are small and creamy-yellow and its light bluish-green foliage droops gently from the tips of its branches.

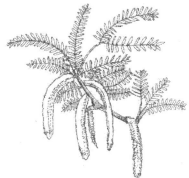

Its flowers are mixed with sugar and used to prevent miscarriage. The ashes are rubbed over the skin to remove hair. The pods of the Shami tree exhibit anti-bacterial properties. Its leaves are used as anti-hyperglycemia, anti-hyperlipidemia, anti-oxidant analgesic, anti-pyretic, anti-depressant and skeletal muscle relaxant. The leaves are also recommended for eye troubles.

The bark is considered to be anthelmintic, refrigerant, anti-diabetic, anti-atherosclerotic and tonic. It is used for treating asthma, bronchitis, rheumatism, piles and muscle tremors.

Did you know?

Lord Agni is the celestial leader of the Vasus (rulers of Dhanishta), and is a Vasu himself. During the ancient Brahmanic period, priests vigorously rub two Shami sticks together to ignite the sacrificial fire. Hence, the Shami tree is acclaimed to be the birth mother of this god of fire, explaining the connection between the Shami tree and Vasu-ruled Dhanishta.

In India, the Shami tree is worshipped for victory and success in battles. Shri Rama revered the Shami tree after his victory over Ravana. In the Mahabharata War, the Pandavas spend 12 years in the forest and safe keep their weapons in a Shami tree. At the end of this period, they remove the weapons from the tree and triumphantly defeat the Kauravas.

The Shami tree is sacred to Goddess Durga. Legend tells that Durga had once engaged in ascetic practices for nine years while sitting in the hollow trunk of a Sami tree. To this day, she is believed to reside in the tree as Shamirama, 'goddess of the Shami tree'. After Navaratri, the Hindu festival that honors Durga and the goddesses, the tenth and final day is Vijayadashami, 'tenth day of victory'. On this day, people exchange Shami leaves and wish each other victory in their ventures.

The Navagraha Van (the planting of a tree for each of the nine grahas) requires the planting of a Shami tree in honor of Shani.[1] If one is under the grips of this graha by dasha or transit, Shami bhasma is recommended. The wood of the Shami tree is used when performing a homa (fire ceremony) in honor of Shani.

---

[1] Refer to Appendix H: "Navagraha Van and Rashi Van".

Shatabhishak: Kadamba
Botanical Name: *Anthocephalus indicus*, Rubiaceae
Other names: Kadamba (H), Kadam tree (E)

Ayurvedic properties of Kadamba, holy tree of Shatabhishak

Parts used	fruits, leaves, bark
Dosha	VPK
Guna	light, rough
Rasa	pungent, bitter, astringent
Virya	cooling
Vipaka	pungent

The Kadamba is an evergreen tree with fragrant spherical, white and yellow flowers that grow in clusters. Its honey-colored flowers open after dark to produce the wine-rich scent that is extracted into perfumed oil. The small, hard ball-like fruits of the Kadamba are sweet and sour to taste. Because of its dense canopy and fragrant flowers, Kadamba trees are cultivated in parks, along avenues and on temple grounds.

An unusual feature of the Kadamba tree is that it releases water vapor into the atmosphere, thereby cooling the local air. Perhaps this explains its association with Varuna, lord of the ocean, and the divine ruler of Shatabhishak.

The dried bark relieves fever and an extract of leaves serve as a mouth gargle. The juice of the leaves is useful in cardiac problems, blood pressure, stomatitis and rheumatism. The juice of the fruit promotes lactation and is a blood purifier, anti-catarrhal and analgesic. Dried stembark is considered febrifugal, antidiuretic and anthelmintic. It is used to treat disorders of the female genital tract and bleeding disorders.

Other medical uses include: fevers, inflammation, snakebites, wounds, conjunctivitis, diarrhea, dysentery, colitis, vomiting, thirst, cough, dysuria, urinary calculi, glycosuria, menorrhagia and poor skin complexion.

Did you know?
The Kadamba tree is intimately connected with Lord Krishna and even referred to as the "Krishna tree". During ancient times, groves of the sweet-scented Kadamba tree grew in Vrindavan, where Krishna spent most of his childhood days.

During these times, Krishna was often seen dancing with his consort Radha and the gopis (milkmaids) under the Kadamba tree. Once, when the gopis undressed to bathe in the local Yamuna River, Krishna takes their clothes and hides them in a Kadamba tree.

In many Indian paintings, Krishna and Radha are shown on a swing suspended from a branch of the Kadamba tree, as gopis circle beneath, singing and dancing. Other times, Krishna is shown playing his flute beneath the shade of this tree.

Women worship the Kadamba in the month of Ashadha (June-July). During the festivities, they join hands and circle around the tree singing devotional songs to Krishna in hopes of an intimate encounter with this divine god of love.

Purva Bhadrapada: Amra (mango)
Botanical Name: *Mangifera indica*, Anacardiacea (heart shaped)
Other names: Am (H), Mango (E)

Ayurvedic properties of Amra, holy tree of Purva Bhadrapada

Parts used	fruits, leaves, root bark, stem bark
Dosha	V+P-K-
Guna	heavy, oily, hard
Rasa	astringent
Virya	cooling
Vipaka	pungent

Grown in India for over 4,000 years, the Mango is one of the oldest cultivated plants in the world. It flourishes in hot and semi-hot hilly regions as well as plains. As the tree ages, it produces an increased number of fruits.

The mango is one of the most sought-after fruits, as it is sweet, contains plenty of vitamin C and is a medicinal tonic. It is the national fruit of India. Each year, an International Mango Festival is held in New Delhi. The festival showcases the numerous varieties of mangos from different parts of India. Many other mango festivals are held in other parts of India at the same time. During the festivals and other auspicious occasions, people tie the green leaves of the Mango together on a string and hang them at the front door as a good omen.

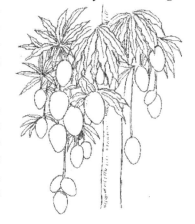

An infusion made from the leaves is used to reduce blood pressure and treat conditions such as asthma, coughs and diabetes. A mouthwash is made from the leaves that hardens the gums and treats dental problems. Its seeds are used for colds, coughs, diarrhea and bleeding piles. The bark is an astringent and helps heal wounds.

Raw mango acts as an appetizer and improves digestion. Ripe mango is a laxative, cardio tonic, hemostatic and improves complexion. The flowers are considered an aphrodisiac and believed to produce longing in the hearts of lovers.

Did you know?

The Mango tree has great mythological value in India. One legend tells that once, long ago, Surya (the daughter of the Sun god) was tyrannized by an evil sorceress. To escape, she jumps into a nearby pond and transforms into a golden lotus flower. Soon, a king wanders by and notices the beautiful lotus. As he reaches for the flower, the sorceress reduces the lotus to ashes.

Saddened, the king carries the ashes back to his palace and deposits them on the grounds. A Mango tree laden with luscious fruit soon appears. As one of its ripe mangos falls to the ground, Surya emerges from its fruit. The king immediately recognizes her as his long-lost wife. The two reunite and, before long, a son is born to the couple.

From this day forward, the Mango tree is a symbol of male progeny. Wives who wish to give birth to sons eat its fruit. Mango leaves are often strung across the doorway of a couple's home to announce the birth of a son.

Uttara Bhadrapada: Nimba (neem)
Botanical Name: *Azadirachta indica*, Meliaceae
Other names: Neem (H), Margosa tree (E)

Ayurvedic properties of Nimba, holy tree of Uttara Bhadrapada

Parts used	flowers, leaves, bark, seed, seed oil
Dosha	V+P-K-
Guna	light
Rasa	bitter, astringent
Virya	cooling
Vipaka	pungent

The Neem is a medium-to-large sized tree, mostly evergreen and with dark, rough bark and reddish wood. It thrives in hot, dry regions. Its small, white flowers produce a delicate, jasmine-like scent. This scent attracts bees, which swarm around the tree during the flowering season. Expelling more oxygen than most other trees, the Neem tree serves as an important air purifier.

The Neem tree is given a very important status in Ayurveda, where it is often referred to as the "village pharmacy" or *"sarva roga nivarini"* (the curer of all ailments). It is used as a bitter tonic herb and is an important detoxifier used to destroy a wide range of parasitic organisms.

The leaves of the Neem tree are applied as a paste to heal smallpox, and often laid on the floor of the room or under the bed of a person affected with smallpox, chickenpox, measles or mumps.

Juice from its leaves is used as a liver stimulant, uterine tonic, syphilis and conditions of excessive mucous and cough. The fruit is a remedy for constipation and various bark decoctions treat jaundice, anorexia, intestinal worms, chronic cough, dysentery, tuberculosis and leprosy. A powder made from the seeds of the Neem tree effectively treats dysmenorrhea and puerperium.

Did you know?
The Neem tree is the abode of Shitala, the 'cooling' goddess prayed to by villagers during an outbreak of smallpox. In Indian villages, leaves of the Neem tree are bound together and displayed outside the front door to warn visitors of a smallpox infestation. Sometimes an image of Goddess Shitala is hung from its leaves.

An old custom in India is the planting of a Neem (considered a female tree and symbolic of the bride) and Asvattha (considered a male tree and symbolic of the bridegroom) together so that they intertwine as they grow. A ceremonial wedding may even be performed to officially marry the two trees. This practice promises a long and happy marriage to a newlywed couple.

Trees are also sometimes married to people. A woman with kuja dosha, an astrological condition that impacts marriage,[1] should first marry an Asvattha or Banyan, both considered male trees, before marrying her husband. This practice satisfies any inauspicious birth chart karma around marriage. A husband without sons is advised to marry a Shami tree (considered a female tree), which is believed to result in male progeny.

---

[1] Kuja dosha forms when Mangala occupies the Lagna, 2B, 4B, 7B, 8B or 12B. Kuja dosha can harm marital life.

Revati: Madhuka (honey)
Botanical Name: *Madhuca nerifolia*, Sapotaceae
Other names: Mahua (H), Butter tree (E)

Ayurvedic properties of Madhuka, holy tree of Revati

Parts used	flowers, leaves, fruit, seeds, seed oil
Dosha	V+P-K-
Guna	heavy, oily
Rasa	astringent, sweet
Virya	cooling
Vipaka	astringent

This medium-sized evergreen tree with its dense, spreading canopy is an endangered plant species. It grows along streams and rivers in the forests of southern India. The oil contained in its seeds is used extensively in cooking and in bakery goods. Hence, it is also known as the Indian Butter tree. Rich in sugars, proteins, vitamins and minerals, the flowers of the Madhuka are eaten raw by the local populace. The sugary nectar of the flowers gives this tree its Sanskrit name: Madhuka, 'honey'.

Nearly all parts of the Madhuka contain medicinal properties. The flowers are used in the preparation of wine and are a reputed aphrodisiac. Juice from the flower is used as a nasya for sinusitis. Mixed with milk, the pulp of the flower is a nervine tonic and when powdered and mixed with ghee and honey, it treats piles. Other floral medicinal applications include the treatment of bronchitis, burning sensations, ear complaints and heart diseases.

The oil extracted from the seeds of the Madhuka fruit is applied to the skin as an analgesic and is also beneficial for skin diseases and rheumatism. A decoction of the bark is used externally to treat skin rash and bleeding gums.

Did you know?
Several folklores relate to the wine made from the flowers of the Madhuka tree. One such tale involves Lord Shiva and takes place in an ancient time before the Madhuka tree existed on earth.

Shiva is concerned, because without the Madhuka tree, the brahman priests are unable to offer the gods wine during their sacrificial ceremony. He summons a parrot, tiger and boar and turns them into Madhuka trees. Soon flowers begin to bloom on their branches. The locals notice that when birds partake of the sweet nectar of the flowers, they chip excitedly in song. Trying it for themselves, they discover the intoxicating honey of this flower and begin making wine out of it. It is said that if a man drinks a small amount of this wine, he becomes a parrot and says the same thing over and over. If he drinks a bit more, he becomes a tiger: he doesn't speak, he roars. If he drinks still more, he becomes a boar and rolls on the ground.[1]

---

[1] *Sacred Plants of India*, Krishna, Nanditha and Armirthalingam, M., pg. 151. Penguin Group, 2014.

Chapter 28: Health Aspects of the Nakshatras

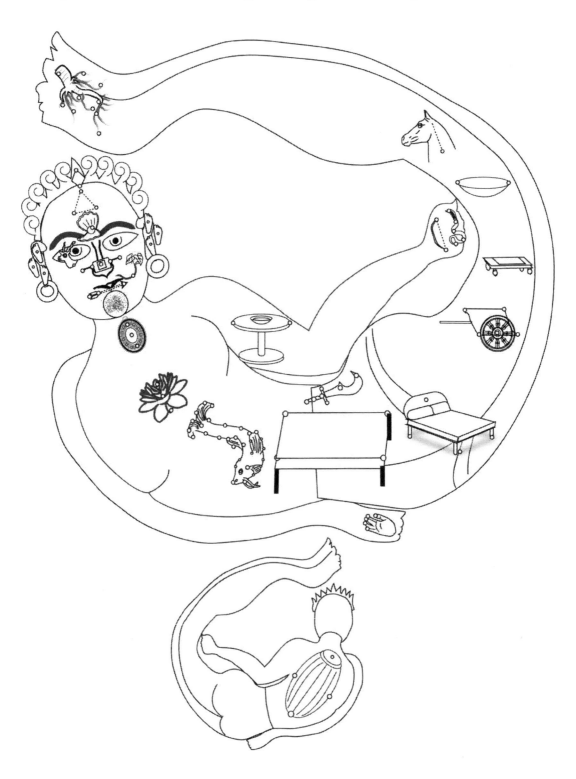

Chapter 28: Health Aspects of the Nakshatras

Nakshatra Purusha

In Chapter 8: "The Kalapurusha of the Birth Chart", the cosmic being in the sky is mapped against the 12 rashis-bhavas of the birth chart. For example, Aries and the Lagna is the head and skull of the Kalapurusha, Taurus and the 2B, the face and throat, Gemini and the 3B, the clavicles, arms and hands, and so on. This concept is instrumental for identifying khavaigunyas, or defective spaces in the body, based on the condition of each of the 12 bhavas and their bhaveshas.

A similar concept is Nakshatra Purusha. In Nakshatra Purusha, Lord Vishnu's body parts are mapped against the 27 lunar nakshatras, sub-groupings of stars that the moon passes through each day of the lunar month. For this reason, there is not a one-to-one rashi-bhava correspondence, as seen with Kalapurusha.

Also unlike the Kalapurusha, the body parts of Nakshatra Purusha are not sequential. For example, Aswhini (the first nakshatra) represents the knees of Nakshatra Purusha, Bharani (the second nakshatra), the head, Krittika (the third nakshatra), the waist, and so on. (See table below) This sequence is based on the Nakshatra Purusha Vrata, a spiritual practice in which the holy body parts of Lord Vishnu are honored and worshipped in a particular order.

Because Nakshatra Purusha is specific to the nakshatras, it is useful for assessing the nakshatra placement of a graha or bhavesha. For example, assume that Rahu occupies Svati, the 15th lunar nakshatra. Notice in the table below that Svati is the teeth of Nakshatra Purusha. Hence, Rahu's placement in Svati can implicate this area of the body as a potential khavaigunya. This is particularly true if the 2B-2B bhavesha are poorly-conditioned and/or Rahu occupies the 2B, which represents the teeth of Kalapurusha. In this case, we have confluence for our Nakshatra Purusha finding. We would also consider vata-type health conditions (Rahu) with the teeth, such as excessive cavities.

For each strong or weak papa graha, weak shubha graha or trik-dusthana bhavesha, check the corresponding Nakshatra Purusha body part and then look for other birth chart indicators as confluence.

Table 13: Nakshatra Purusha[1]

#	Name	Rashi	Degree.Minute	Nakshatra Purusha
1	Aswhini	Aries	0-13.20	knees
2	Bharani	Aries	13.20-26.40	head
3	Krittika	Aries - Taurus	26.40-10.00	hips
4	Rohini	Taurus	10.00-23.20	legs
5	Mrigashira	Taurus-Gemini	23.20-6.40	eyes
6	Ardra	Gemini	6.40-20.00	hairs (top of head)
7	Punarvasu	Gemini-Cancer	20.00-3.20	fingers
8	Pushya	Cancer	3.20-16.40	mouth
9	Ashlesha	Cancer	16.40-30.00	nails
10	Magha	Leo	0-13.20	nose
11	Purva Phalguni	Leo	13.20-26.40	organs of generation
12	Uttara Phalguni	Leo-Virgo	26.40-10.00	organs of generation
13	Hasta	Virgo	10.00-23.20	hands
14	Chitra	Virgo-Libra	23.20-6.40	forehead
15	Svati	Libra	6.40-20.00	teeth
16	Vishakha	Libra-Scorpio	20.00-3.20	arms
17	Anuradha	Scorpio	3.20-16.40	breasts
18	Jyeshta	Scorpio	16.40-30.00	neck
19	Mula	Sagittarius	0-13.20	feet
20	Purva Ashadha	Sagittarius	13.20-26.40	thighs
21	Uttara Ashadha	Sagittarius-Capricorn	26.40-10.00	thighs
22	Shravana	Capricorn	10.00-23.20	ears
23	Dhanishta	Capricorn-Aquarius	23.20-6.40	back
24	Shatabhishak	Aquarius	6.40-20.00	chin
25	Purva Bhadrapada	Aquarius-Pisces	20.00-3.20	both sides of the body
26	Uttara Bhadrapada	Pisces	3.20-16.40	both sides of the body
27	Revati	Pisces	16.40-30.00	stomach

---

[1] *Varahamihira's Brihat Samhita*, M. Ramakrishna Bhat (translator), Chapter CV, p. 934. Motilal Banarsidass Publishers, Delhi, 1982.

Nakshatra Placement of Transiting Moon

The *Atharvaveda* is one of the four Vedas and the oldest medical text in India. It is co-authored by Sage Atharvan and Sage Angiras, two fire priests of different lineages. Its content includes mantras for health and happiness as well as incantations against disease, enemies and competitors.

An important supplementary text to this Veda is the *Nakshatrakalpha Parisistas*. In this scripture, the duration of a disease is determined by the nakshatra position of the transiting moon on the first day of illness.[1] To illustrate, assume you came down with the flu on the day the moon was in Krittika. According to the table below, it takes 10 nights to recover from this condition.

Table 14: Duration of Disease[2]

Name	Duration in Nights	Name	Duration in Nights	Name	Duration in Nights
Ashwini	10	Magha	7	Mula	8
Bharani	15	Purva Phalguni	15	Purva Ashadha	15
Krittika	10	Uttara Phalguni	10	Uttara Ashadha	30
Rohini	20	Hasta	12	Shravana	16
Mrigashira	16	Chitra	10	Dhanishta	15
Ardra	15	Svati	12	Shatabhishak	30
Punarvasu	19	Vishakha	10	Purva Bhadrapada	9
Pushya	12	Anuradha	15	Uttara Bhadrapada	30
Ashlesha	10	Jyeshta	8	Revati	7

Disease Producing Nakshatras

In the ancient Brahmana scriptures, thirty-three gods are invoked by the brahman priests to partake of the soma libation. They are considered the chosen ones, who one after the other drink the soma and are thereby gratified. These thirty-three privileged devatas are identified in the scriptures as the twelve Adityas, eleven Rudras, eight Vasus, Prajapati and Brihaspati. The Adityas are the sovereign rulers of the heavenly realm, the Rudras, the atmospheric realm and the Vasus, the terrestrial realm.

The later Puranic texts acclaim these same thirty-three godheads as the ruling patriarchs of the current manvantara (period of a manu), a period lasting 306.7 million years. As elaborated upon in *The Divine Forces of the Lunar Nakshatras*, a text written by the author,

---

[1] You can determine the nakshatra placement of the moon on any particular day by running the transits for the day using Jyotisha software.
[2] *Parisistas of the Atharvaveda*, edited by George Melville Bolling and Julis Von Negelein, Volume 1, Chapter 1.

twenty-seven of the thirty-three presiding monarchs of the current manvantara are rulers of the lunar nakshatras.

Of interest here is the Rudra category of gods, for their nakshatras are noteworthy for their ability to manifest extreme cases of ill-health. (See table below for listing of nakshatras ruled by a Rudra.) The Rudras are described as fierce atmospheric forces that possess serpentine-like powers. They reign over the tempestuous mid-space, where battles between forces of light and darkness take place.

A graha occupying one of the Rudra-ruled nakshatras should be carefully monitored during its dasha or bhukti periods and when Shani or one of the nodes of the moon transits over the graha. This is particularly true if the graha is poorly-conditioned or influenced by multiple papa grahas or trik-dusthana bhaveshas.

Table 15: Rudra Nakshatras

Name	Ruling Devata	Rashi	Degree.Minute
Ardra	Rudra	Gemini	6.40-20.00
Ashlesha	Nagas (Serpent-snakes)	Cancer	16.40-30.00
Mula	Nirriti	Sagittarius	0.00-13.20
Purva Bhadrapada	Aja Ekapad	Aquarius-Pisces	20.00-3.20
Uttara Bhadrapada	Ahirbudhnya	Pisces	3.20-16.40

Another nakshatra deserving special mention is Shatabhishak (Aquarius 6.40-20.00), a nakshatra notorious for producing severe states of disease. Shatabhishak is ruled by Aditya Varuna, a godhead portrayed as the dark, foreboding nighttime sun. Varuna relentlessly protects the righteous laws of the universe. He is intolerant of those who violent his cosmic ordinaces. In the ancient texts, Varuna is venerated for forgiveness of one's own sins and those of his ancestors. A sinner who refuses to repent must face this unforgiving god and his many fettered net.

Hence, Shatabhishak is reputed as a highly karmic place in the sky. Illnesses caused by a graha occupying Shatabhishak (one hundred physicians or medicines) is said to require a hundred medicines or physicians to cure. These illnesses may manifest on any or all levels: physical, mental-emotional or spiritual. Shatabhishak is also closely associated with addictions, be that food, drugs, sex and so on.

Appendix Material

Appendix A: Summary Graha Condition and Terminology

The following factors of strength and stabilization were presented and discussed in detail in *Your Healing Stars: Volume 1, Fundamentals of Vedic Astrology*.

Table 16: Factors of Strength and Stabilization

Strength		Weakness
bright moon	→	dark moon or eclipsed moon
retrogression	→	combustion
sva rashi or exaltation	→	debilitation
dig bala		
———		———
———		eclipsed sun
———		loser of planetary war
		rashi sandhi

Stabilization		Destabilization
influenced by shubha grahas	→	influenced by papa grahas
flanked by shubha grahas	→	flanked by papa grahas
———		victor of planetary war

A bhavesha possessing one or more factors of strength is considered "strong", while a bhavesha possessing one or more factors of weakness is deemed "weak".[1] If there are factors of strength *and* weakness, the bhavesha is of "mixed condition". Importantly, factors of strength and weakness do not cancel each other out; rather, both factors play out in the individual's life. A bhavesha with no factors of strength or weakness is "ordinary" in condition.

Similarly, a bhavesha possessing one or more factors of stabilization is "stabilized", while a bhavesha possessing one or more factors of destabilization is considered "destabilized". If there are factors of stabilization *and* destabilization, the graha is of "mixed stabilization". Just as factors of strength and weakness do not cancel each other out, the same is true for factors of stabilization and destabilization.

We also need to consider the nature of the bhava that the bhavesha occupies. The kendras (Lagna, 4B, 7B, 10B), trikonas (Lagna, 5B, 9B) and 11B are positive bhavas, while the dusthanas (3B, 6B, 8B, 12B) are negative bhavas. The 2B is considered a neutral bhava. (See chart below.)

---

[1] Principles of bhavesha condition are the same for a graha in its capacity as a karaka.

Bhaveshas that occupy positive bhavas are considered "well-placed", and they manifest the affairs of their bhavas with relative ease. Bhaveshas placed in negative bhavas, especially the trik-dusthanas (6B, 8B, 12B), must deal with challenges and obstacles (6B), upheavals and transformation (8B) and expenditure and loss (12B). These bhaveshas are considered "poorly-placed".

A strong bhavesha has the fortitude to overcome the adversities of a trik-dusthana placement. In contrast, a weak bhavesha may lack the focus, perseverance or courage to surmount the difficulties presented by such placement.

When a bhavesha is strong, stabilized and well-placed, it is considered "well-conditioned". A well-conditioned bhavesha is empowered to manifest the significations of its bhava with relative ease and grace. In contrast, a bhavesha that is weak, destabilized and poorly-placed is considered "poorly-conditioned". A poorly-conditioned bhavesha struggles to produce its bhava's affairs and often requires significant time and effort to do so.

In a similar manner, the condition of each bhava must be evaluated. Shubha graha influences (i.e., an association with or aspect from Chandra (when no a dark moon), Budha, Guru or Shukra) and shubha graha flanking (i.e., at least one shubha graha occupies the bhava on either side of the bhava) stabilize the bhava. In contrast, papa graha influences (i.e., an association with or aspect from Chandra (when a dark moon, Surya, Mangala, Shani, Rahu or Ketu) and papa graha flanking (i.e., at least one papa graha occupies the bhava on either side of the bhava) are destabilizing. When a bhava is stabilized, the job of its bhavesha is greatly facilitated. The person also feels positive about its area of life and associated relationships. However, when a bhava is destabilized, more pressure is exerted on the bhavesha to protect and support the matters of its bhava. Furthermore, the person's attitude or happiness concerning such events is adversely impacted, as are its health aspects and personal relationships.

Always consider the exception to this general rule. A papa graha that influences its own bhava *fortifies* the affairs of the bhava. Still, because of its papa nature, the graha harms the subtle or most sensitive aspects of the bhava, including personal relationships and matters of health.

Figure 15: Bhava-Bhavesha Condition Spectrum

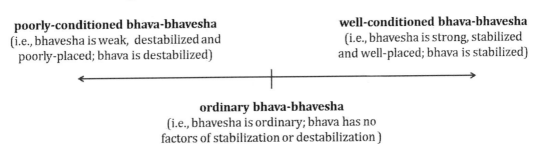

Appendix A: Summary Graha Condition and Terminology

Determine where along the condition spectrum the bhava-bhavesha[2] fall in terms of their overall condition, and adjust your interpretation accordingly. Remember that strength is always more important than stabilization and bhava placement.

---

[2] "Bhava-Bhavesha" is used when referring to the combined condition of a bhavesha and its bhava.

Appendix B: Determining Your Prakruti

Instructions: To determine your prakruti, fill out the form on the next page. Base your choices on what has been most consistent over a long period of your life. Sometimes it helps to additionally have a friend fill in the chart for you, as they may have insight (and impartiality) to offer. Add up the number of marks under vata, pitta and kapha. This will help you discover the ratio of doshas in your own prakruti. Most people have one dosha predominant; a few have two that are approximately equal; even fewer have all three in equal proportion.[1]

---

[1] Based on Lad, BAM&S, MASc, Vasant D. *The Textbook of Ayurveda: A Complete Guide to Clinical Assessment*, Volume Two. 2007, Table 49: *Determining your Prakruti (Constitution)*.

Determining Your Prakruti (Constitution)

Observation	V P K	Vata	Pitta	Kapha
Body frame	V P K	Slim	Medium	Large
Body weight	V P K	Low	Medium	Overweight
Chin	V P K	Thin, angular	Tapering	Rounded, double
Cheeks	V P K	Wrinkled, sunken	Smooth flat	Rounded, plump
Eyes	V P K	Small, sunken, dry, active, black, brown, nervous	Sharp, bright, gray, green, yellow/red, sensitive to light	Big, beautiful, blue, calm, loving
Nose	V P K	Uneven shape, deviated septum	Long pointed, red nose-tip	Short rounded, button nose
Lips	V P K	Dry, cracked, black/brown tinge	Red, inflamed, yellowish	Smooth, oily, pale, whitish
Teeth	V P K	Stick out, big, roomy, thin gums	Medium, soft, tender gums	Healthy, white, strong gums
Skin	V P K	Thin, dry, cold, rough, dark	Smooth, oily, warm, rosy	Thick, oily, cool, white, pale
Hair	V P K	Dry brown, black, knotted, brittle, scarce	Straight, oily, blond, gray, red, bald	Thick, curly, oily, wavy, luxuriant
Nails	V P K	Dry, rough, brittle, break easily	Sharp, flexible, pink, lustrous	Thick, oily, smooth, polished
Neck	V P K	Thin, tall	Medium	Big, folded
Chest	V P K	Flat, sunken	Moderate	Expanded, round
Belly	V P K	Thin, flat, sunken	Moderate	Big, pot-bellied
Belly-button	V P K	Small, irregular, herniated	Oval, superficial	Big, deep, round, stretched
Hips	V P K	Slender, thin	Moderate	Heavy, big
Joints	V P K	Cold, cracking	Moderate	Large, lubricated
Appetite	V P K	Irregular, scanty	Strong, unbearable	Slow but steady
Digestion	V P K	Irregular, forms gas	Quick, causes burning	Prolonged, forms mucous
Taste	V P K	Sweet, sour, salty	Sweet, bitter, astringent	Bitter, pungent, astringent
Thirst	V P K	Changeable	Surplus	Sparse
Elimination	V P K	Constipation	Loose	Thick, oily, sluggish
Physical Activity	V P K	Hyperactive	Moderate	Slow
Mental Activity	V P K	Hyperactive	Moderate	Dull, slow

Appendix B: Determining Your Prakruti

Emotions	V P K	Anxiety, fear, uncertainty	Anger, hate, jealousy	Calm, greedy, attachment
Faith	V P K	Variable	Extremist	Consistent
Intellect	V P K	Quick but faulty response	Accurate response	Slow, exact
Recollection	V P K	Recent good, remote poor	Distinct	Slow and sustained
Dreams	V P K	Quick, active, many, fearful	Fiery, war, violence	Lakes, snow, romantic
Sleep	V P K	Scanty, broken up, sleeplessness	Little but sound	Deep, prolonged
Speech	V P K	Rapid, unclear	Sharp, penetrating	Slow, monotonous
Financial	V P K	Poor, spends on trifles	Spends money on luxuries	Rich, good money preserver
Total				

Appendix C: Determining Your Vikruti

Instructions: To determine your vikruti, fill out the form on the following page. Base your choices on how you have been feeling recently. Sometimes it helps to have a friend ask you the questions and fill in the chart for you, as they may be more impartial. Add up the number of marks under vata, pitta and kapha to calculate the ratio of doshas in your vikruti. If your prakruti is $V_2 P_3 K_1$ but your vikruti shows a ratio of $V_2 P_4 K_1$, this indicates high pitta.[1]

---

[1] Based on Lad, BAM&S, MASc, Vasant D. *The Textbook of Ayurveda: A Complete Guide to Clinical Assessment*, Volume Two. 2007, Table 50: *Determining your Vikruti (Current State)*.

Appendix C: Determining Your Vikruti

Determining Your Vikruti (Current State)

Observation	V P K	Vata	Pitta	Kapha
Appearance	V P K	Thin, bony, emaciated	Medium, intense	Large, sluggish
Weight	V P K	Underweight	Steady	Overweight
Joints	V P K	Cracking and popping	Tender	Swollen
Spine	V P K	Scoliosis tendency	Kyphosis tendency	Lordosis tendency, slipped disk
Muscles	V P K	Tremors, tics, spasms	Tenderness	Swelling
Skin	V P K	Dark, dry, rough, scaly, liver spots	Yellow or red, rashes, pimples, acne	Pale, oily, smooth, swelling
Lymph Nodes	V P K	Narrow	Tender, inflamed	Enlarged, congested
Veins	V P K	Prominent, collapsed	Moderately visible, bruises easily	Full, wide, stagnant
Eyes	V P K	Dry, restless, blinking	Red, burning, hypersensitive to light	Pale, swollen, sticky, excessive lacrimation
Ears	V P K	Ringing (tinnitus)	Pain, infections	Clogged, discharge
Nose, Sinuses	V P K	Dry, crusty	Red, inflamed	Congestion
Lips	V P K	Dry, cracked	Red, inflamed	Pale, oily
Mouth	V P K	Dry, receding gums	Red, inflamed, tender gums	Excessive salivation
Teeth	V P K	Cavities, receding gums, cracked enamel	Yellow, wasted enamel	White, strong enamel
Tongue	V P K	Dry, cracked, tremors, dark coating	Red, inflamed, yellow coating	Pale, thick white coating
Hair	V P K	Dry, knotted, brittle	Oily, graying, bald	Oily, wavy
Nails	V P K	Dry, rough, brittle, cracked, bitten	Soft, sharp, inflamed	Pale, thick, oily
Appetite	V P K	Variable, anorexia nervosa	Strong, unbearable, hypoglycemia	Low, steady
Digestion	V P K	Irregular, gas and bloating	Quick, acid indigestion	Slow, prolonged, indigestion
Metabolism	V P K	Irregular	Hyperactive	Slow
Thirst	V P K	Variable	Strong	Low
Elimination	V P K	Constipation, dry, hard stools	Loose stools, diarrhea, burning	Heavy, oily stools with mucous
Energy level	V P K	Hyperactive, exhausts quickly	Intense, exhausts from excessive thinking	Low, exhaustion due to excess weight
Sex Drive	V P K	Premature orgasm	Painful sex	Low libido
Liver and Spleen	V P K	Palpable (double normal size)	Tender	Enlarged, fatty degenerative changes
Voice	V P K	Dry, exhausted, explosive, whispering, stuttering	Sharp, penetrating, metallic	Deep, hoarse, drum-like

Appendix C: Determining Your Vikruti

Speech	V P K	Rapid, abrupt, unclear ideas	Sharp, determined, premeditated	Slow, monotonous
Breathing	V P K	Nervous, diaphragmatic, (sympathetic nervous system)	Aggressive, intercostals, tight in chest	Slow, abdominal, apnea tendency
Allergies	V P K	Dry wheezing, breathlessness	Hives, rashes, urticaria	Congestion, runny nose
Sleep	V P K	Insomnia, broken	Difficult entering, insufficient	Excessive, drowsiness
Dreams	V P K	Many, active, fearful	Fiery, violent	Watery, romantic
Emotions	V P K	Anxiety, fear, loneliness	Judgement, criticism, anger, hate, jealousy	Attachment, greed, depression
Intellect	V P K	Fast, faulty response	Abrupt, accurate response	Slow, exact response
Memory	V P K	Recent good, remote poor	Moderate, distinct	Slow, remote very good
Total				

Appendix D: Determining Your Mental Constitution

Instructions: To determine your mental constitution it is best to fill out the chart twice. First base your choices on what is most consistent over a long period of your life (your *manas prakruti*), then fill it out a second time responding to how you have been feeling recently in the last month (your *manas vikruti*). Sometimes it helps to have a friend ask you the questions and fill in the chart for you, as they may have good insight (and impartiality) to offer. After finishing the chart, add up the number of marks under *sattva*, *rajas* and *tamas* to discover the ratio of these *gunas* in your *manas prakruti* and *vikruti*. Most people will have one *guna* predominant, a few will have two *gunas* approximately equal. All will have some of each guna.[1]

---

[1] Based on Lad, BAM&S, MASc, Vasant D. *The Textbook of Ayurveda: A Complete Guide to Clinical Assessment*, Volume Two. 2007, Table 51: *Guidelines for Determining your Mental Constitution*.

Guidelines For Determining Your Mental Constitution				
Observations	S R T	Sattva	Rajas	Tamas
Spiritual Practice	S R T	Regular	Irregular	Never
Spiritual Power	S R T	For humanity	Selfish	Destructive
Mental Clarity	S R T	Easy to have clarity	Moderate	Difficult to have clarity
Mental Peace	S R T	Quite often peaceful	Moderate	Rarely peaceful
Satisfaction	S R T	Usually satisfied	Partly satisfied	Seldom satisfied
Behavior	S R T	Gentle	Aggressive	Destructive
Commitment	S R T	Total	Partial	Never
Concentration	S R T	Good	Fluctuating	Poor
Attentiveness	S R T	Good	Fluctuating	Poor, careless
Will Power	S R T	Good	Variable	Low
Knowledge	S R T	Good	Variable	Low
Memory	S R T	Good	Variable	Low
Forgiveness	S R T	Easy	Difficult	Poor, holds a grudge
Cleanliness	S R T	Good	Moderate	Poor
Sexual Activity	S R T	Infrequent, spiritually based	Variable, for pleasure	Excessive, with lust
Donations	S R T	Anonymous	Occasional, with name (attachment)	Rare, only for gain
Love	S R T	Universal, no expectation	Selfish, with expectation	Obsessive
Emotions	S R T	Honest	Denial	Suppression
Attachment	S R T	Rarely, brief	Moderately frequent	Often, longstanding
Fear	S R T	Rarely, brief	Moderately frequent	Often, Longstanding
Anger	S R T	Rarely, brief	Moderately frequent	Often, longstanding
Greed	S R T	Rarely, brief	Moderately frequent	Often, longstanding
Confusion	S R T	Rarely, brief	Moderately frequent	Often, longstanding
Hate	S R T	Rarely, brief	Moderately frequent	Often, longstanding
Grief	S R T	Rarely, brief	Moderately frequent	Often, longstanding
Depression	S R T	Rarely, brief	Moderately frequent	Often, longstanding
Pride	S R T	Little	Moderate	Much
Perception	S R T	Clear	Agitated	Faulty
Facial Expression	S R T	Calm, contented, happy	Mixed, agitated	Dull, gloomy
Eyes	S R T	Calm, clear	Restless, active	Dull, gloomy
Speech	S R T	Clear, calm, peaceful	Fast, restless, agitated	Slow, monotonous

Diet	S R T	Vegetarian, loves all 6 tastes in moderation, 1-2 meals/day	Eats meat sometimes, loves hot, spicy food, 2-3 meals/day	Heavy meat eater, loves sweets, heavy food in excess, 4-5 meals/day
Digestion	S R T	Good, normal	Variable	Poor, slow
Elimination	S R T	Regular	Irregular	Sluggish
Alcohol/Drug Use	S R T	None	Social, occasional	Frequent
Sleep	S R T	Light, brief, satisfying	Interrupted, disturbed, insufficient, unsatisfying	Heavy, deep, excessive
Upon Waking	S R T	Happy, fresh	Disturbed, worried	Drowsy, heavy feeling
Physical Activities	S R T	Movements with awareness	Hyperactive movements	Slow, sluggish, habitual movements
Exercise	S R T	Gentle daily exercise, e.g., yoga, walking, swimming	Aggressive, occasional exercise, e.g., jogging	Heavy, difficult exercise, e.g., weight lifting, hates exercise
Total				

Appendix E: Summary Bhava Classifications[1]

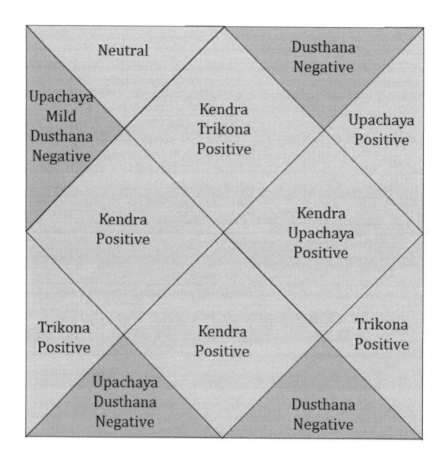

---
[1] Refer to *Your Healing Stars: Volume I, Fundamentals of Vedic Astrology* for a detailed explanation of bhava classifications.

Appendix F: Channels of Nourishment and Elimination[1]

Anna Vaha Srotas & Surya and Mangala

Anna vaha srotas is the channel of digestion, assimilation and absorption of food. It includes the gastrointestinal tract, stomach and small intestines. The organs and processes of this srotas are vast. Thus, multiple grahas serve as karakas.

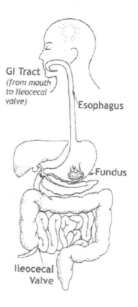

In general, digestion (the process of chemical transformation of food particles by enzymes and bile salts) is a pitta function; absorption (movement of food molecules), a vata function and assimilation (the incorporation of food nutrients into bodily tissues), a kapha function.

Since the stomach is the primary organ responsible for the transformation of food into chyme, Surya and Mangala are the primary karakas for the anna vaha srotas. Surya represents the stomach and gastric fire (i.e., jathara agni) and Mangala the sharp, penetrating digestive enzymes found in the stomach and the bile found in first part of the duodenum.

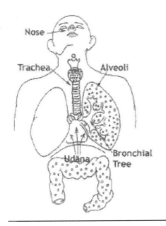

Budha, a vata-pitta graha, represents the small intestine and esophagus that is part of this vaha srotas.[2]

Prana Vaha Srotas & Budha

Prana vaha srotas (respiratory channel) is the channel for prana. Its gunas are light, cool, dry, rough, subtle, mobile and clear. The respiratory tract, bronchial tree, nose and sense of smell are part of this srotas.

Representing the breath and sense of smell, Budha is the primary graha karaka for the prana vaha srotas.

---

[1] Srotamsi pictures in this chapter are reprinted with the permission of the Ayurvedic Institute: Lad, B.A.M.S., M.A.Sc, Vasant D. *The Textbook of Ayurveda: Fundamental Principles of Ayurveda*, Volume One. 2002.

[2] The duodenum, where chemical digestion takes place, is a major pitta site. Vata also plays a major role throughout the small intestines, because of its role of absorption (most nutrient absorption takes place in the small intestines), intestinal peristalsis (contraction of smooth muscles which propels food through the intestines), the opening and closing of the pyloric and ileocecal valves (allowing food to enter the small intestines from the stomach and into the cecum before entering the large intestines) and the production of gases. Hence, Budha, a vata-pitta graha, represents the small intestines. Note that the 6B is the small intestines of the Kalapurusha, and Budha-ruled Virgo, its natural rashi.

This srotas also includes the mucosa lining of the digestive tract. Chandra, a kapha graha, represents this aspect of the prana vaha srotas.

Purisha Vaha Srotas & Shani

Purisha vaha srotas is the channel for elimination of metabolic waste products via the feces. The gunas of this srotas are dry, rough, hard and cool, qualities associated with vata.

As the primary vata graha, Shani is the karaka for this srotas, including the large intestine, sigmoid colon, rectum and anal orifice.

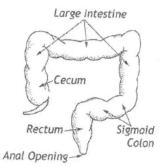

Mutra Vaha Srotas & Shukra

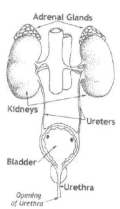

Mutra vaha srotas is responsible for the production of urine, excretion of liquid wastes and regulation of the body's water-electrolyte balance. Its gunas are those of kapha (liquid) and vata (mobile and clear). The mutra vaha srotas includes the kidneys, bladder and urethras.

Shukra, a kapha-vata graha, is the karaka for the kidneys. Chandra, also a kapha-vata graha, is the karaka for the bladder, a holding tank for urine.

Since Budha represents all tube-like structures in the body, the ureters and urethras are governed by this graha.

Ambu Vaha Srotas & Chandra

Ambu vaha srotas is closely related to the mutra vaha srotas. This channel is responsible for water metabolism. Its gunas are those of kapha: cold, slimy, liquid and cloudy.

The ambu vaha srotas includes the kidneys, gastro-intestinal tract mucous membrane and pancreas.

Representing the mucous membrane of the entire gastro-intestinal tract, Chandra is the primary graha karaka for the ambu vaha srotas. In fact, Chandra represents all mucous membranes in the body.

As mentioned under mutra vaha srotas, Shukra is the graha karaka for the kidneys.

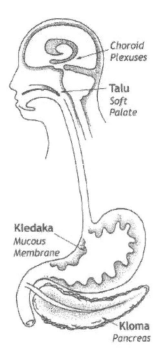

The pancreas is really two glands combined together in one organ. Thus, it is involved in two functions: that of an endocrine gland (producing hormones such as insulin to regulate blood sugar levels) *and* an exocrine gland (secreting pancreatic juices containing digestive enzymes that then pass to the small intestines, where carbohydrates, proteins and fats are further broken done).

Shukra is the primary graha karaka for the endocrine system as a whole. However, each endocrine gland is assigned a more specific graha karaka.[3] Since Guru is responsible for monitoring the blood glucose levels in the body, this graha represents the endocrine function of the pancreas. Mangala, a graha representing sharp, penetrating digestive enzymes, is the graha karaka for the exocrine function of the pancreas.

Sveda Vaha Srotas & Guru

Sveda vaha srotas (channel for sweat) is closely related to the meda vaha srotas. Both include glands (the sebaceous glands of the sveda vaha srotas and sweat glands of the meda vaha srotas) that are responsible for the elimination of wastes via a liquid medium.

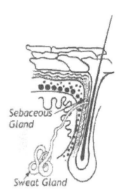

The sebaceous glands secrete sebum, an oily-waxy substance that lubricates the skin and hair. Guru is the graha karaka for the sebaceous glands. In contrast, the sweat glands of meda dhatu secrete primarily a salty-watery substance. Chandra, a watery graha with the rasa of salty, is the graha karaka for the sweat glands.

---

[3] Surya is karaka for the pituitary gland, Chandra, pineal gland, Mangala, adrenals, Budha, thyroid gland, Shani, thymus gland, Guru, pancreas gland, and Shukra, ovaries and testis.

Appendix G: Ayurvedic Significations of the Grahas

Surya Graha Karakas

Sankhya tattva
  Purusha — consciousness

Ayurvedic qualities
  Gunas — hot, sharp, light, penetrating
  Dosha — pitta
  Mental guna — sattva
  Rasa — pungent
  Dhatus-srotamsi —
    Rasa: pituitary gland
    Rakta vaha srota: circulatory system, arteries and heart
    Asthi vaha srota: skeletal system, spinal column
    Anna vaha srota: stomach

Other significations — grey matter of the brain (responsible for comprehension), right side of the body, right eye

Chandra Graha Karakas

Sankhya tattva
  Prakruti — the creatrix or creative force

Ayurvedic qualities
  Gunas — cool, liquid, soft, cloudy, smooth
  Dosha — kapha-vata
  Mental guna — sattva
  Rasa — salty
  Dhatus-srotamsi —
    Rasa dhatu vaha srotas: lymphatic system, spleen, white blood cells and plasma, pineal gland
    Meda vaha srotas: sweat glands
    Artava vaha srotas: womb when pregnant with child
    Prana vaha srotas: mucosa lining of the lungs and phlegm
    Anna vaha srotas: mucous membrane of the gastro-intestinal track
    Mutra and Ambu vaha srotas: bladder

Other significations — white matter of the brain (responsible for memory), lacteal system (including the breasts and breast milk), left side of the body, left eye

Mangala Graha Karakas

Sankhya tattvas
  Jnanendriya — vision, experienced through the eyes
  Karmendriya — the action of walking, performed by the feet

Tanmatra & maha bhuta	form, the quality of the fire element
Ayurvedic qualities	
Gunas	hot, sharp, penetrating, oily, spreading
Dosha	pitta
Mental guna	tamas
Rasa	bitter
Dhatus-srotamsi	Rasa: adrenal glands, venous system and veins
	Rakta vaha srotas: red blood cell production (bone marrow), filtration and removal (liver) and storage (spleen); bile production (liver) and storage (gallbladder)
	Mamsa vaha srotas: the red blood that circulates through the muscles
	Anna vaha srotas: the sharp, penetrating digestive enzymes and bile
Other significations	head, forehead, neck, arms

Budha Graha Karakas

Sankhya tattvas	
Manas	rational mind
Jnanendriya	the sense of smell, experienced through the nose
Karmendriya	the action of grasping, performed by the hands
Tanmatra & maha bhuta	odor, the quality of the earth element
Ayurvedic qualities	
Gunas	cool, light-weight, mobile, subtle, clear
Dosha	vata-pitta
Mental guna	rajas
Rasa	blend of all six tastes
Dhatus- srotamsi	Rasa: thyroid
	Mamsa vaha srota: skin
	Majja vaha srota: nerve impulses and intercellular communication
	Prana vaha srota: respiratory tract (including the nose and sense of smell), bronchial tree, trachea)
	Anna vaha srota: small intestines
Other significations	throat, all tube-like structures in the body (esophagus, ureters, ureteral, bile ducts), hands and fingers

Guru Graha Karakas

Sankhya tattvas	
Jnanendriya	the sense of hearing, experienced by the ears
Karmendriya	the action of speech, performed by the vocal cords
Tanmatra & maha bhuta	sound, the quality of the ether element
Ayurvedic qualities	
Gunas	heavy, slow, oily, smooth, liquid, dense, soft, stable, gross
Dosha	kapha

Mental guna	sattva
Rasa	sweet
Dhatus-srotamsi	Rasa: endocrine function of pancreas
	Meda vaha srotas: omentum, adipose tissue, fat metabolism function of the liver
	Sveda vaha srotas: sebaceous glands
Other significations	thighs, buttocks, vocal cords

Shukra Graha Karakas

Sankhya tattvas	
Jnanendriya	the sense of taste, experienced by the tongue
Karmendriyas	the action of procreation, performed through the reproductive organs
Tanmatra & maha bhuta	taste, the quality of the water element
Ayurvedic qualities	
Gunas	cool, soft, smooth, cloudy
Dosha	kapha-vata
Mental guna	rajas
Rasa	sour
Dhatus-srotamsi	Rasa: hormonal system in general, ovaries and testis, specifically
	Shukra and artava srotas: male and female reproductive organs, respectively
	Mutra vaha srotas: kidneys
Other significations	appendix

Shani Graha Karakas

Sankhya tattvas	
Jnanendriya	the sense of touch, experienced through the skin
Karmendriya	the action of elimination, performed by the anus
Tanmatra & maha bhuta	touch, the quality of the air element
Ayurvedic qualities	
Gunas	cool, dry, rough, hard, lightweight
Dosha	vata
Mental guna	tamas
Rasa	astringent
Dhatus-srotamsi	Rasa: thymus
	Mamsa vaha srota: muscles, tendons, ligaments
	Asthi vaha srota: porous nature of the bones, pelvic girdle, nails and teeth
	Majja dhatu vaha srota: CNS, spinal cord, joints and open spaces in the body
	Purisha vaha srota: large intestines, sigmoid colon, rectum and anal orifice
Oher significations	legs, knees and kneecaps

Nodes of the Moon

Rahu graha karakas
Ayurvedic qualities
- Gunas — extremely subtle, mobile and cool
- Dosha — deranged vata
- Mental guna — tamas

Rahu does not govern any organ or dhatu vaha srotas. Instead, this vata-deranged graha indicates extreme or unusual vata illnesses and diseases, such as paralysis, lameness, Parkinson disease, multiple sclerosis, vertigo and convulsions. On a psychological level, Rahu creates phobias, neurosis, hallucinations and mental disturbances.

Ketu graha karakas
Ayurvedic Qualities
- Gunas — extremely sharp, hot, penetrating
- Dosha — deranged pitta
- Mental guna — tamas

As with Rahu, Ketu does not govern any dhatu or vaha srotas. His dosha is aggravated or deranged pitta. Ketu is associated with smoking, drugs and other pitta-like addictions and health conditions, such as surgery, chronic fevers, accidents from war and other severe pitta disorders and injuries.

Appendix H: Navagraha Van and Rashi Van

Table 17: Navagraha Van

Grahas	Tree	Common Name
Surya	*Calotropis gigantia*	swallow wort
Chandra	*Butea monosperma*	Flame of the forest
Mangala	*Acacia catechu*	cutch tree
Budha	*Achyranthes aspera*	prickly chaff flower
Guru	*Ficus religiosa*	pipal
Shukra	*Ficus glomerata*	cluster fig
Shani	*Prosopis specigera*	Indian mesquite
Rahu	*Cynodon dactylon*	Bermuda grass
Ketu	*Saccharum spontaneum*	cotton-wool grass

Table 18: Rashi Van

Rashi	Tree	Common Name
Aries	*Pterocarpus santalinus*	red sanders
Taurus	*Alstonia Scolaris*	devil tree
Gemini	*Wrightia tinctoria*	dyer's oleander
Cancer	*Butea monosperma*	flame of the forest
Leo	*Ziziphys mauritiana*	common jujube
Virgo	*Mangifera indica*	mango
Libra	*Mimusop elengi*	Indian medaller
Scorpio	*Acacia cateceu*	cutch tree
Sagittarius	*Ficus religiosa*	pipal
Capricorn	*Dalbergia latifolia*	east Indian rosewood
Aquarius	*Prosopis spicigera*	Indian mesquite
Pisces	*Ficus benghalensis*	banyan

Index

10B and Capricorn, 64
11B and Aquarius, 64
12B and Pisces, 64
12B-12B bhavesha, 42
2B and Taurus, 61
3B and Gemini, 61
3B-3B Bhavesha, 113
4B and Cancer, 61
4B-4B Bhavesha, 104
5B and Leo, 62
5B-5B Bhavesha, 112
6B and Virgo, 62
6B-6B bhavesha, 40
7B and Libra, 63
7B-7B Bhavesha, 105
8B and Scorpio, 63
8B-8B bhavesha, 41
9B and Sagittarius, 63
Ajna (command), 151
Ambu Vaha Srotas, 258
Anahata (unstruck), 149
Anapha yoga, 104
Anna Vaha Srotas, 257
Artha sthanas, 127
ashubha yoga, 33
Asthi Dhatu Vaha Srotas, 80
Atharvaveda, 2, 3, 4
Attuning a Mala to your Energy, 165
ava yoga, 31
Bach Flower Essences, 180
Beginning a Mantra Practice, 164
Bheda (destruction), 56
Budha, 23, 111, 163, 181
Budha Aditya yoga, 114
chakras, 143
Chakras and Graha-Rashi Correspondences, 146
Chamara and ava yoga, 31
chamara yoga, 31
Chandra, 26, 100, 184
Chatra yoga, 113
Dharma as Revealed by the Birth Chart, 131
Dharma sthanas, 126
dhatus, 76
Disease Producing Nakshatras, 241
Dr. Edward Bach, 180
dushkriti yoga, 106
Gemstone Evaluation Process, 169
Graha and Rashi Doshas, 14
Graha Combinations, 84
Graha Karaka Confluence, 82
Gunas of the Grahas and Rashis, 94
Guru, 26, 110, 185
How to use essential oils, 186

Important Gemstone Considerations, 177
ishta devata, 134
jaladhi yoga, 105
kahala yoga, 30
Kama sthanas, 128
kama yoga, 106
kapha, 12
Ketu, 45
khavaigunyas, 10, 66
Khavaigunyas and the Birth Chart, 66
Kriyaman karma, 7
kuhu yoga, 105
Lagna and Aries, 60
Lagna-Lagnesha, 29
Lunar yogas, 103
Majja Dhatu Vaha Srotas, 80
Mamsa Dhatu Vaha Srotas, 79
Mangala, 25, 43, 183
Manipura (city of lights), 148
Meda Dhatu Vaha Srotas, 79
Moksha sthanas, 129
mriti yoga, 114
Muladhara (rooted in support), 146
Mutra Vaha Srotas, 258
Nakshatra Placement of Transiting Moon, 241
Nakshatra Purusha, 239
Nakshatra Van, 190
Navagraha Mantra, 166
Navagraha Van, 264
Nicha Bhanga Grahas, 140
pamara yoga, 113
papa kartari yoga, 35
parvata yoga, 30
pitta dosha, 12
Planetary Bija-Mantras, 163
planetary bijas and mantras, 163
Planetary malas, 165
prabhava, 192
Prakopa (provocation), 55
prakruti, 9, 13, 15
Prana Vaha Srotas, 257
prarabdha karma, 7
Prasara (spreading), 55
Pravrajya Yoga, Yogas for Renunciation, 137
Proforma for Disease-Specific Conditions, 86
Purisha Vaha Srotas, 258
purusharthas, 126
Rahu, 45
Rakta Dhatu Vaha Srotas, 78
Rasa Dhatu Vaha Srotas, 77
Rasasashastra, 168
Rashi Van, 264
Sahasrara (thousandfold petal), 152

samprapti, 54
Sanchaya (accumulation), 55
sanchita karma, 7
Sankhya System of Tattvas, 91
Sarasvati yoga, 115
Sattva, Rajas and Tamas, 93
saurya yoga, 114
Shani, 23, 44, 182
Shubha and ashubha yoga, 33
Shubha kartari and papa kartari yoga, 35
shubha kartari yoga, 35
shubha yoga, 33
Shukra, 27, 103, 185
Shukra and Artava Dhatus, 81
Soma, 2
Spiritual Yogas Involving Chandra, 139
Sthana samshraya (localization), 56

Sunapha yoga, 104
Surya, 24, 36, 183
Surya, Graha Karaka for Health, 36
Svadhisthana (dwelling place of self), 147
Sveda Vaha Srotas, 259
Timing Triggers, 119
trik-dusthana bhavas, 39, 45
trik-dusthana bhaveshas, 46
trik-dusthanas, 9
vata, 12
vata dosha, 12
vikruti, 39, 54
vipaka, 192
virya, 192
Vishuddha (pure and clear), 149
Vrikshayurveda, 189
Vyakti (manifestation), 56

Made in the USA
Middletown, DE
15 June 2018